Emmy E. Werner

$10.00
T
2-75
104298

Disadvantaged Children
Health, Nutrition & School Failure

Disadvantaged Children

Health, Nutrition & School Failure

Herbert G. Birch, M.D., Ph.D., and Joan Dye Gussow

HARCOURT, BRACE & WORLD, INC., NEW YORK

GRUNE & STRATTON, INC., NEW YORK AND LONDON

CDEFGHIJ

Harcourt, Brace & World ISBN 0-15-125725-6

Grune & Stratton ISBN 0-8089-0001-3

Library of Congress Catalog Card Number: 78-102443

Printed in the United States of America

ACKNOWLEDGMENTS

The following persons, journals, and publishers have granted permission to incorporate previously published research materials in the body of this book:

Professor Sir Dugald Baird, Dr. F. E. Hytten, Dr. A. M. Thomson, and the *Journal of Obstetrics and Gynaecology of the British Commonwealth,* for Figure 2.5, which appeared in the *Journal of Obstetrics and Gynaecology of the British Empire,* 65:865–876, 1958.

Professor Sir Dugald Baird and the C. V. Mosby Company, Publishers, for Figure 4.8, which appeared in the *American Journal of Obstetrics and Gynecology,* 63:1200–1212, 1952, and for Figure 5.3, which appeared in the *Journal of Pediatrics,* 65:909–924, 1964.

Dr. R. M. Bernard for Figure 5.7, which appeared in the *Edinburgh Obstetrical Society Medical Journal,* 59:2:1–16, 1952, published by Messrs. Oliver and Boyd, Ltd.

Dr. R. Brown and *Developmental Medicine and Child Neurology* for Figures 8.12 and 8.13.

iv

ACKNOWLEDGMENTS

Columbia University Press for Table 10.5, adapted from a table in *The Health of Regionville* by E. L. Koos.

Dr. J. Cravioto, Dr. B. Robles, and the *American Journal of Orthopsychiatry*, for Figures 8.5, 8.6, 8.7, and 8.8, which appeared in the *American Journal of Orthopsychiatry*, 35:449–464, 1965. Copyright © 1965 by the American Orthopsychiatric Association, Inc. Reproduced by permission.

Dr. E. P. Crump, C. P. Horton, J. Masuoka, Donnalda Ryan, and the C. V. Mosby Company, Publishers, for Figures 3.5 and 3.6, which appeared in the *Journal of Pediatrics*, 51:678–697, 1957.

Dr. A. N. Davison, Dr. J. Dobbing, and the *British Medical Bulletin* for Figure 8.9.

Drs. J. F. Donnelly, C. E. Flowers, R. N. Creadick, H. B. Wells, B. G. Greenberg, K. B. Surles, and the C. V. Mosby Company, Publishers, for Figures 3.1, 3.2, 4.2, and 4.6, which appeared in the *American Journal of Obstetrics and Gynecology*, 88:918–931, 1964.

Dr. J. W. B. Douglas and the Editor, the *British Medical Journal* for Table 3.1, adapted from the *British Medical Journal*, 1:2:1008–1013, 1960.

Dr. C. M. Drillien, *Pediatrics Digest*, and E. & S. Livingstone Limited for Table 3.3 and Figure 3.4.

Dr. F. P. Ferguson for W. J. Dieckmann (deceased) and the *Journal of the American Dietetic Association* for Table 6.2.

Dr. G. G. Graham and the *Journal of the American Medical Women's Association* for Figure 8.4.

Dr. W. W. Gruelich and *Science* for Figures 5.4 and 5.5.

Dr. P. A. Harper, Dr. G. Wiener, and the *Annual Review of Medicine* for Table 3.4.

Dr. J. Hiernaux and Wayne State University Press for Table 5.1, which appeared in *Human Biology*, 36:273–293, 1964. Copyright © 1964 by Wayne State University Press. By permission.

Dr. M. L. Hinson, Dr. J. H. Ferguson, and the *Bulletin of the Tulane University of Louisiana Medical Faculty* for Figure 6.1.

Dr. R. Illsley and the Association for the Aid of Crippled Children for Figure 2.1; and Dr. Illsley for Figures 5.3 and 7.1, which appeared in the *Nursing Mirror* and the *Medical Officer*.

Dr. R. L. Jackson and the National Academy of Sciences for Figures 5.1 and 8.3.

Dr. F. J. W. Miller, S. D. M. Court, W. S. Walton, E. G. Knox, and the Oxford University Press, for the Nuffield Foundation, for Tables 10.1, 10.2, and 10.3.

Dr. H. P. Miller and the Thomas Y. Crowell Company, Inc., for Table 2.2.

Professor J. N. Morris, J. A. Heady, and *The Lancet* for Figures 2.2, 2.3, and 4.9.

ACKNOWLEDGMENTS

Dr. S. L. Morrison, J. A. Heady, J. N. Morris, and the Editor, *Archives of Disease in Childhood* for Figure 4.4.

Dr. R. V. Rider, M. Tayback, H. Knobloch, and the *American Journal of Public Health* for Table 3.9.

Dr. R. B. Scott, M. E. Jenkins, R. P. Crawford, the American Academy of Pediatrics, and *Pediatrics* for Table 3.8.

Dr. S. H. Shapiro, H. Jacobziner, P. M. Densen, L. Weiner, the American Public Health Association, and the *American Journal of Public Health* for Tables 2.3, 2.4, and 2.6.

Dr. J. C. Stewart, G. Pampiglione, and *Developmental Medicine and Child Neurology* for Figure 8.14.

Dr. A. M. Thomson, W. Z. Billewicz, and Cambridge University Press for Table 5.2, which appeared in the *Proceedings of the Nutrition Society,* 22:55–60, 1963.

Dr. L. J. Verhoestraete, R. R. Puffer, and the *Journal of the American Medical Association* for Figure 2.5.

Dr. Emmy Werner, the American Academy of Pediatrics, and *Pediatrics* for Figure 3.3.

Dr. W. M. Widdowson, R. A. McCance, the Pan American Health Organization, and the Royal Society for Figures 8.10 and 8.11 and Table 8.2.

The World Health Organization for Figures 8.1 and 8.2, which appeared in an article by K. S. Rao in the *WHO Bulletin,* 20:603–639, 1959.

Dr. A. S. Yerby, the American Public Health Association, and the *American Journal of Public Health* for Table 2.5.

To the Rev. Dr. Martin Luther King, Jr., and to
Senator Robert F. Kennedy,
who cared.

It is bad enough that a man should be ignorant, for this cuts him off from the commerce of other men's minds. It is perhaps worse that a man should be poor, for this condemns him to a life of stint and scheming in which there is no time for dreams and no respite from weariness. But what surely is worst is that a man should be unwell, for this prevents him doing anything much about either his poverty or his ignorance.

G. H. T. KIMBLE

Contents

Preface

W E B E G A N this book three years ago at a time when America
was beginning to "rediscover" its poor. As we bring the volume to a
close, poverty, hunger, and poor health are acknowledged national
problems urgently demanding both present amelioration and, for
the future, basic and permanent solutions. Poverty produces educational failure, and since lack of education reduces opportunities for
employment, it in turn contributes to the perpetuation of poverty,
ill health, and social disadvantage. Poverty and ignorance are thus
mutually reinforcing.

How does poverty produce educational failure? When we began
our work, there was a widespread conviction that poor children
failed in school because their early lives had not offered them certain
experiences fundamental to school success. The nation, having diagnosed educational failure as the product of "cultural" disadvantage,
had prescribed more and earlier educational opportunities for children who were experientially deprived. We were convinced that this
was too narrow a focus. Events have justified our conviction.
Compensatory education, however useful, can not of itself solve the
educational problems of the poor. A serious program for the aboli-
tion of school failure among disadvantaged children must also include improvement in their economic condition, health, and nutritional status.

In this book we examine the relationships between poverty, disadvantage, and educational failure in a more comprehensive and
complex way than is possible when such an examination is based
solely on a concept of cultural disadvantage and defective experience. Children who live in poverty live lives which are not merely
intellectually depressing but physically destructive. Poor children
are exposed to poor food, poor sanitation, poor housing, and poor

medical care. The same homes which lack toys and games are the homes in which hunger and disease abound. To be poor in America, and especially to be poor and nonwhite, is to be assailed by a whole range of physical conditions which, by endangering life, growth, and health, depress mental development and educational potential.

As the richest nation in the world, we have not sought to overcome these handicaps by seriously attacking the complicated problem of poverty. Rather, we have prescribed a large dose of verbiage minimally sweetened with money to whichever aspect of the problem currently forces itself upon public notice. In recent months there has been a growing concern about those children who are hungry and malnourished. Feeding the poor—or talking about feeding the poor —is fashionable, and school failure in poor children is increasingly viewed by many as a consequence of malnutrition.

We welcome this expansion of concern to include hunger and malnutrition as factors which can handicap children as learners. But as we try to make clear in this book, it is not food alone, or compensatory education alone, or health care alone, or improved housing alone which will make the difference between school success and school failure for poor children. One-shot treatments will not overcome handicaps brought on by generations of neglect. A complex and sustained attack will be required to remedy what is a complex and intergenerational problem.

For poor children are not merely born *into* poverty; they are born *of* poverty, and are thus at risk of defective development even before their births. The mothers of these children—exposed during their own childhoods to poor life conditions—come to maturity less well-grown and at greater biological risk as reproducers than do their more fortunate sisters. Beginning too young to bear children, such mothers repeat childbearing too often and continue it too long, through pregnancies in which their health is often poor, their nutrition suboptimal, and their medical care frequently nonexistent.

A child born of such circumstances is likely to be smaller at birth than his more fortunate contemporaries and is more likely to die at birth or before he reaches his second year of life. Both for those who die and those who survive, infancy is more likely to be punctuated by frequent, severe, and persistent illnesses. Throughout the preschool and school years the survivors are likely to be more poorly fed and cared for in their homes, overexposed to disease in their communities, and the recipients of little or no medical supervision. The failure of such children in school is not only not a mystery but is virtually foreordained. Hence a serious attack on school failure must be an attack on the life conditions which characterize poverty wherever it is found.

We have written this book to call attention to the health problems which underlie the school failure of impoverished children. "What do you hope for," someone asked us, "if you write such a book?" What we hope for is the awareness of the size and scope of the danger confronting children born *of* and *into* poverty. What we hope for is a changed system of providing for those who cannot presently provide for themselves. What we hope for is a program that will break the continuous intergenerational chain of poverty. What we hope for is an awareness of the size and scope of the words of Senator Mondale, "authorizing dreams and appropriating peanuts." What we hope for is a change from the wistful notion that expressions of goodwill and a national verbal commitment are sufficient to reduce the spreading problems which are festering along our back country roads, swelling up in our cities, and spreading into our suburbs, problems created by the existence of an impoverished minority—of all colors—which is excluded by ill health and poor education from full participation in American life.

No volume of this scope could have been brought to completion without the substantial help of other persons and agencies. We wish to thank for their encouragement and support our colleagues in the Center for Normal and Aberrant Adaptive Development of the Albert Einstein College of Medicine of Yeshiva University and the organizations which have supported the work of this unit: the National Institutes of Health, the National Institute of Child Health and Human Development; the Association for the Aid of Crippled Children; and the National Association of Retarded Children. Their support, of course, in no way implies their responsibility for the final result—the conclusions we have arrived at are our own. Our thanks go also to Mrs. Ronni Franklin, whose bibliographic exhaustiveness and continued concern with the problem of disadvantaged children did much to make the volume as full as it is. The task of searching out relevant studies would have been considerably more protracted

PREFACE

and considerably less palatable without the resources, both human and bibliographic, of the New York Academy of Medicine. And finally, we wish to express our heartfelt gratitude to Mrs. Ida Hafner, who helped repeatedly to convert an idea into a paragraph and who patiently endured our whims and irritations through numerous agonizing reappraisals of what must have sometimes seemed an endless manuscript.

HERBERT G. BIRCH
JOAN DYE GUSSOW

New York
January 10, 1970

Disadvantaged Children
Health, Nutrition & School Failure

CHAPTER ONE

Health and Learning Failure

Sickness makes people poor; poverty makes people sick.
CHARLES W. MAYO

O F T H E ties that bind the poor to their poverty, many are self-perpetuating. One of these is poor health, another is lack of education. This is a book about poor health and school failure and what they have to do with each other. We have written this book because we, like many others, are concerned about the extent of educational disability that is found among socially or economically disadvantaged groups in all societies. This systematic relationship between social conditions and educational competence is not new, nor even newly discovered; it is a phenomenon which has for years attracted general humanitarian concern and philosophical interest, but only recently assumed the proportions of an urgent problem requiring resolution—an issue of public policy.

A number of factors have contributed to this recent sense of urgency. On a worldwide scale we are faced with the emergence of new nations which require literate populations if they are to move as equals on the stage of history. In our own society ethnically different and economically depressed segments of the population have begun to join in demanding not merely education to a minimum level of employability, but preparation that will allow these previously submerged and subordinated peoples to participate at all levels of an increasingly technical society. These national and international movements have served to convert what was formerly an interesting topic for speculation—a source, at most, of vague unease

—into a problem requiring effective intervention and remediation.

In the newly emerging countries it has been recognized that educational failure is part of a cycle of poverty, social ineffectiveness, and ignorance that is repetitive unless the links which bind its component parts are broken (Cravioto, DeLicardie, and Birch, 1966). In this country, where a burgeoning technology is rapidly eliminating jobs for those with minimal skills, inadequate education is an even more critical link in the poverty cycle. Indeed, Herbert Bienstock (1967), New York Regional Director of the Bureau of Labor Statistics, has ranked lack of education, interrupted education, and educational failure as perhaps the most important causative factor in unemployment.

The likelihood of being caught up in this cycle of poverty and failure is grossly exaggerated for those who are classified as nonwhite. Twice as many nonwhite as white workers in all age groups are unemployed; the unemployment rate for nonwhite teen-agers is two and one-half times that of their white contemporaries, and rates in urban areas are not only high but rising. Between 1960 and 1968 the percentage of unemployed black teen-agers in central city areas went up from 22.7% to 30.4%. And though, in simple numerical terms more whites than nonwhites are poor (in the central cities, for example, more than half the poor are white and nationally almost 68% are), nonwhites and especially nonwhite children tend to be poor in much greater proportion to their total numbers than do those classified as white. More than 34% of nonwhite families compared to only 8.4% of white families were classified as below the poverty level in 1967, and the differential is even greater where children are concerned. Forty-two percent of *all* children classified as poor are nonwhite (U. S. Bureau of the Census, Current Population Reports. Series P-23, No. 27, 1969, and Series P-60, No. 55, August 1968). The median income nationally for the theoretically typical nonwhite couple with 2 children was only 58% of that for a white couple with 2 children; and at a time when overall incomes, even among nonwhites, were steadily climbing, the income of nonwhite families in a number of hard-core slum areas actually declined between 1960 and 1966 (Social & Economic Condition of Negroes in the U. S., 1966).

The excessive educational failure of nonwhites is both cause and consequence of this association between joblessness, poverty, and ethnicity. The reciprocal cycle of cause and effect is the same; it is simply exaggerated where a discriminated-against minority is concerned, producing more joblessness, more poverty, and more educational failure. The extent to which nonwhites and other "white" minorities do not "make it" in school has been well documented in a number of local studies (e.g., McCone Commission, 1965; Havighurst, 1964; HARYOU, 1964) and more recently on a nationwide scale by the Coleman Report on Equality of Educational Opportunity (1967). This national survey of U. S. public schools showed that on nationwide tests of verbal and nonverbal achievement, children from all the principal minority groups (except Orientals) were behind the majority by the first grade, and fell farther and farther behind as their education progressed.

The link between ethnicity and school failure shows up most vividly in a close-up view like Davidson and Greenberg's report *School Achievers Among the Socially Disadvantaged* (1968). Seeking to find a group of children who had "made it" in urban slum schools, in order to discover the qualities which underlay their success, the authors went to the Negro community of Harlem. Though "success" as the study defined it meant nothing more than being up to grade level in reading and mathematics, the investigators had to search the records of 1,331 elementary-school students to find 80 children who met even this modest standard—a ratio of success to failure of 1 in 16.

It is clearly beyond dispute that in this country children handicapped not only by poverty but, additionally, by membership in a depressed minority are at much greater risk of leaving school with an inadequate education than are their less disadvantaged contemporaries. Given their poor education, such children are doomed in young adulthood to either no employment or only marginal employment. As a consequence their poverty is almost certain to persist into their adult life and be handed down to their children who will, more likely than not, repeat their parents' pattern of school failure. "Poverty begets poverty," New York's Health Commissioner George James has said, "is a cause of poverty, and a result of poverty" (1965).

Looking at this cycle of defeat, it has seemed to many that one way to interrupt it was to sever the link between the poverty of parents and the school failure of their children by improving the quantity and quality of their learning experiences both in the school and the preschool years. The nature of the problems raised was such that the first professions to have become involved in this effort were those with primary interests in the structure of society, in the phenomena of learning, and in the organization of instruction. Thus it is that within the last few years the sociologists, the psychologists, and the educators have begun to draw our attention to certain critical distinctions between economically different groups which may help to explain their differential educational achievement. Though there is yet much to be learned, we have come to recognize that in various segments of society children have quite dissimilar opportunities for early social and psychological experience, and are subject to quite dissimilar styles of child care (Richardson, 1966; Wortis et al., 1963). It now seems clear that differences such as these in the "cultural" events to which children are early exposed contribute significantly to a subsequent differential in the ease with which, and the extent to which, they will be able to profit from exposure to common bodies of instruction. But more than "cultural" differences separate economically different groups in this country. Studies have indicated that the same children who are "culturally deprived" in relation to the majority are in a very material sense also educationally deprived. There are differences in the quality and quantity of instruction in the schools as well as in the facilities where instruction is provided, and it is the socially and economically "better-off" children whose education is characterized by better quality, greater quantity, and superior settings for instruction.

Thus the sociologists, the psychologists, and the educators have come up with social, psychological, and educational answers to the question of why so many poor children fail in school. The importance of such factors is unarguable. Their discovery enlarges our understanding of some of the causes of educational failure in the poor, and helps to define certain steps necessary to remedy them. There is some danger, however, that our initial focus on the social and cultural variables relevant to educational achievement may lead us to neglect certain biosocial factors which can directly or indirectly influence the developing child and alter his primary characteristics as a learner. It is inevitable and quite fitting that when the educator, the psychologist, and the sociologist attempt to alter educational achievement they should concentrate on features of curriculum, familial environment, motivation, cultural aspects of language organization, and the patterning of preschool experiences. But the fact is that the child who is both the subject and the object of all this concern, the individual who is interacting with these social, cultural, and educational settings, is a biological organism—a statement the obviousness of which is exceeded only by the extent to which it can be, and has been, forgotten in the face of our fragmented administrative concern with health and with education. As an organism, the child is not only a mind and a personality capable of being unmotivated, unprepared, hostile, frustrated, understimulated, inattentive, distracted, or bored; he is also a body which can be tired, hungry, sick, feverish, parasitized, brain-damaged, or otherwise organically impaired.

It is this physical child to whom we are directing attention. We do not wish to do as some have done (Hunt, 1967) and treat organismic factors as a substitute for experiential opportunity, ignoring the intimate interrelation between the biology of the child and the characteristics of his environment in defining his functional capacities; we would assert merely that society can no longer afford to deal with cultural influences as if they were acting upon a nonmaterial being. The child who is apathetic because of malnutrition, whose sequence of prior experiences may have been modified by acute or chronic illness, whose selectivity as a perceiver and whose organizing ability as a learner may have been affected by previous exposure to risks of damage to the central nervous system, cannot be expected to respond to opportunities for learning in the same way as does a child who has not been exposed to such conditions; for the effective environment of any organism is never merely the objective situation in which he finds himself, but is rather the product of an interaction between his unique organismic characteristics and whatever opportunities for experience his objective surroundings may provide. Thus there is no reason to think that we can fully compensate the child handicapped by an existing biologic disadvantage merely by increasing his objective opportunities for learning in school settings.

In the light of such an understanding, we cannot afford to ignore the biology of the child in educational situations simply because we have already identified a great variety of other variables which are also relevant to educational achievement. This is so because what we come to view as the "causes" of a problem will determine whether we attempt to remedy that problem at all, and what direction our remedial efforts will take. The view that the school failure of the poor is a consequence of a genetically determined intellectual inferiority would, for example, tend to discourage all efforts at educational remediation and encourage us instead to "accept" a low level of achievement from poor children. However, contrary to the impression left by the let's-settle-it-once-and-for-all school of thought (e.g., Ingle, 1964; Shockley, 1966), this particular theory is presently untestable. Even supposing there are genetic differences in "intelligence," it is still the case that all behavior is an interaction between genetic potential and environmental opportunity both within and outside of the womb. Thus the only way to determine whether testable intellectual differences are innate is to fully equalize opportunities for postconceptional development. Although we applaud the notion that this *should* be done, it has not as yet been done. In short, the genetic inferiority theory which many have found insupportable can more properly be described as presently unsupportable, and nonintervention on the basis of such a theory is therefore clearly unjustified.

Inappropriately conceived intervention, on the other hand, is wasteful because it squanders the resources society can allocate to social welfare and education on what may turn out to be noncritical variables. To give but one example: A program of remediation for a child perceived as "unmotivated" would need to be quite different from a program aimed at the child who is listless and apathetic from malnutrition and disease. Even the most sensitive counseling would be unlikely to improve significantly the learning of the hungry child, and the one who is well-fed but unresponsive would gain little except calories from a hot lunch. But it is not only wasteful to ignore health variables in designing programs of remediation, it is actually dangerous. If the factors which have produced a learning disability are misunderstood, programs based on that misunderstanding are unlikely to be successful; and it is unfortunately true that the blame for children's failures in special—albeit inappropriate—

programs usually falls on the children, lending credence to the notion that they are "unable" to learn.

Thus where children have been exposed to exceptional conditions of risk for biologic insult, the damage must be identified and the victims provided not merely with additional educational opportunities but with educational opportunities which are appropriate for them. Since no socially deprived groups can be considered to be homogeneous for organismic disability, such an approach will require the identification of particular subgroups of children for whom special programs of remedial, supplementary, and habilitative education can be devised. The devising of appropriate programs of remediation should not, however, represent the full extent of our concern. A second path of action is implied by the recognition not only that children have been exposed in the past to conditions of biological risk, but that they continue to be so exposed. If these risks can be identified, and if the conditions productive of such risk can be changed for the better, an opportunity exists through the application of public health principles and current biosocial knowledge to reduce significantly the learning handicap of future generations.

It is clear that a society genuinely concerned with educating socially disadvantaged children cannot in good conscience restrict itself merely to improving and expanding facilities for learning, however worthwhile and overdue such improvement and expansion may be. Rather it must concern itself with the full range of factors contributing to educational failure, among which the health of the child is a variable of potential primary importance. In the most general sense, such an argument is not new. The basic relationship between poverty, illness, and educational failure has long been known. What has changed is not merely our understanding of the mechanisms of that relationship, but the nature of the societies in which such grim interactions are occurring; that is, societies in which there is no longer an economic reason for the existence of chronic poverty. As Galbraith (1958) has put it: "To secure to each family a minimum standard as a normal function of society would help insure that the misfortunes of parents, discerned or otherwise, were not visited on their children. It would help insure that poverty was not self-perpetuating. Most of the reaction, which no doubt would be almost universally adverse, is based on obsolete attitudes. When poverty was a majority phenomenon, such action could not be afforded. . . . An affluent society has no similar excuse for such rigor. It can use the forthright remedy of providing for those in want. Nothing requires it to be compassionate. But it has no high philosophical justification for callousness." Thus in an atmosphere of affluence, or of economic growth and development, it becomes possible to approach the problems of poverty as potentially soluble, requiring only that we choose to see them and to solve them.

We wish to argue in this book, therefore, for a formulation of the problem of educational handicap among the poor in which the child is seen as a mind in a body, in a world that is both physically and psychologically hazardous. Not failing to acknowledge the reality of "cultural disadvantage," we would assert that it is but a fragment of the threat which a poor environment offers to the intellectual development of a child; and that the poor, from conception until death, are also at differential risk with respect to a whole spectrum of physical hazards any one of which may be productive of intellectual deficit and educational failure.

In pursuing this line of argument we have examined a vast body of data, very little of which has been *directly* pertinent to our concern. We have not been often opposed by the existing information; we have just not often been helped. For the fact is that there has been little investigation of the specific relationships between the physical status of poor children and either their mental development or their school achievement. We therefore have pursued our argument over some rough and largely uncharted terrain, following trailmarkers when they existed, working point to point like surveyors when no path was visible. Matters of public health seldom yield to careful measurements in the laboratory. Not only are all the variables seldom controlled; often the most significant variables are at any given moment unknown, and later conclusions drawn from the data can at best be only inferential. It has seemed to us, however, that where the inferences are so serious, and where the area of concern is of such critical and immediate importance, that it is not only unnecessary but actually unwise to await the final definitive studies before attempting to convey some sense of the scope of the problem.

What we propose to do in this book, then, is to pursue the trail that has led to our own present concern. We begin our argument by leading from strength, exploring that indicator of social condition which is both the most reliable and the most clearly associated with risk to children: the mortality of infants and their mothers around birth. By looking at the risk of nonsurvival, we will identify both those features of natality which put survivors at risk and those populations in which such features occur to excess. Next we will turn to a direct consideration of conditions in pregnancy and around birth which appear to be associated with hazard to the child, examining in detail—as an exemplar of conditions of reproductive risk—the distribution and the consequences of low birth weight. This in turn will lead us to a consideration of the conditions of life, both past and present, which make certain groups of mothers less efficient childbearers; that is, we will look at certain variables which mediate between social and economic conditions and the lowered effectiveness of mothers as reproducers.

In the remainder of the book we will turn our attention from the hazardous events to which children are exposed during their own production to the character and the effect of the environments in which they must spend their infancies. We will consider first the evidence linking nutrition, disease, and mental development, looking both at experimental studies on animals and at observations of children in areas of endemic nutritional stress. We will then take up the available data on malnutrition, morbidity, and medical care among children of poor families in this country, considering the degree to which the quality of their lives puts these children at risk as learners either by permanently impairing their capacity to learn or by interfering with the orderly acquisition of knowledge.

CHAPTER TWO

Death and Deficit

It is so soon that I am done for,
I wonder what I was begun for.
Epitaph for a three-week-old child

More and more evidence is accumulating that the same conditions that bring death to infants before, during, and soon after birth also may lead to chronic illness and handicap in many infants who survive.

MARTHA ELIOT, 1958

WE SHALL begin our exploration of the relationship between children's social and economic status and their exposure to physiological hazards relevant to education by considering ways in which social class affects the chances of dying in infancy. At first glance, infant mortality statistics may seem quite impertinent to our present concern which is, after all, health in relation to educational failure. Obviously those children whose educational potential engages us are those who do *not* succumb to the hazards of birth and early life. They have survived the perils of entry into the world —what Clement Smith (1951) has called "the valley of the shadow of birth"; they have survived their first day, their first week, their first month, their first year of life. Their very appearance in the schools as objects of educational concern is evidence that they have "come through" the early years alive. Of what significance, therefore, are facts about those who die in infancy in a study of these survivors? Although the deaths of their brothers and sisters and cousins may involve us as humanitarians, of what possible concern are they to us as educators?

There are two reasons for concern: The first is that the rate of infant death in any population is an indicator of the level of health hazard to which that population is exposed. A high infant mortality rate signals the existence of circumstances hostile to life, of an environment in which there are high rates of illness, faulty nutrition, poor conditions for birth, and mothers in poor condition (Butler and Bonham, 1963; Illsley, 1967; Simpson, 1968). So strong is this association between a people's health status and the rate of survival of its infants, that the infant mortality rate of any population and the direction and speed of its change are generally acknowledged to be among the most highly sensitive indicators of the present and future well-being of that group (Hunt, 1966).

The second reason why infant mortality statistics need concern us is that a high rate of infant death, in any population, indirectly suggests survival with increased risk of damage in the survivors. To know which are the killing conditions of life is to suspect which are the maiming ones; for in life as on a battlefield, not all the casualties die. Those children who have come through birth and infancy alive have not necessarily come through unscathed, and it is reasonable to anticipate that the condition of the survivors will surely reflect the relative hostility of the environments to which they have been exposed. Thus in identifying that segment of the general population which is subject to the highest rate of infant loss, we are in effect defining a group in whose surviving children we can expect to find not only a high incidence of present poor health, but a higher-than-average prevalence of primary neurological damage representing the aftermath of excessive exposure to hazards of gestation, birth, and early life.

These are inferred health risks, of course, documentable where data are available but indirectly arrived at nonetheless. Should we wish to dispense with inference, the theoretically best way to discover which groups are subject to the greatest health risks would be to examine population morbidity figures directly. Where we have been able to do this in subsequent chapters, it will become apparent that such data are limited both in extent and in reliability. In contrast to death, disorders compatible with life are subject to observer error and to problems of classification and misreport. The most reliable information we have in the field of public health concerns the rates at which people are born and die, which is the third reason why mortality data are relevant to our investigation into the risk conditions for educational achievement. Given the relationship of mortality rates to various aspects of poor health, and given also the fact that mortality statistics are comparable across studies, across populations, and sometimes across countries, they can be analyzed to add conviction, detail, and refinement to our picture of the effects of social and economic status on health variables.

For an initial look at the effect of social class—unconfounded by significant racial variability—on the survival of infants, it is useful to begin with data from Great Britain, a country in which for many years there was not only relative racial and ethnic homogeneity but also an established system of social classification based on occupation. The most detailed recent information on the deaths of babies to come out of Great Britain derives from the massive 1958 Perinatal Mortality Survey (Butler and Bonham, 1963; Butler and Alberman, 1969), which analyzed the social circumstances of a carefully selected national sample of births producing infants who died sometime between the fifth postconceptional month and the first week of life. Data from the survey are presented in Figure 2.1 (from Illsley, 1967). They show clearly that death rates for babies in the perinatal period increase inexorably as socioeconomic status declines, with perinatal mortality lowest among births to those in the professional class and highest to a marked degree among births to those in the least skilled laboring classes.

But Figure 2.1 shows, in addition, that crosscutting the occupational gradient for perinatal death is a regional one, running from northwest to southeast, and reflecting the state of economic development and general well-being of the respective geographic areas. Perinatal death rates are generally highest for all social groups in the poorer northwest, intermediate in the industrial Midlands, and, in every case, much lower in the relatively more affluent southeast. In some cases the regional differences are sufficiently powerful to reverse the direction of disadvantage between occupational groups from different areas, so that skilled manual laborers in the south, for example, have lower perinatal death rates than professional workers in the poor northwest. Such a finding, although it illustrates the limitation of occupational measures as sole indicators of health risk, adds further weight to the argument that there is a close association between *real* conditions of life and patterns of survival in the young.

Illsley, 1967

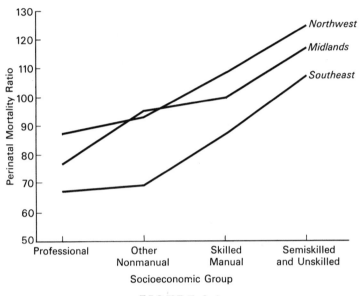

FIGURE 2.1

Perinatal Mortality Rates by Region and Socioeconomic Group, Great Britain, 1958

(Expressed as a ratio of the national rate. Great Britain = 100.)

The same social gradients which affect perinatal death rates persist intensified throughout infancy. Data on neonatal and postneonatal mortality by region and by social class for the year April, 1964–March, 1965, have been analyzed by Spicer *et al.* (1966). They show the same social class and regional gradients; in addition, they show that social factors have an increasing impact on mortality with the increasing age of the infant. The death rate in the first month of life (neonatal) in the two lowest classes is almost one and one-half times the rate for infants in the two highest classes (13.2/1,000 compared to 9.2/1,000). But in the remainder of the first year (postneonatal), though the absolute rate of death is lower, the relative risk is more than twice as great for the infant in the lower classes as it is for his upper-class contemporary. Socioeconomic status is thus clearly associated with increased mortality not only through the first week or the first month of life, but to an even greater extent throughout the remainder of the first year, so that postneonatal deaths emerge as an even more sensitive indicator of socioeconomic differences than deaths which occur in the month after birth.

What is, perhaps, even more distressing than the existence of a marked and persistent social gradient in infant mortality is the fact that despite the global medical advances of the past half-century and, in Great Britain, the universal extension of medical service, the disadvantage of the lower classes, relative to the upper classes, does not appear to have diminished over time. The data in Figure 2.2, compiled by Morris and Heady (1955) from the decennial census reports, allow us to examine the secular trend in infant mortality since 1911. Although there has been a marked absolute reduction in infant deaths over the period considered, there has been virtually

Morris and Heady, 1955

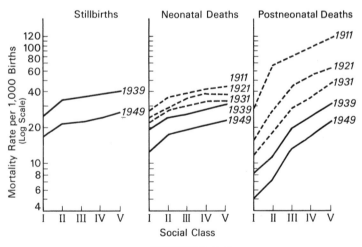

FIGURE 2.2

Social Class Differences in Stillbirth, Neonatal, and Postneonatal Mortality Rates, England and Wales, 1911–1949

no change in the *relationships* between the social groups in any mortality classification. The lower classes have not improved their position vis-à-vis the upper classes; and since they have experienced somewhat less improvement relative to where they started from, they are comparatively worse off.

Using both regular census reports and data from the Perinatal Mortality Survey, Illsley (unpublished) has calculated that between 1938 and 1958, when the stillbirth rates for professional, managerial, and other nonmanual workers fell by 54%, rates for skilled workers fell 47%, and those for unskilled workers only 38%. When the combined stillbirth and neonatal death rates are considered, the decline between 1951 and 1958 amounted to 28% for professional and non-manual workers, while unskilled workers experienced only an 18% improvement over the same period. A similar pattern emerges in relation to postneonatal death even when single occupational groups are compared over time (Figure 2.3).

Morris and Heady, 1955

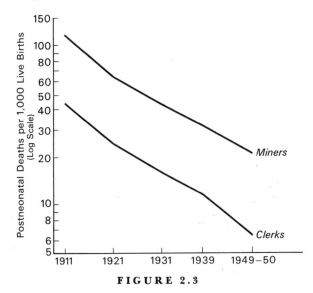

FIGURE 2.3

Occupational Group Differences in Postneonatal Mortality Rates, Children of Miners and Clerks, England and Wales, 1911–1950

(*Legitimate births*)

In sum, then, the British data show: (1) that in a population which is relatively homogeneous ethnically there are social and economic differences among parents which affect the survival of their children; and (2) that although the death rates for infants in all social classes have shown a marked decline over the last 50 years, there has been no tendency during that period for the lower classes to "catch up" with the upper classes where the survival of infants is concerned. Indeed, there has been some tendency for them to fall relatively even further behind.

Since the U. S. is an officially "classless" society where health statistics are not reported in terms of an established occupational classification, a consideration of mortality by social condition encounters more difficulties here than it does in Britain. However, an analysis of available U. S. natality and mortality data by income, areas of residence, ethnicity, and various combinations of these, can be used in order to get at what are very real social and economic differences between groups. Overall, the U. S. infant mortality record is considerably less than outstanding when it is compared with that of Britain and other industrialized countries. The 1966 data show that the United States, the richest nation in the world, tied with Czechoslovakia for sixteenth place in infant mortality, its rate of 23.7 per 1,000 live births placing it below such countries as New Zealand, Japan, and East Germany (Wegman, 1968). If we had Sweden's rate, the world's lowest, 11 more babies out of every thousand born alive in 1966 would have lived past their first birthdays. But the risk of losing an infant in this country, though higher than it should be for everyone, is not democratically distributed in the population. Here as in Great Britain, the death rate of infants is tied to a number of socioeconomic variables.

One such variable is geography. On a state-by-state basis it was more than twice as safe for an infant to be born in Nebraska, where only 18.5 out of every 1,000 infants born failed to survive their first year, than to be born in Mississippi, where the death rate was 37.7 per 1,000 (1966). On a broad regional basis, life expectancy for infants is relatively more favorable—with rates running at or below the national average—in a belt which runs down the Atlantic Coast from Maine to Maryland, then west through the east-north-central region across the northern two-thirds of the country to the Pacific

Coast, and on out to Hawaii. In this vast area there are only 5 states (including Alaska) out of a total of 34 where the infant mortality rate in 1966 exceeded the national average. However, as the map shows (Figure 2.4), things are different in the South. In the

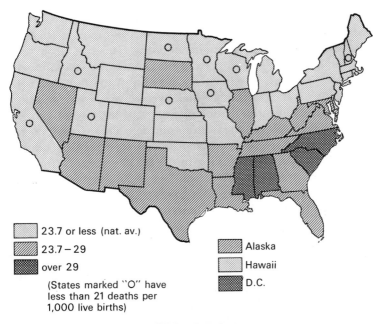

23.7 or less (nat. av.)
23.7 – 29
over 29
(States marked "O" have
less than 21 deaths per
1,000 live births)

Alaska
Hawaii
D.C.

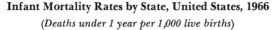

FIGURE 2.4

Infant Mortality Rates by State, United States, 1966

(Deaths under 1 year per 1,000 live births)

southern tier of states, running from Virginia on the east coast to Arizona in the southwest, 15 out of 16 states had infant mortality rates worse than the national average—in some cases shockingly so. Four of the 16 had infant mortality rates of over 29 per 1,000 live births.

This geographic gradient in infant death reflects two kinds of regional differences: differences in economic development, like those which affect mortality rates in Great Britain, and differences in ethnic composition. Although British prosperity declines as one goes north, the geographic gradient in this country reflects an economic differential that runs in the opposite direction. The same 15 southern states with infant mortality rates higher than the national average also have the highest concentration of "hard-core poor," families with incomes under $2,200 a year (Nutrition and Human Needs—Part II, 1969). Mississippi, the nation's poorest state, also has the "dubious distinction," as Wegman has called it (1968), of having the nation's highest infant mortality rate, 37.7 (1966).

The South differs from the rest of the country, however, not only in terms of economic development, but also in the fact that it has traditionally contained a larger than average proportion of groups designated as nonwhite—predominantly the Negroes of the Old South. Although Negro migration to northern urban centers is rapidly altering the balance (between 1940 and 1966 the percentage of the total Negro population living in the South decreased from 77% to 55%—Social and Economic Conditions of Negroes in the United States, 1967), the fact remains that over 50% of all nonwhite births in 1967—and the overwhelming majority of rural nonwhite births— still occurred in just 16 southern states plus the District of Columbia (NCHS, MSVR, Dec. 4, Suppl., 1968). Moreover, on a statewide basis the *concentration* of Negroes in the population of the South is, of course, markedly higher than it is in the rest of the country. The elevated infant mortality rates of the southern states reflect this population pattern, for it is much safer in America to be born a white than a nonwhite child. The nationwide infant mortality rate for nonwhites, 35.4 (1967), was almost twice as high as the white rate of 19.6 for the same year.

More specifically, the child who has had the poor judgment to be born into this nation nonwhite runs a risk of dying in the first month of his life; that is more than one and one-half times the risk run by a white infant. During the remainder of his first year, his risk of dying is well over two and one-half times greater (NCHS, Vital Statistics of the U. S., Vol. II, 1965). He is three and one-half times as likely to die of pneumonia, twice as likely to suffer accidental death, and seven times as likely to expire from "symptoms and ill-defined conditions" as is a white infant (Densen and Haynes, 1967). Given this excessive mortality among nonwhite infants, much of the South's poor showing can evidently be accounted for not merely by the poverty of the region as a whole, but, more specifically, by the heavy concentration of Negroes within its borders.

But race and economic conditions are interlocking variables. The "ethnic" classification "nonwhite" is really a crude socioeconomic classification rather than a strictly racial one, a statement which can best be clarified by an examination of some of the alternate classifications. Income is one of these. When viewed on a broad geographic basis, infant death rates, as we have seen, appear to be responsive to average income level: In the 17 states having the lowest per capita income (1963), the average infant mortality rate was 19% higher than the national average (Hunt and Huyck, 1966). We actually have no other national data on differential infant mortality rates according to income (NCHS, PHS 1000, 3:6, March 1967); but as it turns out, income alone is not a particularly valid measure of actual economic status anyway. A father earning $6,000 a year, for example, with a family of 6 children, will almost certainly be poor, while a father with a similar income who has only 1 child will probably not be.

Official acknowledgment of this fact has radically altered the statistical composition of the poverty population. The old "poverty line" of $3,000 was based solely on income. The first year that the new "poverty index" of the Social Security Administration (which takes family size into account) was utilized it increased by 4 million —to a total of 15 million—the number of children believed to be living in poverty in the U. S. (New York Times, 1965). Nor is present income a reliable indicator of social or educational status. There is, for example, a considerable difference between a poor graduate student and a poor tenant farmer—in past history as well as in potential income—though they may presently be living on the same per annum cash allowance.

A more useful classification which has been used to divide groups by socioeconomic status in this country is the census tract of residence. Crude as it is—and it is particularly crude in circumstances where discriminatory housing practices inhibit freedom of choice of residence among certain groups—census tract information can sometimes be used to make gross socioeconomic distinctions. Moreover, in the North, where Negroes tend to be concentrated in urban ghettos, we can use census data to observe at closer range, on a neighborhood scale, the same interlocking of economic and ethnic differences which operate to affect mortality on a regional scale. The information in Table 2.1 derives from a study which used

TABLE 2.1

Relationship of Income, Other Social Variables, and Infant Mortality, Chicago

Decile	Income Range	Education Score	Occupation Score	Social Rank	Average Percentage Nonwhite	Infant Death Rates
1	$8,400–19,999	75.5	70.8	73.1	3.0	15.5
2	7,800– 8,399	62.3	46.6	54.4	2.6	18.5
3	7,400– 7,799	57.1	43.6	50.3	2.5	18.6
4	7,000– 7,399	55.7	44.0	49.8	5.4	23.2
5	6,650– 6,999	49.5	34.1	41.8	3.3	20.8
6	6,300– 6,649	45.1	28.4	36.7	7.4	28.5
7	5,900– 6,299	43.8	27.1	35.4	17.8	24.1
8	5,250– 5,899	42.9	26.8	34.8	30.6	27.9
9	4,250– 5,249	42.4	28.7	35.5	73.3	39.8
10	2,000– 4,249	34.0	26.0	30.0	88.1	36.9

Adapted from Bedger *et al.*, 1966

census tract data to investigate the relationship between income and various indices of health in the Chicago area (Bedger *et al.*, 1966). Dividing census tracts into ten equal groups according to income range, the researchers found a very regular relationship between income and such other social variables as parental education, occupation, and social rank. It is apparent that income level, when area of residence is kept as a constant, may reflect real socioeconomic status with more accuracy than income alone. What is also important to notice in Bedger's data, however, is the huge absolute increase in the percentage of nonwhites *and* in the rate of infant mortality in the lowest two income deciles.* The percentage of nonwhites

* The usefulness of census tract data in making socioeconomic discriminations is highly dependent on local conditions—e.g., the size and concentration of the "poor" population, the availability of improved housing for upwardly mobile

goes from 7.4% in the sixth decile to 30.6% in the eighth; and then, abruptly, it more than doubles to 73.3% in the ninth and 88.1% in the tenth deciles. In other words, as income declines beyond a certain minimum level, there is a sharp increase in the percentage of nonwhites in the population considered. But just at the point where the percentage of nonwhites suddenly increases, the regular trend of increase in the risk of infant death which accompanies declining income also makes an abrupt upward jump. The groups in the ninth and tenth income deciles, who are not only poor but also preponderantly nonwhite, have infant mortality rates more than twice those of the highest income groups. Bedger's data thus clearly illustrate the tendency for low socioeconomic status and race to be confounded in U. S. health data. They also reflect the degree to which separating data by skin color, as is done in many official health records, will almost always tend to separate groups by economic status as well.

To use ethnicity as a classification, however, does not automatically homogenize for social class. You do not *have* to be poor if you are nonwhite—Bedger observed, for example, that in the highest income area in Chicago there were two census tracts which were 98.6% nonwhite—nor do you need to be nonwhite to be poor. Just as there are nonwhites in each of the Chicago income deciles, including the highest, so there are whites in each decile including the lowest. As we have earlier pointed out, however, and as the Chicago data confirm, there is a strong link between poverty and minority ethnic status in this country; sufficiently strong, in fact, that whenever comparisons can be made between nonwhites of all incomes and poor people of all colors in such poverty-related variables as education, health, and housing, the nonwhites come off worst.

It should perhaps be made explicit that the term "nonwhite" does

---

families from the lower classes, and so on. Failure to find marked or significant social class differences in infant mortality rates on the basis of census tract data (e.g., Willie, 1959; Stockwell, 1963) has been interpreted to mean that "the infant mortality rate is no longer the extremely sensitive index of difference in socioeconomic status that it was in the past" (Stockwell, 1963). A more appropriate interpretation of the findings might be that census tract data do not always "get at" socioeconomic differences. Thus negative findings are merely negative for a given community. They are irrelevant in the more usual circumstances, such as Bedger's, where very real differences are found.

not here refer exclusively to Negroes, nor does it include all the ethnically different and disadvantaged groups in the population. The naming of statistics with respect to ethnic, racial, or color groups is an Augean stable. One is never sure in the face of the term "non-white" whether the designation is merely a euphemism for American Negroes, or whether it includes other "differently colored" groups such as Orientals, Puerto Ricans, American Indians, or Mexican-Americans. The range of color designated by the term under the latter circumstances may range from pale blond (in the case of some Puerto Ricans) to deep ebony (in the case of some Negroes). The safest rule of thumb is to assume that the term "nonwhite" refers to various specifically identified segments of the population which differ from the predominantly European-derived majority in social and ethnic characteristics and, all too frequently, in economic characteristics as well.

Among these minorities, the largest group by far—21.5 million people who constitute 11% of the total population of the United States—is made up of a people with an acknowledged portion of ancestors of African origin. In national vital statistics, this numerical dominance of the Negroes obscures the separate contributions to health statistics of Indian, Eskimo, Philippine, Oriental, Hawaiian, or other groups classified as "nonwhite," just as the numerical dominance of those who are socially and ethnically integrated into the white majority obscures the statistical significance of births and deaths to persons of Mexican, Puerto Rican, or Cuban origin who are usually included in the "white" group (NCHS, Vital Statistics of the U. S., Vol. II, 1965). Although the social and economic problems of these other minorities may differ in detail from those of the Negroes, the limited data available suggest that in terms of the issues we are raising, their similarities outweigh their differences. Data drawn by Miller (1964) from the 1960 census show, for example, that where income is concerned the Negroes are somewhat better off than the Puerto Ricans and the Indians and somewhat worse off than the Spanish-Americans of the Southwest, but that all are well below the white median. Table 2.2 shows the median income of various ethnic groups in 5 southwestern states with non-Negro nonwhite groups separated out. Obviously the composition of the nonwhite population markedly affects income level. Orientals,

TABLE 2.2

Median Incomes by Color, Five Southwestern States,
United States, 1959

Color	Arizona	California	Colorado	New Mexico	Texas
White	$2,996	$3,583	$2,876	$2,961	$2,632
Negro	1,622	2,528	2,289	1,751	1,167
Spanish-American	1,944	2,835	1,929	1,912	1,536
Other nonwhite	1,034 (⅔ Indian)	3,014 (Oriental)	2,361 (Indian, Oriental)	1,378 (¾ Indian)	1,943 (Indian, Oriental)

Miller, 1964

though somewhat lower in mean income than the whites, are highest of all nonwhite groups; Indians are lowest.

These economic patterns are reflected in rates of infant loss. In 1963, when the national nonwhite infant mortality rate (predominantly Negro) was 41.5, the rate for the overall nonwhite population in Arizona was 56.2 (predominantly Indians), and the rate in Alaska was 46.7 (predominantly Aleuts and Eskimos). In California, on the other hand, the relatively low infant mortality rate among nonwhites (28.3) is a reflection of the relatively high proportion of Orientals among the nonwhite population (NCHS, PHS 1000, 20:3, Sept. 1966).

It is evident, then, that much of the excessive mortality of the nonwhites reflects the widespread and often profound poverty which exists among them. This being so, it should follow that within the nonwhite group, as within the white group, differences in economic status will produce differences in infant loss. Indeed, Bedger found that nonwhites living in high income census areas had infant loss rates "comparable to those of the white population living in the same areas."

A more specific comparison comes from a special study of health care conducted by the Chicago Board of Health (1965), in which the city was dichotomized into "poverty" and "nonpoverty" areas on the basis of such characteristics as income, education, housing, proportion of the population on public assistance, and rates of unemployment and juvenile delinquency. The classification was crude enough, as the authors pointed out, so that many of the city's poor lived in "nonpoverty" areas, and, conversely, many of those living in "poverty" areas were not poor. Nevertheless, the study showed that the nonwhites living outside of identified poverty areas of the city had an infant mortality rate in 1964 of 29.6, a figure markedly below the national nonwhite rate for that year of 41.1. Nonwhites living in "poverty areas," however, experienced a rate of infant loss of 45.5. Thus even the rough dichotomization of nonwhites into "poverty" and "nonpoverty" groups revealed a significant difference in their rates of infant loss.

The more clearly the *combined* effects of both ethnic and economic inequality are revealed, the more marked the mortality differential grows. As we have seen, nonwhites as a group are 87% worse off than the whites; and the people of the poorest southern state are 117% worse off than those of the best of the northern states. According to Bedger, the largely nonwhite poor of Chicago are more than 140% worse off than the largely white "non-poor." But that is not the whole story. Where populations have been segregated by prejudice and circumstance into an almost entirely nonwhite poverty population and an almost entirely white nonpoverty population, even more shocking differences in mortality appear. Yerby (1965) points out that although the infant mortality rate in one nonwhite poverty area of New York City in 1962 was 49.5, "in Kips Bay-Yorkville, a middle-class white community about one mile away, the infant mortality rate was 14.7." Nor is the extreme expression of the problem confined to the teeming urban slums. The rate for Mississippi's largely rural nonwhite population was 57.6 in 1965, and rates as high as 62/1,000 live births have been reported for single Mississippi Delta counties. The infant mortality rate for Indians in Arizona in 1963 was 62.4, compared to a rate of 24.4 for all other races combined in that state.

But the excessive mortality among nonwhite infants must reflect something more than their parents' poorer present economic status. In the Chicago Board of Health Survey (Chicago Board of Health, 1965), the infant mortality rate of whites living *in* poverty areas was only 25.1, a rate significantly below the figure of 29.6 for nonwhites who lived *outside* of poverty areas. In fact, the rate for all nonwhites in the city was higher than the combined rates for all "poverty area" residents. This is confirmation on a local level of the national reality that nonwhites in general have a worse record than "all poor people." That fact is merely a fact, however. It should not be taken to indicate that some racial weakness rather than life circumstance is elevating nonwhite mortality rates.

The fact is that poverty does not appear to weigh equally on white and nonwhite; just as income fails fully to reflect real economic status, so a comparison of whites and nonwhites of apparently equal economic status fails to take into account the impact of an often overt discrimination on life circumstances. It is quite likely, for example, though difficult to prove, that the double handicap of discrimination and poverty exaggerates for nonwhites such natural hazards of slum life as getting less of everything while paying more (e.g., Schrag, 1968; New York Times, July 24, 1967, and August 11, 1968). The authors of the Chicago Board of Health Survey concluded from their data that "the impact of residence in the poverty areas, although by no means negligible for the white population of the city, was far greater on the nonwhite population . . . that is, the disabilities associated with membership in a minority group, including, for example, discrimination, inability to obtain access to adequate medical care, etc., fell relatively most heavily on the nonwhites residing in the poverty areas."

It needs also to be recognized that income is merely a reflection of a family's present situation. Among nonwhites who have often moved to the urban slums from an even more appalling poverty in the rural South, poor reproductive performance in the mother, as we will subsequently show, is less likely to reflect present economic status than it is to reflect the mother's own past history as a growing organism (Baird, 1949; Thomson, 1959; Thomson and Billewicz, 1963).

Perhaps the best evidence that it is an environmental-ethnic rather than a biological-racial component which accounts for the excess of deaths among the poor who are also nonwhite is the way in which mortality ratios between white and nonwhite infants change in the period around and after birth. We have earlier observed, in the British data, that socioeconomic differences are more apparent in the postneonatal death rate than in deaths occurring closer to the time of birth. It is generally recognized that mortality of children beyond the first month of life is predominantly sensitive to their immediate environmental circumstances (Verhoestraete and Puffer, 1958; Hammoud, 1965). On the other hand deaths around birth, through the first week and to a lesser extent through the first month of life, are more heavily influenced by biological factors; i.e., the physical status of the mother, her efficiency as a childbearer, and thus the intactness and vitality of the infant.

In newly developing countries the effect of improved environment is felt first in a reduction in the death date of children aged 1 to 4 years, next in declining postneonatal deaths, and much more slowly in perinatal and neonatal deaths. The relative immunity of perinatal mortality rates to immediate environmental influences has been dramatically illustrated by data from the Netherlands (Verhoe-

Verhoestraete and Puffer, 1958

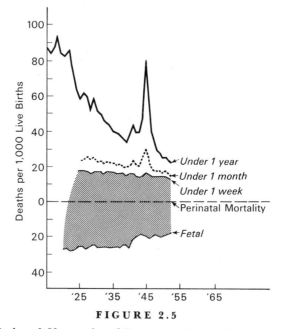

FIGURE 2.5

Perinatal, Neonatal, and Postneonatal Mortality Rates,
the Netherlands, 1915–1952

28

straete and Puffer, 1958). Figure 2.5, which presents mortality data covering the period 1915 to 1952, shows that the marked increase in infant mortality in the Netherlands during the last 5 months of World War II was reflected to a much lesser extent in neonatal mortality and not at all in the mortality of infants under 1 week of age.

In these first days of life the human being, whether rich or poor, black or white, faces a greater risk of death than at any other period—a fact which reflects the presence in the newborn population of large numbers of infants born alive but too damaged or too immature to survive. In the U. S. almost two-thirds of the infants who will not survive the first year of life die within the first week (64% in 1965), after which time the odds on survival begin to improve.

Now although nonwhite mortality rates are higher than white rates throughout infancy, it is in this first week after birth—when, as we have seen, the immediate environment appears to exert the least effect—that there is the least difference between the rates at which white and nonwhite babies die. Table 2.3 gives data by age at death for white and nonwhite infants in the U. S. in 1965. As the figures show, in the first 24 hours after birth, when mortality rates are high for all infants, the nonwhite death rate is 55% higher than the white rate. In the next two days the differential actually declines so that by the second day after birth excess mortality among non-whites is down to 23%. As the environmental factor becomes increasingly potent, however, the differential begins to increase once again so that by the time a nonwhite infant is 6 days of age he is more than twice as likely to die as a white infant of the same age; and by the time he is into his fourth month of life the odds against him are almost 3 to 1.

The malignant effects of postnatal environment are even more clearly illustrated when the survival of low birth weight infants is considered (Erhardt et al., 1964). Rates are much higher among non-whites; but at equally low birth weight, nonwhite infants actually have a somewhat *better* chance for survival during the first month of life than white infants. Data in Table 2.4 (Shapiro, 1954) show that under 2,500 grams the nonwhite infant has a higher survival rate than a white of equal weight; and, as data in Table 2.5 show, until the age of 36 weeks after conception, the same advantage

TABLE 2.3

Infant Mortality Rates by Age, Color, and Sex, United States, 1965

(Rates per 100,000 live births in specified group)

Age	Total			White			Nonwhite		
	Both Sexes	Male	Female	Both Sexes	Male	Female	Both Sexes	Male	Female
Under 1 year	2,469.6	2,772.1	2,151.7	2,151.1	2,436.9	1,849.4	4,032.7	4,438.8	3,615.2
Under 28 days	1,766.3	1,998.2	1,522.5	1,608.3	1,829.1	1,375.2	2,541.6	2,839.5	2,235.3
Under 1 day	1,016.5	1,142.9	883.6	930.1	1,048.4	805.2	1,440.5	1,613.3	1,263.0
Under 1 hour	193.9	205.6	181.6	182.0	189.4	174.1	252.5	286.1	217.9
1–23 hours	822.6	937.3	702.0	748.1	858.9	631.1	1,188.1	1,327.2	1,045.0
1 day	258.3	291.8	223.1	240.0	275.4	202.6	348.3	373.5	322.4
2 days	158.9	187.0	129.3	152.9	181.7	122.5	188.1	213.2	162.2
3 days	66.4	80.2	51.9	61.9	76.4	46.7	88.3	99.2	77.1
4 days	37.4	41.2	33.3	33.0	36.2	29.6	58.9	66.3	51.3
5 days	28.9	32.7	24.8	24.3	27.1	21.3	51.2	60.8	41.4
6 days	20.7	23.6	17.7	17.7	19.8	15.5	35.5	42.5	28.4
7–13 days	83.2	93.3	72.5	69.4	78.0	60.4	150.8	169.5	131.6
14–20 days	53.2	58.4	47.7	43.8	47.6	39.9	99.1	112.2	85.7
21–27 days	42.9	47.0	38.6	35.2	38.6	31.6	80.8	89.0	72.3
28–59 days	170.1	191.2	148.0	130.0	150.0	108.9	367.0	395.8	337.4
2 months	130.4	147.5	112.5	100.9	117.5	83.4	275.3	296.6	253.3
3 months	103.5	116.4	90.0	80.5	91.6	68.9	216.3	239.9	192.1
4 months	74.3	80.5	67.9	56.1	61.9	50.0	163.9	173.0	154.5
5 months	52.1	56.9	47.1	39.3	43.2	35.1	115.2	124.9	105.1
6 months	41.7	43.5	39.9	32.1	33.4	30.7	89.1	93.6	84.4
7 months	33.8	34.8	32.8	26.0	26.5	25.4	72.3	75.9	68.5
8 months	28.1	30.7	25.4	21.7	24.2	19.1	59.4	62.9	55.8
9 months	25.6	25.6	25.6	20.9	21.5	20.3	48.7	46.2	51.3
10 months	21.8	22.8	20.7	17.4	18.5	16.2	43.4	44.0	42.7
11 months	21.8	24.1	19.3	17.9	19.6	16.1	40.7	46.5	34.7

NCHS, Vital Statistics of the U.S., 1965

TABLE 2.4

Neonatal Mortality Rates by Sex, Birth Weight, and Color, United States, January–March 1950

(Single births)

Deaths Under 28 Days, per 1,000 Live Births

Birth Weight in Grams	White		Nonwhite	
	Male	Female	Male	Female
1,001–1,250	731.7	589.3	648.6	603.4
1,251–1,500	579.4	412.3	464.6	412.0
1,501–1,750	583.0	246.0	252.9	228.0
1,751–2,000	246.0	147.7	206.2	131.5
2,001–2,250	117.1	59.5	104.6	62.0
2,251–2,500	55.8	30.2	50.8	35.1
2,501–2,750	23.8	13.2	25.6	13.4
2,751–3,000	11.6	6.8	15.7	9.7

Adapted from Shapiro, 1954

TABLE 2.5

Infant Mortality Rates by Color and Duration of Gestation, United States, January–March 1950

(Single births)

Deaths Under One Year per 1,000 Live Births

Gestation Period in Weeks	White	Nonwhite
Under 28	793.5	718.3
28–31	374.3	332.4
32–35	119.7	108.9
37 or more	7.9	13.1
Total live births	717,133	120,653

Adapted from Shapiro, 1954

accrues to nonwhiteness when prematurity is defined in terms of gestational age. After the gestational age of 36 weeks, however, the nonwhite mortality rate is higher. Though the data are old, Shapiro *et al.* (NCHS, PHS 1000, 3:4, Oct. 1965) concluded that "the associations have not changed materially since this study."

Some have argued that this higher survival rate reflects a greater physiologic maturity among underweight or underage Negro babies compared with their white counterparts. But Erhardt has pointed out that for each birth weight interval nonwhites have a lower mean duration of pregnancy, so that survival cannot be related "to their advanced maturity if the latter is measured by length of gestation" (Erhardt *et al.*, 1964). At least a partial alternate explanation is suggested by some findings of Rider *et al.* (1957) in a study evaluating the effect of hospital adherence to standards for premature care on the survival of such infants. He found that the five hospitals which ranked highest in meeting recommended standards of care were the larger medical-school-affiliated institutions serving a major proportion of the Negro population, and that these same hospitals had the highest survival rate for prematures. Sixty-two percent of the prematures in the highest ranking hospitals were nonwhite, whereas at the smaller, often private, hospitals which ranked lower in quality of care, fewer than 20% of the premature infants were nonwhite.

Such a finding lends support to Harper and Wiener's (1965) suggestion that the lower mortality rate among nonwhite prematures can be at least partially explained by the fact that the Negro in the North, being primarily an urban dweller, is cared for in better hospitals. This may well be, for when the premature infant goes home the situation changes. After the first month of life, and throughout the rest of infancy, death rates for nonwhites are higher for infants of every birth weight except for those infants weighing 1,000 grams or less at birth (who usually remain in the hospital for more than 30 days). For Baumgartner (1965) this observation strongly suggests that "inadequate medical care, inadequate maternal supervision, inadequate housing, and associated socioeconomic deprivations are exerting unfavorable influences on the later survival of those nonwhite babies who initially appear the more favored. It is apparent that socioeconomic factors not only influence the incidence of low birth weight in all ethnic groups, but greatly influence survival after the neonatal period."

It should not be assumed, however, that socioeconomic factors do not also have a marked, if somewhat less direct, effect on survival during the perinatal period. As we have earlier pointed out, except for infants under the gestational age of 36 weeks or under a birth weight of 2,500 grams, mortality rates are persistently higher for nonwhites even in the period immediately surrounding birth when biological influences are uppermost. Such a differential probably reflects the fact, suggested earlier, that the mother of the child has both an immediate environment and historical antecedents, each of which is capable of influencing her reproductive performance. Clearly there are factors in the immediate environment which act on the mother's biology—her nutritional status, her age and parity, her antenatal and obstetrical care—which can affect the outcome of the pregnancy and the survival of the infant in the immediate postnatal period. In this respect it may be relevant to observe that 28% of the white and 46% of the nonwhite infant deaths in 1963 occurred in the 17 states which, as a group, had not only the lowest per capita income, but also a physician ratio per 1,000 population that was 30% below the national average (U. S. Dept. HEW, Reference Facts on Health, Education and Welfare, 1967).

However, as data from Yerby (1966) and Shapiro et al. (1960) show, the white-nonwhite mortality differential may not entirely disappear even when an adequate income and superior medical care are available to the nonwhite group. Yerby's table (Table 2.6) shows a perinatal mortality rate among Negro professionals in New York City almost as high as the rate for whites in the laboring classes; and Shapiro's data (Table 2.7) demonstrate that although prepaid medical care reduced the rate of perinatal mortality among nonwhites in the city, it did not bring it down to the level of white rates. What we are probably seeing here are the effects not of the immediate but of the past environment, that in which the mother grew to adulthood. The "biological" factors in infant mortality—that is, the health of the mother and the vitality of the child—are to a very large extent a reflection of the life experiences of the mother during her growing years; and the persistent higher mortality rates among nonwhite infants (and, as we shall see, among their mothers as well) are evi-

TABLE 2.6

Perinatal Mortality Rates by Occupation and Color, New York City, 1961–1963

(All births)

Occupational Group	Perinatal Mortality Rate	
	White	*Negro*
Professional, managerial, or technical workers	16.7	24.2
Clerical and sales workers	20.8	31.5
Craftsmen and operatives	20.9	32.9
Laborers and service workers	25.9	36.6

Adapted from Yerby, 1966

TABLE 2.7

Perinatal Mortality Rates by Color, New York City and HIP (Adjusted), 1955–1957

Perinatal Mortality Rate per 1,000 Live Births and Fetal Deaths [a]

Ethnic Group	New York City [b]	HIP (Adjusted) [b]	Standard Error of Difference	P [c]
Total (Excluding Puerto Rican)	27.9	23.1	1.2	<0.01
White	27.3	22.7	1.3	<0.01
Nonwhite	43.8	33.7	5.0	0.05

[a] Perinatal mortality rate is defined as infant deaths under seven days plus fetal deaths, 20 weeks gestation or more, per 1,000 live births and fetal deaths.

[b] New York City rates are observed rates for deliveries of women of all ages excluding those under 20 and age not stated.
HIP rates are adjusted to age of mother and ethnic distribution of New York City deliveries (excluding deliveries to women under 20 and age not stated).

[c] "P" represents the probability that NYC-HIP difference is due to chance factors.

Shapiro *et al.*, 1960

dence that the consequences of a life of poverty cannot be immediately overcome.

What is particularly ominous about the mortality differential between white and nonwhite infants is not merely that it shows the minority groups to be at a significant disadvantage with respect to the majority of the population, but that it indicates a secular trend for the worse in their relative standing compared to the "whites." As Figure 2.6 shows (Hunt, 1966), national infant mortality rates for both whites and nonwhites have generally declined over the last 50 years, though at a slowing rate and with fluctuations up and down. But in percentage terms the white rate has tended to drop more, despite the fact that it began its decline from a much lower base. Between 1950 and 1965 the white infant death rate declined 19.8%, while the nonwhite rate dropped only 9.4% during the same period. Thus the nonwhite rate in 1950 was 66% higher than the white rate, but by 1965 it was 87% higher and in absolute terms at the level of the white rate prior to 1942.

Shapiro has pointed out, moreover, that although regional differences in white infant death rates tended to level out during the 1950s, no such equalization took place among nonwhite births (NCHS, PHS 1000, 20:3, Oct. 1965). In regions where white mortality rates were highest at the beginning of the decade—namely, the east, west-south-central, and mountain divisions—dramatic reductions in deaths after the first month of life tended to bring the overall white infant mortality rate in these regions closer to that in the rest of the country, where death rates were lower to begin with and declined less during the decade. In 1949–1951, death rates for white infants in the postneonatal period ranged from a low of 5.6 (in the New England region) to a rate more than twice as high, 12.3 in the west-south-central region. By 1959–1961, the range was only from 5.0 to 6.8.

For nonwhites, on the other hand, there were no such impressive decreases in regional differential except in the mountain division (where nonwhites are predominantly Indian). Here the total infant mortality rate dropped from an appalling 94.4 in 1949–1951 to a slightly less appalling 48.7 in 1959–1961. (The 1965 rate of 37.7 was still over one and one-half times the white rate for the region.) The postneonatal mortality rate for mountain division nonwhites—an

Hunt, 1966

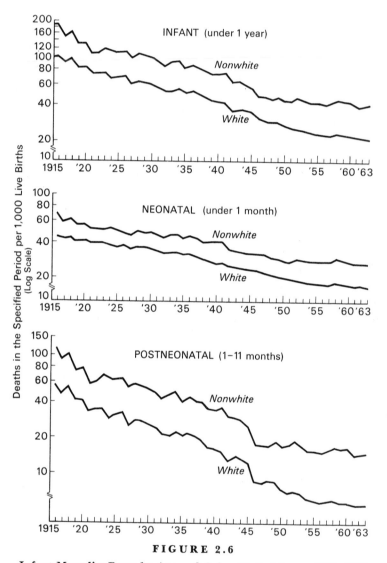

FIGURE 2.6

Infant Mortality Rates by Age and Color, United States, 1915–1963

even more sensitive indicator of environmental beneficence or hostility—dropped from 107 in 1939–1941 to 60.2 in 1949–1951, and to 20.1 in 1965, at which point it was still more than three times the white rate for the region—the highest white rate in the nation. Omitting the "improved" mountain division, then, there has been no tendency for the geographic gap between regions of low and high nonwhite mortality to close. Indeed, for deaths after the first month of life, as Shapiro has pointed out, the range between low and high rates actually widened during the 1950s, not only because there was little change for the better in areas with the worst records and a considerable change for the better in the region with the best record (rates for the Pacific area once again reflecting the advantaged status of the Oriental group), but also because in the east-south-central region, comprising the states of Kentucky, Tennessee, Alabama, and Mississippi, there was an *absolute* increase (from 18.9 to 19.8) over the decade in the rate of postneonatal death among nonwhite infants.

Available data for the first half of the 1960s show a continued tendency for things to get even worse so far as nonwhites are concerned. Once again the east-south-central region showed an absolute increase in infant mortality; the 1965 rate of 47.3 is thus higher than the rate in the same area at the end of the 1940s. And since there was an actual decrease in the rate of deaths in the first month of life, the higher overall rate for the whole first year reflects a considerable increase (from 19.8 in 1961, to 20.9 in 1965) in the risk of death for nonwhites in the postneonatal period. The mortality rate for nonwhite infants also increased in the New England and in the east-north-central regions, reversing the downward trend of the 1950s. Other areas showed small declines in the first half of the 1960s, with the only substantial improvement occurring once again in the mountain region. It is interesting to note that infant mortality in Puerto Rico, a rapidly industrializing society, declined between 1964 and 1966 from 51.6 to 36.7, while in Mississippi during the same period it went from 39.4 to 40.6 and then to 37.7. It should also be noted that, with the exception of a few urban areas, there is no single region in the U. S. in which mortality rates for *white* babies—infant, neonatal, and postneonatal—did not go down between 1961 and 1965 (NCHS, Vital Statistics of the U. S., Vol. II, 1965).

As we have noted earlier, the discouraging pattern of excessive nonwhite mortality applies not only to babies but to their mothers as well. Despite a large secular decline in absolute rates of death for both white and nonwhite mothers, the presently large differential in maternal risk reflects a relative worsening of the status of nonwhites. In 1967, the maternal death rate among nonwhite women

NCHS, PHS 1000, 20:3, 1966

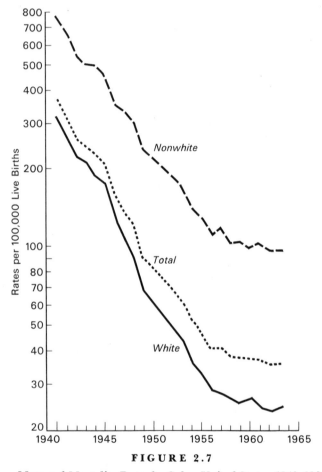

FIGURE 2.7

Maternal Mortality Rates by Color, United States, 1940–1963

was 69.5 per 100,000 live births, while the white rate was 19.5 (NCHS, Advance Final Mortality, 1967, MVSR, March 25, 1969). As Figure 2.7 (NCHS, PHS 1000, 20:3, Sept. 1966) shows, the rates for both groups have been dramatically reduced from the rates of 25 years earlier when the white rate was 439.9 and the nonwhite rate was 875.5; but the relative difference between the groups over the period has increased markedly.

Before World War II, nonwhite rates generally tended to be double the white rates. Since 1955, puerperal death rates among nonwhite mothers have run about four times those of whites. Thus on a national level, the present white-nonwhite differential for maternal mortality is even more substantial than that for deaths among infants. That this is, like the variation in infant mortality, at least partially a reflection of social and economic differences is demonstrated by the fact that when maternal mortality rates are considered by geographic region they follow, in exaggerated fashion, essentially the same pattern as did the infant mortality rates. In the low per capita income group of states, maternal mortality is 40% higher than the national average (Hunt, 1966); and the highest rate is once again found in the poorest state, Mississippi. Once again, however, in every state except Hawaii, nonwhite rates are higher, frequently many times higher, than white rates, as Table 2.8 shows.

The implication of these high rates of maternal death among depressed populations is twofold. In a direct sense the deaths of mothers leave children motherless, and, where fathers are often absent, frequently orphaned. But deprivation or orphaning through puerperal fatality actually affects a relatively small number of children. In 1965, for example, total maternal deaths numbered 1,189, compared with 87,453 fetal deaths, 92,866 infant deaths, and 312,110 premature births (NCHS, Vital Statistics of U. S., 1965). Of more ominous significance is the fact that a high maternal mortality rate invariably represents merely the visible top of an iceberg of maternal morbidity.

In considering the large white-nonwhite differential in rates of maternal death, however, we cannot ignore the fact that there are differences in the composition of the white and nonwhite childbearing populations in this country which may account for it; that is, compared to white mothers as a group, nonwhite mothers

Maternal Mortality Rates by Color, United States and

(Rates per 100,000 live

Division and State	Total	White	Nonwhite
United States [a]	35.9	24.2	98.1
New England			
Maine	21.9	20.7	112.6
New Hampshire	33.4	33.6	—
Vermont	14.6	14.6	—
Massachusetts	19.4	17.2	71.7
Rhode Island	12.7	9.5	88.6
Connecticut	23.6	21.2	51.9
Middle Atlantic			
New York	46.3	32.0	131.5
New Jersey	34.8	—	—
Pennsylvania	28.2	19.3	99.6
East North Central			
Ohio	24.5	19.8	64.0
Indiana	31.7	24.6	111.1
Illinois	28.0	21.5	60.3
Michigan	36.2	25.7	120.9
Wisconsin	26.0	23.8	77.7
West North Central			
Minnesota	11.2	11.0	20.2
Iowa	17.0	17.3	—
Missouri	34.4	29.3	66.3
North Dakota	27.3	24.2	97.6
South Dakota	25.2	21.1	72.6
Nebraska	20.7	17.6	81.9
Kansas	27.0	21.5	104.7
South Atlantic			
Delaware	31.7	21.6	71.8
Maryland	31.1	18.3	75.7
District of Columbia	64.3	5.7	88.4
Virginia	44.7	25.1	105.6
West Virginia	50.0	44.1	165.8

[a] Figures by color exclude data for residents of New Jersey for 1962 and 1963.

2.8

Each State, by Division, 1961–1963
births; 3-year average.)

Division and State	Total	White	Nonwhite
South Atlantic (cont.)			
North Carolina	50.5	22.1	112.6
South Carolina	65.2	18.4	131.2
Georgia	49.8	28.0	89.3
Florida	42.7	21.2	102.7
East South Central			
Kentucky	44.9	36.1	138.9
Tennessee	44.8	31.1	93.2
Alabama	74.8	27.1	155.3
Mississippi	84.1	29.3	131.9
West South Central			
Arkansas	49.1	24.9	108.5
Louisiana	41.9	21.4	73.5
Oklahoma	33.5	23.7	92.5
Texas	45.6	35.1	105.2
Mountain			
Montana	20.0	13.0	103.6
Idaho	31.1	31.7	—
Wyoming	24.8	21.5	110.9
Colorado	26.0	25.6	37.3
New Mexico	51.8	48.3	77.7
Arizona	38.4	24.5	111.2
Utah	24.5	21.1	158.2
Nevada	22.9	13.0	97.3
Pacific			
Washington	18.3	17.3	35.2
Oregon	19.2	16.1	105.9
California	28.4	22.8	70.6
Alaska	56.8	19.5	133.9
Hawaii	20.6	24.4	18.9

tend to be not only poorer but also younger when they start and older when they finish childbearing, more frequently unmarried, and less likely to have prenatal care. It may well be that these practices in the nonwhite population rather than any more general association between poverty and poor health explain the excessive mortality among nonwhites.

Age at childbirth does have a significant effect on maternal mortality (women aged 45 or older are more than ten times as likely to die in childbearing as are women in the 20–24 age group), and it is possible that the acknowledged differences in age distribution of white and nonwhite mothers accounts at least in part for the elevated risk associated with nonwhiteness. In fact nonwhites turn out to be at excessive risk at every age. As Table 2.9 shows (NCHS, PHS 1000,

TABLE 2.9

Maternal Death Rates by Age and Color, United States, 1963

(*Rates per 100,000 live births*)

Age	Total	White	Nonwhite
Under 20	23.1	14.6	51.0
20–24	18.9	13.6	50.1
25–29	28.2	17.2	90.4
30–34	52.6	35.1	146.9
35–39	96.8	65.1	277.0
40–44	137.1	99.8	343.7
45+	202.8	178.7	343.2

Infant, Fetal and Maternal Mortality, 1963; NCHS, PHS 1000, 20:3, 1966

20:3, 1966), nonwhite women aged 45 or older are twice as likely to die from reproductive complications as are white women of the same age. At younger ages the discrepancy is even worse. Death rates among nonwhite mothers are never less than three and one-half times white rates; and a nonwhite woman in the most fecund age group (25–29) has five times the chance of dying in the course of reproduction as does a white woman. When deaths are divided by cause, or even by cause and age, the same situation obtains. For every cause but one, at every age but one (risk rates for dying of hemorrhage under 20), the risk of dying from the bearing of a child is consistently and markedly higher for nonwhite than for white mothers.

Another possible basis for the differential risk among the white and nonwhite populations is their different rates of illegitimate birth. Childbearing out of wedlock is clearly more prevalent (even if inadequacies of reporting are taken into account) among nonwhites. In 1965 the reported rate for first illegitimate births for unmarried nonwhite women was 44.4/1,000 compared to a rate of 7.8/1,000 for unmarried white women. Unmarried status, moreover, strongly affects mortality, even when abortion is discounted as a cause. Pakter *et al.* (1961b) found death rates for all causes four times as high among unmarried as among married women in New York City, and when abortion deaths were eliminated, the ratio was still two to one. But unmarried pregnancy had a much more profound effect on maternal death rates among mainland whites, and even among Puerto Ricans, than it did among nonwhites. Unmarried whites had the *highest* rates of puerperal fatality—27/10,000 births; married white women had the lowest rate—3/10,000, a ratio of 9 to 1. Among Puerto Ricans the puerperal death rate for unmarried mothers, though much less elevated by their marital status, was still almost two and one-half times that of married mothers; but among nonwhites the rate for unmarried mothers was only about one and one-half times the rate for married mothers (19.9 compared with 12.5), and the absolute rate for unmarried nonwhites was lower than that for unmarried whites. So it is clearly not their unmarried state that accounts for excessive maternal mortality in the nonwhite population.

There are also significant differences in the extent to which white and nonwhite populations get prenatal care, another factor that may explain some of the excess deaths among mothers in the nonwhite group. There are, in fact, few data which can be used for comparing the effect of prenatal care or lack of it on maternal death; but Whitridge and Davens (1952) did a comparison of rates of survival between women who attended county maternity clinics in Maryland and a group of women of unknown history who represented the remainder of the population of the affected counties. The Negro clinic group, all of whom received prenatal care, had a maternal mortality rate of 16.4/10,000, a substantial decrease from the rate of 24.8 among nonclinic patients. But not only was the white rate lower to begin with; clinic care apparently made much more of a difference among whites. Nonclinic white women had only 8.6 deaths per 10,000 births, and white clinic patients had no deaths among 2,377 births. Although it is difficult to assess the overall comparability of the clinic and nonclinic groups, it seems clear that it is not simply differences in the extent of prenatal care, just as it is not simply differences in the age or marital status, of the nonwhite population that explain its relatively high risk of death. Rather, the different death rates in the white and nonwhite groups are the consequence of a constellation of factors in which the depressed population differs from the majority.

Thus the data we have examined in this chapter tend to confirm for the U. S. what was earlier found in Great Britain: that there is a socioeconomically depressed segment of the population which experiences markedly higher rates of infant loss (especially after the first month of life) than the average. We have found that in this country a high infant risk rate is also accompanied by a high rate of maternal mortality, and that excessive risk is associated with ethnicity as well as with depressed socioeconomic status, so that segments of the population which are both poor *and* nonwhite experience the highest rates of infant and maternal loss. Finally, we have observed that despite vast improvements in medical technology and medical treatment over the past decades, the survival rate of this depressed segment of the population not only has failed to improve as rapidly as has that of the more privileged minority, but has in some cases become worse. Thus, while nonwhites in most of the country are only relatively worse off than they were 5 years ago, there are some parts of the country where they are absolutely worse off than they were a generation ago.

If these high rates of death are taken as indicators identifying populations in which the surviving children are at risk of deficit, then on further analysis we would anticipate finding at least two things to be true: First, in populations where rates of death around birth are high, we would expect to find an excessive incidence of pregnancy and birth complications, with elevated levels of risk for abnormal development in the children who survive. Second, in the light of the excessive rate of postneonatal death among these populations, we would expect to find conditions of life among them which are compatible with neither the health nor the optimal growth and development of surviving children. It is the first of these expectations which we shall explore in the following chapter.

CHAPTER THREE

Low Birth Weight and Handicap

We live, move, have a being, and are subject to the actions of the elements and the malice of diseases in that other world, the truest microcosm, the womb of our mother.

SIR THOMAS BROWNE

In the past we have not been greatly worried over . . . premature infants once they outlived the threat of respiratory distress by surviving 4 or 5 days and thus notified us they were probably going to go on living . . . but now pediatricians have begun to insist on survival with subsequently normal mentality, school performance and the ability to acquire that college education now considered the right of every child.

CLEMENT A. SMITH

I T W A S our anticipation in the previous chapter that when we came to look at events associated with pregnancy and birth we would find direct evidence that surviving children in the lower social classes, especially those classified as nonwhite, had an elevated rate of exposure to conditions of risk for later maldevelopment, commencing at least as early as their conceptions. As we now begin to examine the available data on the events of reproduction, it will become clear that our anticipation was correct, and that almost every complication of pregnancy, labor, delivery, and the perinatal period which is potentially damaging to children is excessively prevalent among economically depressed populations (Illsley, 1967), and particularly among those further handicapped by ethnic differences.

Pasamanick, Knobloch, and Lilienfeld (1956), in reexamining some earlier data on a group of randomly selected hospital births, found that the incidence of reproductive complications increased

as one moved from the white upper economic fifth through the
white lower economic fifth to the nonwhite group. The "important" complications (in terms of risk to the fetus) of bleeding and
toxemia increased from 5% to 10% to 21.8%, and the total complications increased from 5% to 14.6% in the two white groups and
then jumped to 50.6% in the nonwhite group. More recent data from
Donnelly *et al.* (1964), as seen in Figures 3.1 and 3.2, show the occurrence in two white and two nonwhite hospital populations (representing about 29,561 births) of various reproductive complications.
Except for blood incompatibilities, there is a clear increase for both
single and total complications from the upper-class white to the
lower-class nonwhite.

It has been long acknowledged that exposure to disturbances
of the reproductive process is associated with the risk of serious
physical or intellectual handicap for at least some of the children

Donnelly *et al.*, 1964

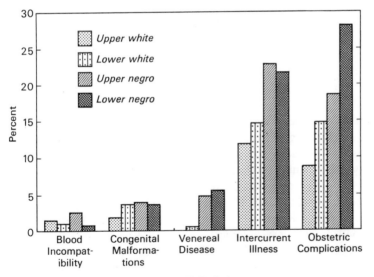

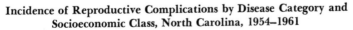

FIGURE 3.1

**Incidence of Reproductive Complications by Disease Category and
Socioeconomic Class, North Carolina, 1954–1961**

(University hospital births)

Donnelly *et al.*, 1964

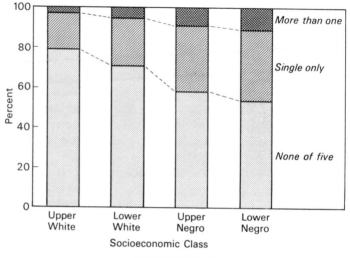

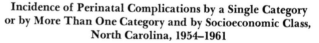

FIGURE 3.2

**Incidence of Perinatal Complications by a Single Category
or by More Than One Category and by Socioeconomic Class,
North Carolina, 1954–1961**

(*University hospital births*)

who survive such exposures (Little, 1862). In the past two decades, however, a suggestive series of studies by Pasamanick and his associates has advanced a somewhat broader notion, namely that these abnormalities may produce a "continuum of reproductive casualty," including disorders which range all the way from the catastrophic to the relatively minor. It must be viewed as a possibility, they have argued, that all men are conceived equal and that later differences in neurological, psychological, and intellectual status derive from exposure to risks of maldevelopment in the periods before, during, and after birth. Noting that there was a pattern of pregnancy and birth complications associated with fetal and neonatal death due to brain injury, Pasamanick and his group hypothesized that among the surviving infants "there must remain a fraction so injured who do not die, but, depending on the degree and location of trauma, go on to develop a series of disorders extending from cerebral palsy, epilepsy, and mental deficiency, through all types of behavioral and learning disabilities, resulting from lesser degrees of damage sufficient to disorganize behavioral development and lower thresholds to stress" (Pasamanick and Knobloch, 1960).

In a series of retrospectively organized studies these investigators found a significant excess of prematurity and/or complications of pregnancy and birth in the histories of individuals afflicted with cerebral palsy, epilepsy, mental deficiency, behavior disorders, reading disabilities, strabismus, hearing disorders, and autism. Of the various conditions examined in these studies, only tics, childhood accidents, and juvenile delinquency showed no significant excess of pregnancy or perinatal abnormalities when "cases" were compared with control groups. (Lilienfeld and Parkhurst, 1951; Lilienfeld and Pasamanick, 1955—cerebral palsy. Pasamanick and Lilienfeld, 1954, 1955; Lilienfeld and Pasamanick, 1955—epilepsy. Pasamanick and Lilienfeld, 1955; Lilienfeld and Pasamanick, 1956—mental deficiency. Pasamanick, Constantinou, and Lilienfeld, 1956—speech disorders. Pasamanick, Rogers, and Lilienfeld, 1956—behavior disorders. Pasamanick and Kawi, 1956—tics. Kawi and Pasamanick, 1958—reading disorders. Knobloch and Pasamanick, 1963—strabismus, childhood accidents, autism, juvenile delinquency.)

Although there are a number of difficulties both statistical and methodological (see McMahon and Sowa, 1961) which complicate any straightforward cause-and-effect interpretation of these data, the studies as a group provide support to the broadest possible view of the problem which concerns us; that is, that exposure of the fetus to abnormalities of pregnancy and the birth process may be associated not only with devastating handicap to the child but also with a range of lesser handicaps, including some psychological abnormalities (e.g., behavioral difficulties) in which there has been traditionally no necessary assumption of a damaged soma underlying a malfunctioning psyche.

It is not our intention in the present chapter, however, to consider this full range of socially distributed abnormalities of the reproductive process. Rather we are electing here to examine at some length the risks associated with, and the distribution of, the single most prevalent abnormality associated with natality—low birth weight. The rationale for such a decision is quite simply the fact that prematurity,[*] as a disturbance in outcome rather than a complication of pregnancy or the birth process, is associated in practice with a whole host of major reproductive complications—multiple birth, placenta previa, premature separation, severe bleeding, chronic hypertension, heart disease, preeclampsia, eclampsia, induced labor, precipitate delivery, cesarean section, neonatal anoxia, to name the most significant—so that an examination of the epidemiology of prematurity alone allows us not only to avoid uneconomical repetition in our presentation, but also to draw a reasonably accurate picture of the overall distribution of the significant reproductive abnormalities (Eastman, 1947; Eastman and DeLeon, 1955; Turnbull and Walker, 1956; Thurston *et al.*, 1960; Freedman *et al.*, 1961; Raiha, 1962; Lubchenco *et al.*, 1963; Dann *et al.*, 1964; Heimer *et al.*, 1964; Donnelly *et al.*, 1964.)

The very interrelationships with other complications of the reproductive process which make prematurity a representative entity, of course, introduce complications into any assessment of its importance as a "cause" of damage. Under some circumstances, prematurity may represent the appropriate termination of a pregnancy complicated by an already imperfect relationship between mother and fetus, for fetuses which are primarily defective or otherwise in trouble *in utero* are more likely to be born before term, often following a complicated pregnancy, than are those infants not so threatened in the womb. On the other hand, infants who are born prematurely, even when no history of complications is present and no congenital abnormality is visible, are more liable to abnormal development than are infants born at term.

Whether, in any given case, prematurity is causal or merely symptomatic is often difficult to determine except where preexisting damage is clearly evident at the time of birth. Most malformation

<hr />

[*]We are not unmindful of the fact that infants weighing under 2,500 grams at birth can be separated into those who are indeed "premature" in arriving and those who are full-term but underweight. The term "prematurity" is here used to denote both, because risk apparently attaches to the condition (e.g., Gruenwald *et al.*, 1963; Jantzen *et al.*, 1968) whether it is defined by the weight of the child at birth or by the maturity of certain of its physiologic functions or by its gestational age (the most difficult definition to utilize with any accuracy in practice for lower socioeconomic groups).

clearly occurs early, at the time when the organs and tissues are differentiating and developing most rapidly. Anoxia too may be early and chronic. In neither case can damage in the infant be counted against the events at birth. Yet as Baird (1959) among others has pointed out, infants in trouble in the womb may be particularly vulnerable to perinatal stress, so that premature birth in already stressed infants may be productive of further or more extensive damage. When a series of abnormal reproductive events has terminated in the birth of a damaged infant, it is, of course, diagnostically and theoretically critical to determine which event produced that damage; but it is of limited significance to the issues we are raising. We are arguing only that populations which experience a higher-than-average incidence of premature births have children who were exposed to higher-than-average rates of risk for damage—whatever its cause.

Of all the known complications of pregnancy and parturition, no single condition is more clearly associated with a wide range of insult to the nervous system than the too early expulsion into the world of a child scarcely able to function as an independent organism. Survivors, especially those in the lowest birth-weight ranges, are at much greater risk than full-term infants of severe neurological, mental, sensory, or other defects. Cerebral palsy is one of these, a malady for which, it has been observed, prematurity "is the one etiological factor which has been established peradventure" (Eastman and DeLeon, 1955). Prematurity has also been implicated in such other serious handicaps as epilepsy (Lilienfeld and Pasamanick, 1954), severe mental retardation (Ascher and Roberts, 1949; Pasamanick and Lilienfeld, 1955; Lilienfeld and Pasamanick, 1956; Fairweather and Illsley, 1960; Drillien, 1965), autism and other serious mental illness (Knobloch and Pasamanick, 1962a; Zitrin, 1964; Pollin et al., 1966), and blindness (McDonald, 1962; Dann et al., 1964).

In addition to these devastating handicaps, there is evidence from a variety of recent anterospective studies that premature children are also subject to a number of somewhat lesser physical, sensory, and neurological defects. Harper and Wiener (1965), reviewing these studies, found them in general agreement that prematures were persistently shorter and lighter than full-term controls, tended to be more often hospitalized for illness, and suffered from a high incidence of "visual, hearing, and other defects," with the deficit increasing as birth weight declined. Data from a long-term study in Baltimore, for example, showed impaired hearing in 3.6% of the prematures as compared with less than 1% of a matched group of full-term children (Harper and Wiener, 1965). Goldstein et al. (1967) found low birth weight, especially birth weight under 2,001 grams, to be much more common among children with strabismus than among a group of matched controls; and Drillien, in Edinburgh, found strabismus in 5% of children weighing above 4½ pounds at birth, in 11% of those weighing between 3½ and 4½ pounds, and in 16% of those very small babies of birth weight 3½ pounds or less.

Four studies of very small babies (maximum allowable weights ranging from 1,000 grams to 1,800 grams) by Drillien (1964, 1965), Dann et al. (1958, 1964), Lubchenco et al. (1963), and McDonald (1962, 1963, 1964) show a striking level of "visible" damage among these smallest babies. Drillien (1965) found that of 72 children weighing 3 pounds or less at birth who had passed school entering age, 75% had some congenital defect or mental retardation. Dann et al. (1964) found a 59% incidence of serious visual impairment, but a relatively low incidence of other disorders among 100 very small infants whom they followed up. However, among 83 infants whose parents did not make them available for follow-up, only one-third of the 60 on whom data were available were "normal" at 6 months, and 32 were known to be defective mentally. Lubchenco et al. (1963) found 43 of 63 children in their study to be handicapped in some respect by defects of the eye or the central nervous system or both (26 children had multiple handicaps). McDonald (1962), who alone included children up to 4 pounds and was therefore likely to find the lowest proportion of gross damage, judged 22% of the children in her sample to have some degree of neurologic or ophthalmic defect. Thus the recent studies of very low birth weight children support the conclusion that there is a very high incidence of neurological and physical defect among them.*

* Data on eye defects among such children prior to 1953 are complicated by the presence of retrolental fibroplasia (RLF), a serious visual defect which cannot be "counted against" prematurity per se because it is apparently related to dam-

LOW BIRTH WEIGHT AND HANDICAP

Substantial numbers of such very small infants are born in this country every year. In 1965, 1.3% of the total number of births in the U.S.—some 49,000 infants—were under 1,500 grams at birth (NCHS, Vital Statistics of the U.S., 1965). Thus the poor odds for the intact survival of such children represent a health problem of considerable proportions. Nevertheless, from a strictly numerical standpoint, it is neither the visible defects nor the lowest birth weight babies (whose high mortality rate presently eliminates large numbers of them from further consideration) which most concern us. From the standpoint of education and public health, the far more critical area of concern is the fate of that great number of low birth weight children most of whom are not so small or so obviously damaged. The issue is whether there is, in fact, a continuum of damage such that the impact of prematurity, which is so evident and so potent in the lowest birth weight ranges, extends its effects, though perhaps to a lesser degree, up through the higher weight ranges, producing more subtle and widespread damage and resulting in a generally reduced level of mental functioning among those survivors who are not grossly handicapped.

The question is critical enough to have been asked for decades. Thirty years ago, Benton (1940) reviewed the literature then available, and found the evidence contradictory. "Some authors maintain that, as a group, prematurely born children are radically inferior to the average in their mental development, and others insist with equal vigor that the mental development of these children compares favorably with that of full-term children." He noted, however, that

---

agingly high incubator oxygen levels—i.e., to inappropriate management rather than to prematurity itself. Four-fifths of the serious eye defects reported by Lubchenco, and more than three-quarters of those recorded by McDonald, were related to RLF; and Dann (1964) found that among 11 very low birth weight children born after 1955, only 5 had any eye defects: 4 with strabismus and 1 with myopia. It should be noted, however, that since prematurity by definition requires "management," the premature is particularly subject to the kind of errors which can produce damage. Moreover, as Harper and Wiener (1965) point out, there are some small infants who appear to need high oxygen levels or for whom prolonged O_2 therapy is apparently needed to reduce the risk of cerebral palsy. "Managing" such an infant offers a Hobson's choice, suggesting that at present the womb may be the only place where some fetal infants can be appropriately managed, and emphasizing once again that the premature is an infant at special risk.

most of the studies up to that time were marred by rather serious defects in technique. Intelligence was often estimated by the method of "clinical impression," based on noncomparable or nonstandardized tests or calculated from the reports of parents. Children were ranked by such nonquantifiable qualities as "leaving something to be desired," a pejorative which some observers might wish to apply with varying implications to most children. In many of the studies there was no normal comparison group, and there was usually insufficient concern for the economic status of the children.

Social status and economic level are critical variables where prematurity is concerned; for if one is to demonstrate an association between low birth weight and subsequent intellectual impairment in the child, one must take into account the acknowledged associations between depressed social and economic status and reproductive abnormalities, on the one hand, and depressed social and economic status and lowered IQ scores on the other. It is possible, in other words, that what depresses the mean IQ scores of groups of premature children is merely the excessive representation among them of poor children whose IQ scores are lowered in any event.

The data Benton reviewed did not permit a judgment on this score. But more recent anterospective data on several groups of prematures followed since birth make it possible to conclude that even when grossly damaged infants are eliminated from consideration, groups of children born prematurely have somewhat lower mean IQs than do *economically comparable* groups of children born at term. Wiener, reviewing two decades of studies since 1940, concluded that "of 18 studies reporting measures of IQ only one failed to find premature subjects at a disadvantage" (1962). Harper and Wiener found that data available by 1965 confirmed the lowered intelligence test scores of children of low birth weight, and that "three major studies using large numbers of children note progressively lower intelligence test scores with increasingly low birth weight." In pursuing our investigation of the hazard associated with premature birth we will examine these three studies and a number of others, beginning with one other large British study, that of Douglas, which includes data on the school achievement of prematures.

Douglas followed a group of prematures, selected from the British

TABLE 3.1

Scores on Tests of Mental Ability
and School Achievement, at Age 8 and 11

	Controls	Prematures	Difference
Tests at 8 years (408 pairs)			
Sentence completion	50.9	47.9	−3.0*
Reading	51.0	48.0	−3.0*
Vocabulary	50.0	48.3	−1.7*
Picture intelligence	50.5	47.7	−2.8*
Tests at 11 years (355 pairs)			
Reading	50.1	47.1	−3.0*
Vocabulary	50.3	47.3	−3.0*
Arithmetic	50.4	46.6	−3.8*
Mental ability	51.1	46.9	−4.2*

* Each of these differences is statistically highly significant when tested by Student's t-test.

Douglas, 1960

National Maternity Survey of March 1946, until they were 11 years of age. The infants were matched, shortly after birth, with full-term infants from the same cohort on the basis of age, sex, position in family, type of home background, age and social class of parents, and (where possible) locality of residence. Intelligence data on the children have been reported in two papers (Douglas, 1956, 1960) based on tests given to 407 matched pairs (of the original 675) when they were 8 years old, and a second set of tests given to 309 pairs when they were 11. Table 3.1 shows the test scores of the prematures and their controls for both test periods. On both occasions the prematures made significantly lower scores, with a decline in their general level between the first and the second set of tests. Douglas concluded, however, that as a consequence of changes in family circumstances children who had been properly matched at birth were no longer so well matched at the ages of testing. He therefore discounted the results on the ground that there had been inadequate control of factors relevant to intellectual stimulation. His reanalysis, based on a rematching of groups on these factors, will be considered later.

School-age IQ data are also available from what is perhaps the best-controlled study, that of a group of prematures first reported on by Knobloch *et al.* (1956) when they were infants. This was a balanced sample of 500 prematures born in Baltimore in 1952 and, like the Douglas sample, matched individually with full-term control infants by race, age, parity of mother, hospital, season of birth, and socioeconomic status (based on census tract of residence and maternal education). When the children were between 6 and 7 years old, a recomparison of just under 400 pairs of cases and controls remaining in the study on a variety of measures of maternal attitude and social class showed that the original matching had effectively controlled for economic and social variables (Wiener *et al.,* 1965). As was the case with Douglas' scoring, the Baltimore data included only apparently "normal" children, excluding all those who were blind or otherwise grossly handicapped or uncooperative, or who had IQ scores of less than 50. Examinations of the prematures at ages 3–5 showed them to be intellectually retarded relative to their controls and less likely to be either physically or neurologically normal (Knobloch *et al.,* 1959; Harper *et al.,* 1959). Subsequently Stanford-Binet scores for these children at ages 6–7 and their WISC scores at ages 8–10 have become available (Wiener *et al.,* 1965; Wiener *et al.,* 1968). At both testing periods lower birth weights were associated with lower test scores, the term controls scoring a mean 95.6 on the Stanford-Binet and a mean 94.7 on the WISC. Children whose birth weights had been between 1,500 and 1,999 grams scored on the average 5 points lower on the Stanford-Binet when they were between 6 and 7 years old, and 6.2 points lower on the WISC when they were between 8 and 10.

Two other large studies which have used group rather than individual controls have obtained results somewhat discrepant with those of the Baltimore group. McDonald (1964) has published IQ data on the infants in her earlier mentioned study of very low birth weight infants in which she concluded that when twins and children with cerebral palsy, blindness, deafness, or IQs below 50 were excluded, the mean IQ of her prematures did *not* differ from the mean IQ of the general population. Her sample is large, consisting of all those surviving infants of birth weights up to 4 pounds admitted over a year-and-a-half period to one of 19 premature units in various British hospitals. One hundred and sixty-six of 1,128 children discharged alive were located when they were between 6 and 8 years of age, and 905 of them were tested (721 single births) on the Stanford-Binet by psychologists or local school officials in their districts. Since their social class distribution (based on fathers' occupations) appeared consistent with that of the population at large, their scores were compared with those of whole population samples. Omitting 90 single children who had cerebral palsy or were blind or deaf, 6 in whom testing was unsatisfactory, and 11 others in whom the IQ was under 50, McDonald found the average IQ score of the whole group to be 102.4—not significantly below that of the national comparison samples. Actually, as Harper and Wiener have pointed out, the two groups are difficult to compare since there is no evidence that the IQ tests were equivalently administered and scored or that the total population sample had been similarly selected—i.e., had omitted all damaged children. More to the point, perhaps, is the fact that within the low birth weight group, children with lower birth weights were impaired relative to those with higher birth weights; those in the birth weight group 3 pounds or less having a mean IQ of 98.6 compared to a mean IQ of 103.4 for those 3.1 to 4 pounds.

Drillien (1964) found much larger differences in IQ associated with reduced birth weight in a longitudinal study involving 251 low birth weight singletons, 127 low birth weight twins, and 212 infants (119 singletons, and 93 twins), each with a birth weight of over 5½ pounds. Since prematurity in Edinburgh, as in the U. S., is associated with lower economic status and since the control group was randomly chosen—from births following directly after premature births—lower classes are somewhat overrepresented in the premature group, a fact which may affect Drillien's overall comparisons. Drillien found significant differences in development associated with birth weight at all ages up to 5, with the least difference by birth weight occurring at 18 months. At 4 years mean developmental quotients (DQs) were 106.7 for full-term controls, 99.2 for children between 4½ and 5½ pounds, 96.8 for those between 3½ and 4½ pounds, and 80.2 for infants under 3½ pounds at birth.

Table 3.2 compares the results from Drillien and McDonald with those of the Baltimore group at two ages. Drillien's results ob-

TABLE

Scores on Mental Development Tests

	Pounds	Grams	Pounds	Pounds
	3 or less	>1,500	>3–3½	3½ or less
Drillien				
4 years, DQ				80.2
Baltimore				
6–7 years, SB		88.9		
8–10 years, WISC		84.7		
McDonald				
6–9 years, SB	98.5		103.0	

viously show the most marked decline of IQ with birth weight of any of the studies. Drillien, of course, included twins and did not exclude severely defective children from her means, a fact which helps to explain the differences between hers and other findings. It should be noted, however, that as Table 3.3 shows, the effect of including twins is to lower the DQ scores of both standard and low birth weight groups, not merely to increase the differences between them. On the other hand, Drillien's inclusion of 35 children judged mentally retarded or neurologically damaged does tend to lower the scores of the low birth weight children as a group.

TABLE 3.3

Mean DQs at Age 4 by Birth Weight, Singletons and Twins

	Weight in Pounds			
	3½ or less	>3½–4½	>4½–5½	>5½
Singletons	82.5	97.3	100.1	108.7
Twins	73.3	95.9	97.0	103.5

Drillien, 1964

3.2

at Various Ages by Birth Weight

Grams	Pounds	Grams	Pounds	Pounds
1,501–1,999	>3½–4½	2,000–2,500	>4½–5½	>5½
	96.8		99.2	106.7
90.6		93.0		95.6
88.5		90.8		94.7
	103.8			

Present evidence, then, supports the notion that even when the effects of social class on IQ and prematurity distribution are controlled, groups of premature children are likely to achieve somewhat lower mean DQ scores in their preschool years and somewhat lower mean IQ scores at school age than are full-term children, and that scores within the premature group will tend to decrease with decreasing birth weight. It is entirely possible, however, that the data so far presented, showing only a moderate IQ decline with declining birth weight, vastly underestimate the actual impact of premature birth on children in the lowest social classes, especially on what is the specific focus of our concern: the school achievement of children in these groups. For one thing, IQ alone is only a partial measure of the consequences which may attach to low birth weight. For another, it is quite possible that even on strictly IQ measures the impact of premature birth may not be equal for children raised under quite unequal social conditions.

Table 3.4 from Harper and Wiener (1965) presents data relevant to the second of these issues and suggests that prematurity may be a handicap to children in all classes. When the Drillien, McDonald, and Baltimore data are looked at by social class, prematurity does appear to have affected the IQ among all groups except the upper-class children in McDonald's study. Characteristically, IQ scores

TABLE 3.4

Comparison of Mental Development Data from Three Longitudinal Studies

DRILLIEN (1964): *Mean DQ scores at 4 years*

Birth Weight	SOCIAL CLASS			All Cases	
(pounds, ounces)	Upper	Middle	Lower	Mean	Number
<3–9	97.1	72.8	63.6	80.2	40
3–9–4–8	102.2	93.1	84.0	96.8	77
4–9–5–8	103.8	101.4	87.8	99.2	123
>5–8	110.2	102.7	95.3	106.7	126

MC DONALD (1964): *Mean Stanford-Binet IQ scores at 6–9 years of age*

Birth Weight			SOCIAL CLASS					
	Upper		Middle		Lower		All Cases	
(pounds, ounces)	Mean	Number	Mean	Number	Mean	Number	Mean	Number
<3–1	106.7	29	98.4	64	92.3	38	98.5	131
3–1–3–8	121.6	16	102.7	95	98.2	56	103.0	167
3–9–4–0	111.8	54	104.2	161	98.1	86	103.8	301

BALTIMORE (Wiener *et al.*, 1965): *Mean Stanford-Binet IQ scores at 6–7 years of age*

Birth Weight			SOCIAL CLASS					
	Upper		Middle		Lower		All Cases	
(grams)	Mean	Number	Mean	Number	Mean	Number	Mean	Number
<1,500	95.9	12	88.1	23	81.6	9	88.9	44
1,500–1,999	101.1	10	88.8	31	88.7	27	90.6	68
2,000–2,500	103.3	73	91.9	142	86.1	86	93.0	301
>2,500	104.9	116	93.4	184	89.3	109	95.6	409

F ratio for birth weight: 7.77, 3, and 810 df, p < .001

| Birth Weight | SOCIAL CLASS | | | | | | | |
| | Upper | | Middle | | Lower | | All Cases | |
(grams)	Mean	Number	Mean	Number	Mean	Number	Mean	Number
<1,500	88.6	13	81.1	18	86.0	10	84.7	41
1,501–1,999	91.7	15	91.8	32	82.7	27	88.5	74
2,000–2,500	94.8	93	89.1	110	89.0	99	90.8	302
>2,500	98.0	145	94.7	158	89.9	102	94.7	405

F ratio for birth weight: 10.84, 3, and 810 df, p < .001

show a double gradient, declining as expected with social class regardless of birth weight, and declining with birth weight within each social class group so that the most extreme differences within the premature groups occur between the IQ scores of the heaviest infants in the upper class and the lightest infants in the lowest class. In the case of Drillien's subjects there is a difference of more than 46 points between these extremes. But although the data seem to support the idea that there may be an effect of prematurity in every social class, they do not really allow for a judgment on the corollary question of whether prematurity is an equivalent * risk condition in every social class. In Drillien's and McDonald's studies, the deficit is clearly more marked among lower-class children. In the Baltimore study, however, the percent of IQ decline from the highest to the lowest birth weight groups is almost identical for upper and lower social classes at ages 6–7; and at older ages greater relative deficit appears to be associated with membership in the higher economic groups. Since white and Negro data are not separated it is impossible to tell whether this finding may not be an artifact of a reported marked decline in DQ among the Negro controls (Knobloch and Pasamanick, 1961), beginning sometime after the 40-week examination and resulting, by the time of the 3–5 year examination,

---

* Even an equivalent IQ decline would not imply equivalent handicap, since a 10% reduction in IQ from 120 to 108 would undoubtedly have less profound effects on the future of a middle-class child than would a comparable reduction, from 100 to 90, on the prospects of a lower-class child.

in a mean difference of almost 14 points between white and Negro DQs (110.9 compared to 97.4).

Given these difficulties with the available American data, the most suggestive findings on the interaction of prematurity and social class are from a study in Aberdeen, Scotland (Illsley, 1966), dealing with a total population of births of known social class and relative ethnic homogeneity. These data show clearly that the relationship between low birth weight and IQ is affected by social class. The IQ scores of the children from the lowest social classes appear to have been seriously depressed by their birth weight status, poor economic circumstances having apparently potentiated the risk associated with premature birth. In the upper classes, on the other hand, birth weight appears to have had little effect on IQ scores, suggesting that

Adapted from Werner *et al.*, 1967

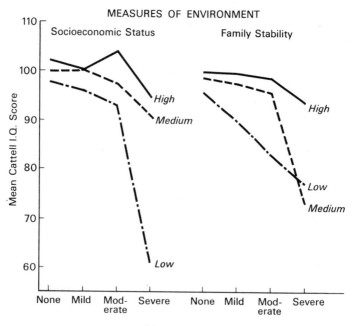

FIGURE 3.3

Mean Cattell IQ Scores at Age 2 by Severity of
Perinatal Complications and Estimates of Two Environmental
Measures, Kauai, Hawaii, 1955

a beneficent postnatal environment is capable of compensating almost fully for whatever initial handicap is associated with underweight at birth. Since we have argued earlier that prematurity can be used as a generalized indicator of reproductive risk, it is interesting to observe the similarities between the Aberdeen low birth weight data and Figure 3.3 which presents data from the Kauai pregnancy study on children exposed to varying levels of complication around birth (Werner et al., 1967). As was true among the Aberdeen babies, even severe perinatal stress appeared to be compensable in good postnatal environments; for children from the poorest homes, however, the interaction between reproductive and environmental hazards represented a cumulative risk which had a profound effect on IQ levels of those lower-class children exposed to the severest perinatal stress.

Such biosocial interactions have been observed in several of the premature studies. Figure 3.4 presents Drillien's IQ data for her prematures at ages 5–7. As can be seen, there is little actual handicap among the children from the best homes except at birth weights under 3½ pounds. In other social groups, however, decreasing birth weight was associated with a marked increase in the number of backward and seriously handicapped children. Drillien has concluded that prematures in the weight range 4½ to 5½ pounds from advantaged homes run by competent mothers are not seriously handicapped relative to full-term infants from the same kinds of homes; but that where children are from poor homes, even this moderate degree of prematurity is likely to be handicapping. Dann et al. (1964), in their follow-up of infants with birth or postnatal weights of 1,000 grams or less, found the greatest IQ change after the age of 4 years in a pair of premature male twins one of whom increased 13 points (from 82 to 95) and the other 15 points (from 96 to 111) for no apparent reason other than the fact that they lived in an "intellectually and socially stimulating environment."

These results are not surprising. It is obvious that, between the time of birth and the time when IQ can be reliably tested, children are exposed to a variety of factors in the postnatal environment which may be either hostile to or supportive of development. In a subsequent chapter we will be exploring the characteristics of the postnatal environment of poor children. What the prematurity data

Drillien, 1964

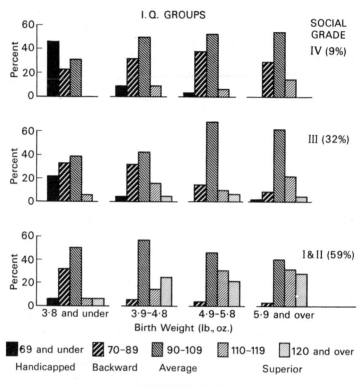

I. Q. GROUPS

SOCIAL GRADE
IV (9%)

III (32%)

I & II (59%)

Birth Weight (lb., oz.)

■ 69 and under ▨ 70–89 ▧ 90–109 ▨ 110–119 ☐ 120 and over

Handicapped　Backward　Average　　　Superior

FIGURE 3.4

**Intellectual Ability at Age 5 to 7 by Birth Weight and
Social Grade, Edinburgh**

(*Percentage of total population*)
Social grades I, II = middle class and superior working class;
III = average working class; IV = poor working class.

tell us is that circumstances which may adversely affect all poor
children (the declining DQs among the Baltimore controls?) are
especially noxious for the premature child whose need for a fostering
environment is apparently maximal.

It would appear, then, that there is a differential risk associated
with prematurity in terms of the social class in which it occurs, and

that the interactions between prematurity and environment are complexly mediated and affect the prospects of the premature child both before and after birth. When added to the stresses of being poor and lower-class, premature birth is a cumulative condition of risk— so far as measurable IQ is concerned—not merely uncompensated for by events succeeding natality, but exacerbated by the adverse circumstances in which the lower-class child lives.

Thus far we have been considering the outcome of low birth weight in terms of such general measures as IQ, DQ, and evidence of neurologic damage. However, as Harper and Wiener (1965) have pointed out, global IQ scores may tend to obscure "the degree to which low birth weight is a correlate of mental impairment. . . . Generally accepted psychiatric theory would lead to the prediction that mild neurologic deficit would be associated with aberrations in perception, perceptual-motor integration, abstract reasoning, short attention span, to name but a few possibly relevant variables." The Baltimore group examined this hypothesis by testing their prematures at ages 6–7 on a variety of psychological measures and found a correlation between birth weight and impairment on five of the six measures (all except the Goodenough IQ). The best predictors in discriminating normal from abnormal development proved to be the Bender-Gestalt test of visual-motor coordination and an evaluation of perseveration trends, ability to comprehend instructions, and concreteness of thinking which they called "thinking mode" (Wiener et al., 1965). Data subsequently reported on the WISC given to the children at 8–10 years of age showed that the abstract verbal reasoning (similarities) and perceptual-motor integration (block design, object assembly) subtests were more affected by low birth weight than was the total IQ score (Wiener et al., 1968).

But premature children are not only impaired intellectually— whether grossly or subtly; they have also been found by virtually all investigators to be more subject to personality disturbances than children of higher birth weight, a fact not without its significance for performance. Wiener, in his 1962 review, found that of ten studies reporting on personality development only Pasamanick and Kawi's (1956) study of children with tics failed to find prematures overrepresented among groups of individuals with personality disorders. Pasamanick et al. (1956) found prematurity three times as often in the histories of white children with behavior disorders, and three and one-half times as prevalent among behaviorally disturbed Negro children as among their respective control groups.

Drillien (1964), too, found that at school age prematures had more difficulty adjusting to the school routine than maturely born children of equal intelligence from similar types of homes; and decreasing birth weight was associated with an increasing proportion of children judged "unsettled or maladjusted" by their teachers. Moreover, environmental disadvantage appeared to increase the impact of biological handicap. Drillien found that severe familial stress in the absence of other adverse factors produced "borderline to obvious maladjustment" at school age in less than 10% of the maturely born controls. However, such stress produced maladjustment in almost half of those who had been subjected to complications before or during birth, and in more than half of those who had both complications and a birth weight of less than 4½ pounds.

Wortis also found a high level of deviant behavior among a group of Negro prematures from lower-class families assessed at 2½ years (Wortis et al., 1964). Both the degree of prematurity and the overall deviant behavior scores were correlated with a diagnosis of neurologic abnormality. But though there were significant differences between brain-injured and non-brain-injured children in the various personality deviations mentioned, a high percentage of all the prematures were recorded as having sleeping or eating difficulties. Whether or not such behavioral difficulties are associated with a reduced IQ score, they are quite capable of affecting school performance. Drillien found, for example, that among children from the "best" homes twice as many children of birth weight 4½ pounds or less were working *below capacity* in school as were their mature controls (26% vs. 13%), apparently largely because of behavior problems.

Thus it is clear that the impact of premature birth on the future prospects of infants is not limited either to the risk of gross defect or—in the remaining children—to some small reduction in IQ scores (British Medical Journal, 1964), but is expressed rather in a constellation of small and large defects, the impact of which it is difficult to assess except in terms of society's ultimate goals for these children. If these goals include acceptable levels of achievement at school age, then we must be concerned not only with the small proportion of premature children considered severely handicapped or, in the traditional sense, "brain-damaged," but with all those children who —vulnerable as a result of circumstances attending their entry into the world—come to suffer minor disorders of perception and cognition, an increase in impulsivity or distractibility, a delay in the mastery of certain body functions, or any of the handicaps associated with physical impairment. All together, such abnormalities may directly or indirectly interfere with the normal intellectual development and school achievement of a sizeable number of premature children, especially those raised under poor material conditions.

Drillien's findings on the disposition of her very low birth weight babies at school age are revealing. Of the 72 children who had entered school, only 29% were working in a regular school in classes appropriate to their age; and only 10% (7 children) were working at average or above average levels for their class and age. Another 43% (31 children) were in normal school but receiving special treatment (19 were already from 1 to 3 years retarded for their age). On the basis of these findings, and of her examinations of the children who had not yet reached school age, Drillien concluded that of the children who weighed 3 pounds or less at birth, "over one-third of the total group are ineducable in normal school for reason of physical or mental handicap or both. Over one-third are dull children who will probably be retained in normal school but will require special educational treatment, and less than one-third are low average or above average in ability. These figures should be compared with those for Scotland generally, according to which about 3% of the population require special schooling for mental, physical or psychological handicap and probably no more than 10% require special educational treatment in normal schools." Even when intelligence was normal, Drillien noted, prematurely born children in this group, like the larger prematures, "were more likely to be working below their intellectual capacity in school than were maturely born children of like intelligence from similar homes" (1965).

Lubchenco et al., who studied 63 children whose birth weights were 3 pounds 4 ounces or under, found a "troublesome lack of correlation between intelligence quotients and school performance, particularly in children of normal intelligence" (1963). Twenty of

35 children with normal intelligence had experienced difficulties in schooling (11 had repeated one or more of the first three grades); and though the authors concluded that the specific reasons for the failures were not clear, subtle brain damage, specific reading problems, and hearing losses appeared to play a part.

These studies, of course, concern the smallest babies. School achievement data on the Baltimore prematures have not been published, but Wiener *et al.* (1968) have reported that prematures and controls were separable on a "composite psychological efficiency ranking," and that data have been collected showing that prematures have impaired school achievement at age 13. Some of the most interesting data, on a sample of prematures heavily weighted with infants over $4\frac{1}{2}$ pounds, come from Douglas (1960). He found that on an academic selection exam given at age 11 for admission to secondary school, the premature group scored lower than their socially matched controls; only 9.7% of them gained a place in the more selective grammar schools compared with 22% of their controls. Moreover, the prematures received more adverse comments from their teachers when the latter were asked to "assess their powers of concentration, attitude to work, and discipline."

Douglas, however, rematched the prematures and controls in an attempt to fully equate background variables relevant to achievement. Three groups of significant environmental variables were identified: (1) social and educational background of both parents; (2) maternal care and management; and (3) interest of parents in school progress. Prematures whose backgrounds were superior on one, two, or three counts were scored +1, +2, or +3; and −1, −2, or −3 ratings were given where controls had superior backgrounds. The following data show the effect of separating the children on these measures in terms of the percentages who were admitted to the selective grammar schools.

Superiority in background factors clearly improved the achievement of the premature; but regardless of the degree of superiority (as measured in this study), premature children were unable to gain a *significant* advantage in terms of school placement. A poorer family background, on the other hand, even in terms of a single factor (−1), produced a highly significant relative decline in the proportion of premature children who were able to score sufficiently high for grammar school placement. Thus, so far as school achievement is concerned, prematurity once again represents a potential risk, differentially realized according to the environment in which it occurs. A poor environment is, then, a special threat to a premature, and prematurity is a special threat to a child from a poor environment.

Ratings of background factors		Difference in % of children receiving grammar school placement	
favorable to premature	+3	+25.0	
	+2	+11.1	not significant
	+1	+ 2.5	
equal		− 4.9	
favorable to control	−1	−22.6	
	−2	−26.6	highly significant
	−3	−47.6	

Having established the risk associated with low birth weight, especially for children born into lower-class groups, we are now ready to examine the frequency with which births of under 2,500 grams occur among different social groups in this country. As the Pasamanick data have suggested, the risk of producing a low birth weight baby is not regularly distributed throughout the childbearing population; prematurity, in whatever society it has been studied, inevitably occurs to excess in the lower social strata and among the most significantly disadvantaged peoples. Since the data in the last chapter led us to conclude that the most disadvantaged group in the U. S. will generally be found among those classified as nonwhite, it is no surprise to find that it is the nonwhite population which experiences the highest rates of prematurity.

In Table 3.5 are data on the birth weight distribution by ethnic group of 3,760,358 live births in the U. S. in 1965. For the population as a whole, the percentage of live births weighing 2,500 grams or less was 8.3% of the total. Among the white majority the proportion was lower; 7.2% of babies fell into this weight range. Among nonwhite infants, however, 13.8% weighed 2,500 grams or less, with

TABLE 3.5

**Distribution of Live Births by Birth Weight
and Color, United States, 1965**

(3,760,358 live births)

Birth Weight (grams)	All Births	White	Nonwhite
1,000 or less	0.6%	0.5%	1.1%
1,001–1,500	0.7	0.6	1.2
1,501–2,000	1.6	1.3	2.7
2,001–2,500	5.5	4.8	8.8
2,500–3,000	19.6	18.3	26.2
3,000–3,500	38.3	38.5	37.3
3,500–4,000	25.6	27.1	17.8
4,001–4,500	6.8	7.4	3.9
4,500–5,000	1.2	1.3	0.9
5,001 or more	0.2	0.2	0.1
	100.0%	100.0%	100.0%
Percentage under 2,500 grams	8.3	7.2	13.8
Median weight (grams)	3,290	3,320	3,130
Number of live births	3,760,358	3,123,860	636,498

Number of nonwhite births under 2,500 grams, 87,836

NCHS, Vital Statistics of the U. S., 1965.

their frequency at all levels of low birth weight being twice as great as that of white infants.

Where length of gestation can be calculated—in those parts of the country where birth certificates carry "last menstrual period" (LMP) information—nonwhites appear to be at an even more significant disadvantage than when a judgment of prematurity is based on birth weight. In 1962, 19.5% of the nonwhite babies born in New York City had a gestational age of 36 weeks or less in contrast to 9.5% of white babies; and in Baltimore, where LMP data are also available, 25.3%, or more than one-fourth of nonwhite infants, compared to 10.3% of whites, were delivered at a gestational age of 36 weeks or less (NCHS, PHS 1000, 21:1, 1964).

It is a poor enough record, but the long-term trends are even worse. Although the mortality data which we have already examined might have prepared us to accept a *relative* worsening of the non-whites' position resulting primarily from a somewhat more rapid decline in white prematurity rates, the reality is more alarming. Nonwhites *are* relatively worse off, but it is because white prematurity rates have remained constant while nonwhites have experienced an absolute increase in their rate of premature birth—not merely in a few local areas as is the case with nonwhite mortality, but nationally.* The chart (Table 3.6) shows the long-term trend in low-birth-weight births between 1950 and 1967. The percentage of immaturity among white births remained relatively stable, but the percentage of nonwhite births 2,500 grams or under increased from 10.8 in 1951 to 13.6 in 1967. Because the white rate in 1967 was precisely the same as it was in 1951, the overall increase in premature births during the period (from 7.6 to 8.2) is entirely due to the changing weight among nonwhite births. If the 1951 rate had been maintained, almost 17,000 fewer nonwhite babies would have been born weighing under 2,500 grams in 1967.

It has sometimes been argued that the consistent finding of an excess of low birth weight babies among nonwhites is an ethnic phenomenon: that Negroes "naturally" give birth to smaller babies, and that their high rates of prematurity merely reflect this difference.

---

* Since premature birth is the single most important cause of death among infants—infants who weigh 2,500 grams or less at birth account for two-thirds of the total neonatal deaths in this country (NCHS, PHS 1000, 3:4, 1965)—there is an apparent inconsistency between an overall increase in prematurity among nonwhites accompanying an overall decrease in neonatal mortality. Their excess prematurity does account for a high proportion of the excess mortality among nonwhites; but between 1950 and 1965 the percentage of nonwhite births taking place in hospitals rose from 57.9% to 89.8% (NCHS, Vital Statistics of the U.S., 1965), a situation which has inevitably led to more complete reporting of premature births and higher survival rates for premature infants. In general, it will be recalled, and for reasons not fully understood (p. 29), nonwhite survival rates at equal degrees of prematurity are better than those of whites, though there is no evidence that survival rates in given birth weight groups are presently increasing (NCHS, PHS 1000, 3:4, 1965).

TABLE 3.6

Births Under 2,500 Grams by Color, United States, Selected Years 1951–1967

(percentage of total births)

	White and Nonwhite	White	Nonwhite
1967	8.2%	7.1%	13.6%
1965	8.3	7.2	13.8
1961	7.8	6.9	13.0
1959	7.7	6.8	12.9
1957	7.6	6.8	12.5
1955	7.7	6.9	11.8
1953	7.7	7.1	11.4
1951	7.6	7.1	10.8

Adapted from Natality Statistics Analysis, 1962; NCHS, Vital Statistics of the U. S., 1965; Advance Report, Final, 1967.

Although it is difficult to conceive of a "natural difference" that would increase its penetrance by more than three percentage points over a period of 15 years, the view that Negro babies are "naturally" small has a long if not always scientifically distinguished history. Bivings (cited by Crump *et al.,* 1957) wrote in 1932: "There is a good deal of evidence which would lead one to believe that the pigmented skin of the Negro filters out much of the available ultraviolet light, thus probably playing a part in the production of weakness and lessening birth weight." Meredith (1952), bringing together available data from 1896 to 1951, comparing height, weight, and selected other measurements for white and Negro infants, concluded that "the average North American Negro infant is . . . nearly 4% lighter at birth than the average North American white infant [while] stature at birth is shorter for North American Negroes . . . by about . . . 2%."

For such data to reflect ethnic differences, however, would require that the white and Negro populations involved be equated on other variables which appear to affect birth size and weight, such as maternal height and weight, age and parity, prior pregnancy experience, and, most important, the crosscutting variable of socioeconomic status. Some data from Llewellyn-Jones (1965) suggest the deceptive nature of birth weight comparisons by ethnic group where social class is exerting complex effects. Examining births to 8,555 women at the General Hospital in Kuala Lumpur, Llewellyn-Jones found that although mean birth weights varied significantly for Indian, Malay, and Chinese babies born to lower-class mothers, there were no significant differences by racial stock in the birth weights of infants born to upper-class Indian, Chinese, and Malay mothers. Specific maternal variables are not controlled in the studies Meredith cites; and it should be recalled that since national birth weight statistics did not become available until 1950, birth weight data prior to that time are usually derived from rather specialized and unrepresentative populations. Moreover, so far as socioeconomic status is concerned, Crump (1957) pointed out that there was little or no careful control among the studies, and Meredith himself conceded that "the combined Negro groups typify a slightly lower economic level than the white groups."

National birth weight statistics show that the median nonwhite birth weight is indeed lower by a considerable amount than the

TABLE 3.7

Median Birth Weight by Color, United States, Selected Years 1950–1967

(in grams)

Year	White	Nonwhite
1967	3,310	3,130
1965	3,320	3,130
1964	3,320	3,130
1962	3,320	3,140
1960	3,340	3,150
1957	3,330	3,170
1955	3,330	3,190
1950	3,320	3,250

NCHS, PHS 1000, 21:1, 1964; NCHS, PHS 1000, 21:11, 1967; NCHS, Vital Statistics of the U.S., 1965; NCHS, MSVR, Dec. 4, 1968.

white median, reflecting the much higher proportion of low birth weight babies among nonwhites. The respective figures for 1967 are 3,130 grams for Negro infants and 3,310 grams for whites. Moreover, as Table 3.7 shows, the nonwhite birth weight has undergone an absolute decline of 120 grams over the period 1950 to 1967, while the mean white birth weight has remained remarkably constant. Since it is difficult to argue for a change in the ethnic makeup over the period, the more likely explanation is that there has been a decline in the economic status of the childbearing nonwhite population, or, alternatively, a relative increase in the childbearing of the most economically depressed segment of that population. In either case the explanation for white-nonwhite birth weight differences, like that for ethnic group differences in infant mortality, is largely a socioeconomic one.

The implication of such a statement is that birth weight would vary with socioeconomic status within the nonwhite group. It does. Figure 3.5 shows the birth weight distribution of a group of 1,572 Negro infants divided into four groups according to their socioeconomic status (Crump et al., 1957, 1961). It is clear that throughout much of the weight range there is a very regular effect of socioeconomic classification on birth weight distribution. In fact, one of Crump's findings sheds an interesting light on the relationships between birth weight, ethnic group, and status. Crump (1961) analyzed skin color in 661 newborn Negro infants and their parents and found that lighter mothers did tend to have heavier babies, a finding which would suggest that the "ethnic" argument had some cogency. However, Crump also found that among Negro mothers skin color was really a socioeconomic indicator: that the greater proportion of darker Negroes were in the lower socioeconomic groups, and that the proportion of unmarried mothers was four times as great among those who were dark in color as among those who were light (32.5% compared with 8.8%). Moreover, further doubt was cast on the racial basis of the weight variation by the fact that there was no consistent relationship between the infant's *own* skin color at birth and his birth weight.

Further evidence on the relationship between economic status and birth weight comes from Scott, Jenkins, and Crawford (1950) who analyzed the birth weights of 11,818 Negro infants delivered at Freed-

Crump *et al.*, 1957, 1961

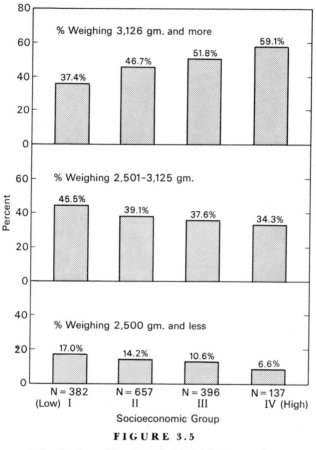

FIGURE 3.5

**Distribution of Specific Birth Weight Categories
by Socioeconomic Group**

man's Hospital in Washington, D.C. As Table 3.8 shows, during the period between 1939 and 1947, when the economic status of the District population, including Negroes, was better than that of the rest of the country, the average birth weight of full-term Negro infants was 3,337 grams—higher than that previously reported for

TABLE 3.8

Relation of Birth Weight to Income, Washington, D.C., 1939–1947

(11,818 Negro births)

Year	Average Male Birth Weight (grams)	Standard Deviation	Average Female Birth Weight (grams)	Standard Deviation	District of Columbia Per Capita Income
1939	3,319	300	3,231	539	$1,031
1940	3,396	431	3,242	409	1,080
1941	3,196	372	3,223	227	1,079
1942	3,401	427	3,279	540	1,212
1943	3,279	286	3,273	499	1,296
1944	3,459	539	3,232	400	1,309
1945	3,428	404	3,337	413	1,376
1946	3,482	518	3,369	418	1,548
1947	3,469	295	3,396	427	1,632

Scott, Jenkins, and Crawford, 1950

Negroes. Moreover, during the four-year period from 1944 to 1947, when the District's per capita income showed a progressive increase, the average full-term birth weights were "suggestively though not consistently higher" than those during the previous 5 years. Though birth weights for these nonwhite infants approached it, they did not reach the norm for American white infants. However, at least half of the infants under scrutiny in the study were classified as indigent. When Scott *et al.* (1950) analyzed the weights of 654 Negro infants seen in private practice who came from lower-middle-class families, the mean birth weight was 3,300 grams (7.20 pounds) for females and 3,500 grams (7.66 pounds) for males, figures which compare favorably with the average for whites.

Higher socioeconomic status is associated not only with a generally higher mean birth weight, but with a specific and marked reduction in the proportion of low birth weight babies in a number of populations where it has been studied. Thomson (1963) found a strong association between prematurity and social class even in a population of relative ethnic homogeneity in Aberdeen. And Drillien (1964) confirmed the importance of social status "even in a relatively prosperous community such as Edinburgh, during a period when little gross poverty existed," finding marked differences in the proportion and in the birth weight distribution of underweight babies related to social class and socioeconomic background. In this prosperous country, at a period when gross poverty *does* exist, it is perhaps even more to the point to note that lower social status within both the white and the nonwhite groups appears to relate significantly to a higher incidence of premature births.

In Table 3.9, data on white premature births in Baltimore during

TABLE 3.9

**Prematurity Rates by Socioeconomic Tenth,
Baltimore, 1950–1951**

Socioeconomic Tenth	Number of Births	Number of Premature Births	Percent Births Premature (Observed)	Percent Births Premature (Adjusted) [a]
Total White	27,979	1,894	6.8	6.8
Highest	3,447	176	5.1	5.0
9	2,382	146	6.1	5.7
8	2,814	162	5.8	5.6
7	2,587	169	6.5	6.6
6	2,526	169	6.7	7.0
5	2,704	191	7.1	7.1
4	2,646	212	8.0	7.9
3	3,075	240	7.8	7.6
2	2,735	206	7.5	7.4
Lowest	3,063	223	7.3	7.6
Nonwhite	14,298	1,621	11.3	11.4

[a] Adjusted for birth order and age of mother

Rider *et al.*, 1955

the years 1950 and 1951 are arranged in deciles according to socioeconomic status (Rider *et al.*, 1955). When the rates were adjusted for age and parity, Rider found that the rate of prematurity increased from 5% in the highest income decile to 7.6% in the lowest;

and though the increase in rate was not uniform, "the trend is quite evident that prematurity is inversely related to economic status." But the study as designed does not dispose of the issue of excessive nonwhite prematurity, since the rate for nonwhites—unclassified as to economic status—was 11.4%, a rate markedly above that of even the poorest whites. This difference, Rider suggested, might be associated with a corresponding difference in socioeconomic level. Fortunately there are data, though not in this study, to support his hypothesis. Crump, in the earlier cited study (1957), examined the effect of social class on prematurity within a Negro group in Nashville, Tennessee. Among 1,572 Negro births he found a mean percentage of prematurity of 13.3, somewhat higher than that found by Rider. But Crump, who was able to classify his subjects economically, also found a "striking" influence of socioeconomic status on the rate of prematurity. When the women were classified into four major economic groups on the basis of marital status, parental educational level, and the father's (or mother's) occupation, the rate of births below 2,500 grams increased from a low of 6.6% in the highest socioeconomic group (a rate comparable to that of whites in the seventh income decile of Rider's study) to a high of 17% in the lowest economic group. When the women were distributed on a scale of 1 to 10, the effect of social class was even more obvious. Prematurity rates ranged from a high of 23.3% in the lowest socioeconomic group to 5.3% in the highest (Figure 3.6).

It is clear from the studies cited that a higher socioeconomic status is correlated with a higher mean birth weight and a lower rate of premature births among both whites and Negroes in this country. Thus any hypothesis which argues that the excess of Negro babies below 2,500 grams can be fully accounted for by an ethnically related shift downward in birth weight distribution is not only questionable, but, as Pasamanick et al. (1956) have suggested, unparsimonious as well. Indeed, until socioeconomic differences between ethnic groups are eliminated over several generations, it will be virtually impossible to discover whether there are any ethnically determined differences in birth weight distribution between U. S. Negroes and whites. In the meantime, the most likely explanation for the persistently high rate of prematurity among American nonwhites is the persistently low level of their overall social and economic status.

Crump *et al.*, 1957

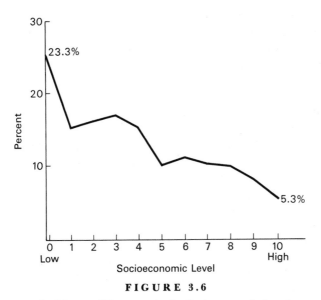

FIGURE 3.6

Incidence of Prematurity by Socioeconomic Level

What we have learned in this chapter, then, is that pregnancy complications of all kinds are found excessively in populations characterized by a low economic status and/or membership in a depressed minority. When we have examined this distribution at close range, using prematurity as a generalized measure of reproductive risk, we have seen that the likelihood that children will be exposed to reproductive abnormality increases with depressed economic status and is even further increased with minority status. We have not yet considered the reasons *why* there is such an association between excessive reproductive failure and depressed social and economic status, a topic to which we shall turn in the following chapters.

For the moment, it should be noted that a whole congeries of intervening variables may be involved. Some of them are immediate and short-term, reflecting the frequently self-destructive social patterns associated with lower-class life; Pakter (1961*b*), for example, found that illegitimacy added to the risk of prematurity within the nonwhite ethnic group. But a mother's competence as a reproducer is influenced not only by her adult life, but also by her life history. Drillien (1957), for example, found that "for any social class of father, prematurely born babies are more likely to have mothers of poorer social origin than the maturely born." The lower-class mother as a reproductive organism is thus the product of the cumulative effects of a lifetime of stress associated with poverty which have attendant effects on her growth and development, effects which—as the data in the next chapters will demonstrate—are reflected in higher rates of pregnancy and birth complications. The finding of Rider in Baltimore that the incidence of prematurity increases from 5% to 7.6% to 11.4% as one moves downward (from the white upper economic fifth through the white lower economic fifth to the Negro population) could thus be explained by the degree to which a variety of factors associated with increased prematurity tend to pile up in the most disadvantaged segments of the population, so that reproductive failures, as Pasamanick *et al.* (1956) have written, tend to increase "exponentially" below a certain socioeconomic threshold.

Just as we have learned in this chapter that exposure to prematurity and other reproductive risks increases with declining social status, we have also learned that the degree to which this exposure has consequences—that is, the extent to which the potential hazard of prematurity is realized in reduced levels of performance at school age—appears also to be, at least partially, a function of social class. Thus the subpopulations in which the risk of low birth weight is greatest are the very ones in which low birth weight has a significant influence on subsequent growth and behavioral development.

As we turn in the chapters immediately following to a consideration of various factors which contribute to the high rate of reproductive failure among poor mothers, we need to keep in mind the extent to which such factors, acting through the mother, significantly affect the level of risk to which the child himself is exposed.

CHAPTER FOUR

Too Young, Too Old, and Too Often

It is time to consider a fifth freedom—freedom from the tyranny of excessive fertility.   DUGALD BAIRD

ALTHOUGH lawyers and theologians may dispute the day and hour at which a fertilized human ovum assumes legal rights and a soul, there is no moment between conception and birth when the life and health of an unborn child are not intimately associated with the well-being of his mother. It is the mother's body which holds, nurtures, and finally ejects the child. Therefore the fact that abnormalities of the reproductive period which may result in intellectual deficit in children occur most frequently in certain social groups leads us naturally to consider the ways in which social circumstances may have contributed to such abnormal reproductive performances. We turn our attention, then, in this and in the following chapters, from the infants to their mothers, stepping back from the risk conditions of the prenatal and perinatal periods in order to explore some of the antecedents which may have produced them.

In demonstrating an association between excessive reproductive risk, on the one hand, and poverty, low social status, and minority group membership on the other, we have shown merely that disadvantaged mothers and their children are at risk. We have proffered no explanation for this association. To get at the "causes" of reproductive casualty, "we must look for elements inside the concept of social status which may, theoretically at least, have a direct influence upon the course of pregnancy and the growth of the foetus" (Thomson, 1963).

More than a decade ago Guttmacher (1953) wrote that the patient most likely to have a premature infant was the young Negro woman "in her first pregnancy who has received little or no prenatal care, who comes from an underprivileged group, who works hard and eats badly." As this statement implies, the mother who appears to be at greatest risk usually *is* so for multiple reasons. Indeed, Thomson (1963) has argued that "attempts to isolate single factors in the socioeconomic spectrum may simply obscure the true state of affairs: that prematurity, like many other aspects of ill-health, depends on the cumulative effect of successive or simultaneous social and physiological injuries rather than upon any single cause."

As with prematurity, so with other reproductive complications; no "cause" from which they arise need be singular or simple, and any consideration of single causes is unavoidably somewhat misleading. However, in this and the following chapters we will be taking up one by one a number of factors which affect reproductive risk. We will look at women's age and parity, their growth, their diets, and their obstetrical care in order to examine the contribution which each of these makes to reproductive performance. Yet we do this fully aware that all these "causes" are interrelated, not only to one another but to a number of other variables which we shall not here consider in detail—a woman's smoking habits, for example (Simpson, 1957; Frazier et al., 1961; Herriot et al., 1962), her housing conditions (Thompson, 1968), her relative opportunity to terminate pregnancy (Hall, 1965; Gold et al., 1965), the physical and emotional demands of her life (Wortis and Freedman, 1962), and so forth. Thus it must be understood that when we deal with "causes" singly, and as simply as the information permits, it is always within the understood context of a reality in which they are complex and interacting.

The most general maternal factors affecting pregnancy outcome—and those to which an obstetrician would from the first direct his attention—are the mother's age and her history as a reproducer. It is not surprising that the age of the mother and the number and frequency of her previous pregnancies should have an effect on her efficiency as a reproducer. Even among laymen it is a commonplace that first babies seem to give more trouble getting born, that late pregnancies are especially risky, and that women who have a large number of children in rapid succession are more likely to have complications in the current pregnancy. In the most general terms, these commonplaces sum up the pattern of risk associated with variations in age and parity: relatively high risks of complication for the never-before-pregnant or the young too-often-pregnant mother, relatively lower risks for those in their twenties bearing second, third, or fourth children, and rapidly increasing risk for mothers who are over 30

NCHS, PHS 1000, 3:4, 1965

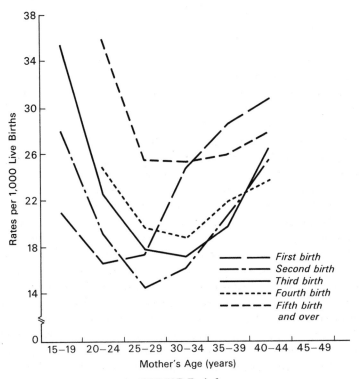

FIGURE 4.1

Neonatal Mortality Rates by Maternal Age and Birth Order, United States, January–March 1950

or of parity over 4 (Yerushalmy *et al.,* 1938, 1940; Butler and Bonham, 1963).

Figure 4.1, taken from national data for the year 1950 (NCHS, PHS 1000, 3:4, 1965), shows the typical U- and J-shaped curves which appear when age and parity are considered together. The pattern of risk varies somewhat for specific infant outcomes; but the trends for stillbirth and prematurity are quite similar to that for neonatal death shown here. Thus it is clear that there is excessive risk of complication and poor outcome in pregnancy when the mother is at either extreme of age or parity. What does this pattern of risk have to do with the unfavorable reproductive experience of the lower-class woman? A great deal, for as we shall show, mothers in lower-class populations are characteristically overrepresented in these high-risk groups.

The mother who is poor differs from those who are not so poor in the early age at which she begins her reproductive life, in the late age at which she ends it, and in the total number of pregnancies which she completes during her whole period of fertility. The pattern has been well documented in various studies of total populations of births in England and Scotland (e.g., Baird, 1946; Illsley, 1956; Baird, Hytten, and Thomson, 1958; Baird, 1965; Russell *et al.,* 1963). In Aberdeen, for example, it has been shown that women from the lower social classes are younger at marriage and at the time of first delivery than are those in the higher classes. Since families tend to be largest when the mother is under age 20 at marriage, it is the lowest-class mothers who have the most children. In Aberdeen in 1955, 15.3% of births in the two lowest classes were fifth or subsequent pregnancies, compared with only 4.6% of such births in the two highest classes. Russell (1963), in Newcastle-upon-Tyne, found a similar pattern—an increasing prevalence of very high parity with declining social class. Women who had already borne 4 or more children accounted for only 8% of the births in social classes I and II, 12.2% of the births in class III, and more than twice as many (24.7%) of the births in classes IV and V.

Although we have been unable to find national data in this country directly relating social class to age at childbearing or pregnancy number, the relationship can be initially approached through two related kinds of statistics: one which shows numbers of children ever born to mothers according to their income level, and the other which relates income to family size. These sets of figures are useful so long as it is kept in mind that both will tend to underestimate the number of pregnancies in lower-class populations having high rates of spontaneous abortion and fetal loss; and that family size data, excluding as they do children who died in infancy, will produce an even larger underestimate of total completed pregnancies. Data from the 1960 census show that mothers aged 35–39, in families with annual incomes of $2,000 or less, averaged 3.7 children compared with an average of 2.5 children for those with incomes of over $7,000. When data are divided by race, the trends remain the same: rising income is associated with a decline in the number of children for both whites and nonwhites at all childbearing ages.

The effect of such a differential can be demonstrated by considering data on income in relation to size of family. In 1963, fully 34% of all poor family units contained no children at all; but a low-income family with any surviving children was almost two and one-half times as likely to have 6 or more as was a high-income family. Nearly 1 out of every 3 families with 6 or more children had an income of $3,000 or less a year, compared with 1 in 10 of two-child families. Median income was highest for families with 2 children ($6,900), lower for families with 4 children ($6,500), and lowest ($5,000) for families with 6 or more children (Population Reference Bureau, 1965). By the Social Security Administration yardstick, which realistically recognized that families with 6 children can be poor at more than $3,000 a year, 26% of families with 5 children or more, and 35% of those with 6 children or more, were poor in 1967 (Current Population Reports, August 5, 1968). Thus it is perfectly clear that it is the families with the least money who have the most living children; and if we keep in mind that these data underestimate total pregnancies, it is legitimate to infer that it is the poorest women who, as a group, are pregnant most frequently.

Since the poorer women not only have larger completed families, but have more children than the well-off even at the earliest childbearing ages, it is obvious that they begin childbearing sooner. Where populations of women can be examined by social class, such a hypothesis is confirmed. Donnelly *et al.* (1964), for example, studying factors associated with prematurity among almost 30,000 births in three North Carolina hospitals between 1954 and 1961, divided their population into four groups: a "most favored" and "least favored" white group and a "most favored" and "least favored" nonwhite group. They found that among the "most favored" white mothers only 3% fell into the teen-aged under-20 group. But over 20% of the "least favored" white mothers were teen-agers; and a similar proportion of very young mothers was found in both the most and least favored nonwhite group. In fact, as Figure 4.2 shows, 56% of all the lower-class Negro women were either under 20 or over 30 years of age.

. Donnelly *et al.*, 1964

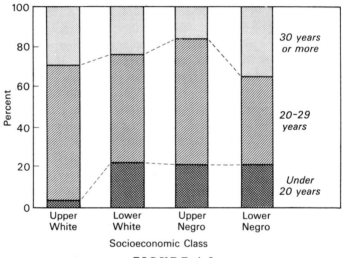

FIGURE 4.2

Distribution of Single Live Births by Maternal Age and Socioeconomic Class, North Carolina, 1954–1961

(*University hospital births*)

As we have seen earlier, the classification "nonwhite" can be used in this country as a rough indicator of socioeconomic status; and though national data on age and frequency of childbearing are not available in the U. S. by social class, they are, like other vital

TABLE 4.1

Birth Rates by Maternal Age, Live Birth Order, and Color, United States, 1967 [a]

Live Birth Order and Color	Birth Rates by Age of Mother (years)							
	15–44[b]	10–14	15–19	20–24	25–29	30–34	35–39	40–44	45–49
Total	87.6	0.9	67.9	174.0	142.6	79.3	38.5	10.6	0.7
First child	30.8	0.8	51.1	75.3	26.5	6.6	2.2	0.5	0.0
Second child	22.6	0.0	13.6	59.5	40.2	12.3	3.8	0.8	0.0
Third child	13.9	0.0	2.7	25.0	34.4	17.1	6.1	1.3	0.1
Fourth child	8.3	—	0.5	9.4	20.4	15.3	6.7	1.6	0.1
Fifth child	4.8	—	0.1	3.4	10.6	10.7	5.6	1.4	0.1
Sixth and seventh child	4.5	—	0.0	1.4	8.3	11.2	7.3	2.1	0.1
Eighth child and over	2.7	—	0.0	0.1	2.1	6.2	6.8	2.9	0.3
White	83.1	0.3	57.3	168.8	140.7	76.5	36.6	9.8	0.6
First child	29.7	0.3	45.3	76.6	27.4	6.7	2.2	0.5	0.0
Second child	22.1	0.0	10.3	59.2	41.9	12.5	3.8	0.8	0.0
Third child	13.5	0.0	1.5	22.7	35.4	17.7	6.3	1.3	0.1
Fourth child	7.9	—	0.2	7.4	19.8	15.6	6.9	1.6	0.1
Fifth child	4.3	—	0.0	2.1	9.3	10.4	5.6	1.4	0.1
Sixth and seventh child	3.7	—	0.0	0.7	5.9	9.7	6.8	2.0	0.1
Eighth child and over	1.8	—	0.0	0.1	1.0	3.9	4.9	2.2	0.2
Nonwhite	119.8	4.1	135.2	212.1	155.9	99.1	52.4	16.8	1.2
First child	38.4	4.0	88.2	65.6	20.2	6.0	2.0	0.5	0.0
Second child	25.9	0.2	34.1	61.7	28.1	10.7	3.7	0.8	0.1
Third child	16.8	0.0	10.1	41.2	27.8	12.8	4.9	1.3	0.1
Fourth child	11.5	—	2.3	23.9	24.8	13.2	5.4	1.2	0.1
Fifth child	8.1	—	0.4	12.1	20.1	12.6	5.5	1.3	0.1
Sixth and seventh child	10.1	—	0.0	7.0	25.2	21.4	10.7	3.1	0.1
Eighth child and over	9.0	—	0.0	0.7	9.7	22.3	20.0	8.7	0.7

[a] Based on a 20% to 50% sample of births. Rates are live births per 1,000 women in specified age and color groups, estimated as of July 1; live birth order refers to number of children born alive to mother. Figures for age of mother not stated and birth order not stated are distributed.
[b] Rates computed by relating total births, regardless of age of mother, to women aged 15–44 years.

NCHS, MVSR, Dec. 4, 1968

statistics, available by race. They show that with one exception—women over age 30 bearing first babies—there is a consistent over-representation of nonwhite mothers in all age and parity groups in which disturbances of pregnancy and its outcome are most frequent.

Where age is concerned, for example, nonwhite birth rates are higher than white rates at all ages; but the differential is lowest during the ages of minimum risk (20–29) and begins to ascend on either side of that age range. As Table 4.1 shows (NCHS, MVSR, Dec. 4, 1968), during the two most fertile 5-year periods, 20–24 and 25–29, the age-specific nonwhite birth rates are respectively about 26% and 11% higher than white rates. However, for women 40–44, 45–49, and 15–19 the age-specific nonwhite birth rates are respectively 1.7 times, 2 times, and 2.4 times white rates, and the rate for nonwhite girls under 15 is almost 14 times higher than that for white girls.

Because nonwhite women commence childbearing earlier on the average than white women, nonwhite births at each age level are of higher birth order. Moreover, not only are nonwhite women younger for every birth order than white women, but as Table 4.2 shows, they

TABLE 4.2

Median Maternal Age by Live Birth Order and Color,
United States, 1965

Live Birth Order

	Total	*1st*	*2nd*	*3rd*	*4th*	*5th*	*6–7th*
	Median Age of Mother (in years)						
White	25.9	22.2	24.4	27.3	29.2	31.0	32.7
Nonwhite	25.0	20.2	22.8	24.4	26.4	27.9	29.8

NCHS, Vital Statistics of the U. S., 1965

are also increasingly younger with each succeeding live birth—a fact which reflects a tendency for pregnancies to be more closely spaced among nonwhites. Thus the average nonwhite woman is only 2 years younger than the average white woman at the time she has her first child, but she is almost 3 years younger by the time she is having her fourth child. She is also considerably more likely than the white woman to have that fourth child, and, as Figure 4.3 shows, even more likely to have even later children (Lunde, 1965). In 1963 only 28% of all white births were of fourth or subsequent children, but 43% of all nonwhite births in the same year were of similar rank.

Lunde, 1965

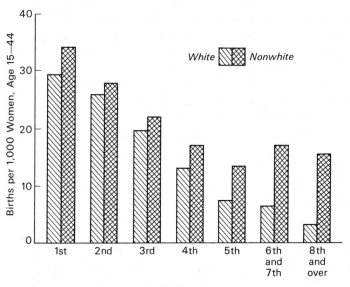

FIGURE 4.3

Birth Order by Color, United States, 1963

Indeed, almost one-third of all nonwhite births were of fifth or higher rank.

Actually a rather marked underestimate of the number of births to very poor nonwhites results from a white-nonwhite dichotomization, which treats the nonwhite population as homogeneous in both social class and reproductive pattern—which it is not. Even a rough division into income groups shows that although nonwhites have more births than whites at all income levels, there are marked differences by income in childbearing patterns within the nonwhite population. Data from the 1960 census on women in the age group 45–49 show that among nonwhites making under $2,000 a year the mean number of children ever born was 4.8, but at incomes between $7,000 and $10,000 the number was just under 3 (Lunde, 1965).

But educational level is often an even better indicator than income of real social status; and better-educated Negroes, as it happens, have a reproductive pattern not dissimilar from that of educated whites. Negro women who have completed high school have approximately the same number of children as white high school graduates, and Negro college graduates actually have fewer children than similarly educated whites (Lunde, 1965). Based on data from the 1960 Growth of American Families Study, Campbell (1965, 1966) concluded that Southern farm background was the characteristic associated with the greatest excess fecundity among nonwhites in this country; and that "by the time nonwhite couples are one generation or more removed from the rural south, their fertility is very much like that of the white population" (1966). Thus figures on mean numbers of pregnancies which include the relatively small families of educated nonwhites tend to minimize the frequency of childbearing in the most disadvantaged families.

Among women presently on farms or recently in-migrant to the cities, fertility is much higher. Campbell (1966) noted that farm women in the Growth of American Families Study expected to have a mean of just under 6 children. That they may, in fact, produce even more by the time their childbearing days are finished is suggested by Darity's (1963) finding that the average number of children already produced by a group of low-income mothers attending a birth-control clinic in Charlotte, North Carolina, was 4.8, and the women's mean age was only 29 so that they had many years of fertility ahead of them. Browning and Northcutt (1961) found a strikingly similar pattern among Negro migrant families in Florida. The mean number of pregnancies per patient for 719 women was 4.8; and of the 525 mothers on whom records were available, 48.8% became pregnant again within 12 months following delivery. When Northcutt et al. (1963) subsequently compared the migrants with a group of nonmigrant women of similar economic class, they found that the pattern of childbearing was not associated with mobility, that the nonmigrant groups also had a mean of 4.8 pregnancies per woman, and that 9.9% of the migrants, compared to 11% of the nonmigrants, had been pregnant ten or more times. Thus poor women viewed as a group, and especially poor nonwhite women (of whom the great majority in the childbearing population are Negro), begin childbearing younger, repeat it more rapidly than the better-off and white women, and are more likely to continue it into the older ages and higher birth orders where the rates of complication are strikingly high.

The data thus far considered, then, indicate a clear association between low social status, on the one hand, and, on the other, childbearing begun early, repeated rapidly, and continued to a relatively advanced age. We have earlier pointed out that it is precisely this pattern of childbearing that is associated with a high level of reproductive risk. These associations permit at least two interpretations. One is that the factors of high parity, extreme youth and age, and close spacing of pregnancies are themselves productive of risk. The other interpretation is that frequent childbearing extending over a long span of years does not of itself constitute a risk, but becomes associated with poor outcomes merely because such a large proportion of the women who behave in this fashion come from the most deprived groups and thus have other characteristics which put them at reproductive risk.

In other words, given the tendency among the poor to an earlier initiation of childbearing, it is inevitable that groups of women bearing babies when they are teen-agers will include a high proportion of lower-class mothers, among whom there is an excess of illegitimacy, untreated disease, poor health practices, and other factors associated with poor reproductive outcome. Similarly, women bearing fifth children will tend to be characterized by a different set of social and economic characteristics than will women bearing second children. "Each combination of age and parity," as Illsley has pointed out (1967), "acquires a specific social composition," and such social segregation must necessarily be controlled for if we are to assess the specific contribution of age and parity to reproductive risk.

Let us consider for a moment the two groups representing perhaps the most extreme examples of the social segregation process: one consisting of very young women having second or later pregnancies, and the other of women over 30 having their first pregnancy. Both of these groups of women have very high stillbirth and prematurity rates, apparently reflecting the effect of biologically inappropriate relationships between age and parity. The postneonatal death rates of the two groups, however, appear at first glance to reflect their different social status: very young women of high parity who tend to come predominantly from the lower classes have one of the highest postneonatal death rates of any age or parity grouping, and women over 30 having first children tend to come predominantly from the upper classes and to have the lowest postneonatal death rates. But Morrison *et al.* (1959) have shown that the patterns of postneonatal loss persist across social classes. In every class the "later infants of young mothers" constitute a highly vulnerable group, probably for largely environmental reasons; and, as Figure 4.4 shows, mothers

Morrison *et al.*, 1959

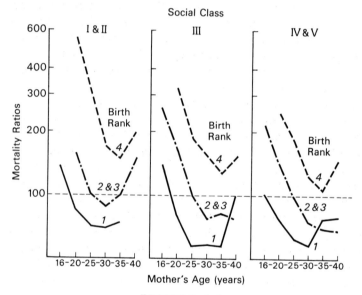

FIGURE 4.4

Postneonatal Mortality Ratios by Birth Rank, Maternal Age, and Social Class, England and Wales, 1949–1950

(Single, legitimate live births)

having their first babies between the ages of 30 and 34 have the lowest postneonatal death rate in classes IV and V as well as in classes I and II.

So although the piling up of groups of women in particular age and parity groupings is a social phenomenon, there are within any social class particular aspects of the relationship between age, number of prior pregnancies, and the mother's efficiency as a reproducer which are relatively independent of her social status and reflect instead certain underlying organismic characteristics. Thus there is a hazard associated with first births, and it is both independent of age (first babies just seem to have more difficulty getting born) and at the same time affected by age (first babies, as we have seen, have even more trouble getting born if their mothers are over 30). There also appears to be a biological hazard specifically associated with aging, most dramatically illustrated by abnormalities arising from age-induced alterations of the chromosomal material, but evidenced as well in an increasing tendency to dizygotic twinning (Hytten and Leitch, 1964).

As the preceding analysis has made clear, the reproductive habits associated with poverty interact with the biological risk associated with certain age and parity relationships in such a way as to produce an increased risk in childbearing for women in the lower social classes. In Newcastle-upon-Tyne, for example, Russell (1963) found that in the three highest social classes only 19.4% of all perinatal deaths were accounted for by women in their fifth or subsequent pregnancy, although such grand multiparae accounted for 48% of perinatal deaths in the two lower classes. Even when social class is held constant, however, the pattern of risk associated with particular age and parity relationships tends to persist; grand multiparae are at risk in any class.

Yet given the demands which pregnancy imposes, it would be surprising indeed if groups of women growing up and raising families under very unequal conditions should respond equally to the challenge of childbearing at whatever age or level of fecundity. They do not. Thus Figure 4.5 (Baird, Hytten, and Thomson, 1958) illustrates clearly that the increased risk with increasing age of producing a stillborn child, though evident in all social classes, is higher at every age for those in the least favored economic groups. Figure 4.6, based on the data of Donnelly et al., shows a similar differential for the incidence of prematurity among 22,000 white births in North Carolina; prematurity rates for each age and each birth number were higher among women in the less economically favored groups. Figure 4.7, drawn from U. S. Vital Statistics data, shows the same excessive rate of risk at each age when nonwhites as a group are compared with whites.

The fact that lower-class and/or nonwhite women experience an excessive risk of reproductive failure at every age and parity is not surprising in the light of the multitude of other factors which, as we have earlier suggested, tend to pile up against them. Some of these adverse influences will be the subject of succeeding chapters. There are also, however, some less evident aspects of the age and parity relationships among these women which help to explain their poorer reproductive performance. So far as the average mother is concerned,

Baird, Hytten, and Thomson, 1958

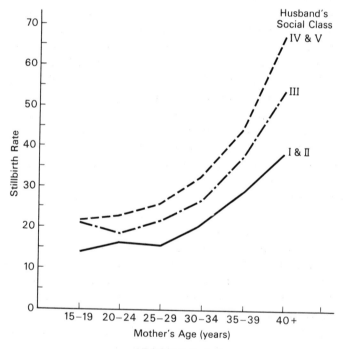

FIGURE 4.5

Stillbirth Rates by Maternal Age and Social Class,
Scotland, 1950–1956

Donnelly *et al.*, 1964

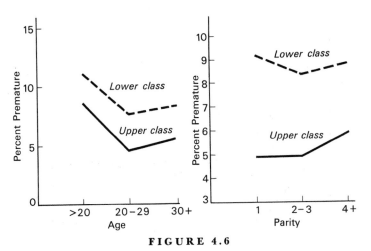

FIGURE 4.6

**Prematurity Rates by Maternal Age and Social Status (left)
and by Parity and Social Status (right), North Carolina, 1954–1961**

(22,126 university hospital white births)

poor women have added to the already heavy demands of advanced age and parity a life of greater physical and emotional strain. Drillien (1956) found that multiparae in poorer homes in Edinburgh had a rising prematurity rate after the second birth, while middle-class mothers tended to maintain their low prematurity rate for all births after the first. Data from the Perinatal Mortality Survey (Butler and Bonham, 1963) show a similar class variation where perinatal mortality is concerned, death rates tending to rise after the third birth except in the highest social class where they do not begin to increase until after the fourth birth. These findings suggest that a poorer general physical condition among lower-class women may result in their showing more quickly than their relatively more affluent sisters the effects of repeated pregnancies. This may be of particular pertinence for older nonwhite women in this country; between 1950 and 1962, fifth or subsequent babies accounted for from 75% to 79% of all live births to nonwhite mothers aged 40–44, while among white women in the same age group the percentage of

NCHS, Vital Statistics of the U.S., 1965

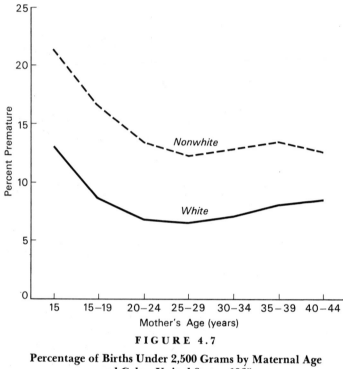

FIGURE 4.7

**Percentage of Births Under 2,500 Grams by Maternal Age
and Color, United States, 1965**

mothers of high parity was much lower, ranging from 47% to 54% (NCHS, PHS 1000, 21:1, 1964).

The excess of risk associated with youth presents a somewhat different problem. In purely physiologic terms, reproduction appears to be most efficient when it commences soon after the attainment of physical maturity (Baird, 1952). Baird, in an investigation of the process of labor in 1,792 married primiparae in Aberdeen, found that labor was most "normal" in the group of women 15–19 years old. Of this age group, 80.3% delivered spontaneously in less than 24 hours, but, as Figure 4.8 shows, the incidence of various deviations from this normal pattern increased with increasing age—even for the

Baird, 1952

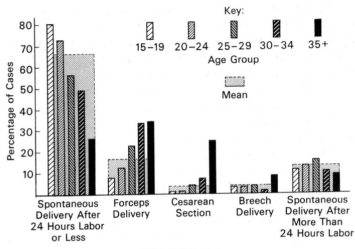

FIGURE 4.8

Variation in Process of Labor by Age, Aberdeen

(1,792 married primiparae)

group of women in their twenties, the period in which all studies show the rates of reproductive casualty are lowest. The forceps-delivery rate rose from 7% in the youngest mothers to 36% in those aged 35 and over. Moreover, the higher incidence of intact perineum (55%) in women under 20 (compared with 36% in women aged 20–24, and 20% in women 30–34) supported the notion that "normal labor" among primiparae occurred most readily before the age of 20, and that the physiologically "ideal" age for childbearing was somewhere around 18. Similar conclusions have been reached by various authors in this country; indeed, Marchetti and Menaker (1950) judged the obstetrically optimum age to be closer to 16.

But as Baird *et al.* (1958) point out, such a finding does not necessarily argue for the early initiation of childbearing: "In the complex society in which we live, there may be very good reasons why women should not start childbearing too early. The biological advantage of physiologically efficient reproduction may be less important than the social advantages of adequate knowledge and experience, and of high aims for children." Actually something more than high aims appears to be involved, for despite the advantage of youth, very young mothers as a group have consistently higher rates of infant loss, the risk inherent in youthful parturition being apparently much more serious for the child than for the mother. This was Yerushalmy's conclusion when he found that young mothers who were themselves at the lowest risk of maternal death had infants who were at excess risk (Yerushalmy *et al.*, 1940). The notion that extreme youth in childbearing may be harder on the infant than on the mother gains further support from the finding of Baird *et al.* (1954) that stillbirth rates associated with preeclampsia were almost three times as high among primigravidae under 20 as among those in the age group 20–24, even though there were no significant differences by age in the prevalence of either preeclamptic toxemia or severe preeclampsia. Such a result, they argue, reflects the lesser "vitality" of the fetuses of younger primiparae who come, in Scotland as in the U. S., predominantly from the lower social classes.

The special vulnerability of infants of very young mothers is emphasized when multiple births are considered. As Figure 4.9 shows, there was a risk of approximately one in six that an infant who was the product of a multiple birth to a woman under 20 years of age would die in the first week of life (Morris and Heady, 1955). Baird (1960) has pointed out further that although such "maternal problems" as uterine dysfunction and prolonged pregnancy are seldom seen among very young primiparae in Aberdeen, such "infant problems" as prematurity and central nervous system malformation—both of them conditions which may have little relation to actual performance in labor—are much more common in this group. In the U. S., young women under 20 years of age have a higher percentage of low birth weight babies than any other age group.

Even here, however, there is an excessive risk attaching to the economic-ethnic classification "nonwhite" over and above that attaching to youth; prematurity rates for very young nonwhite mothers are almost twice as high as those for very young white mothers. Repeated pregnancy is also much more frequent among nonwhite girls in this age range.

Table 4.1 shows that although the birth rate for nonwhite girls 15–19 years old having their first babies was approximately twice

Morris and Heady, 1955

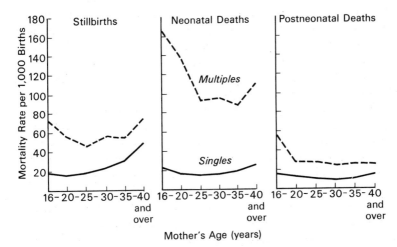

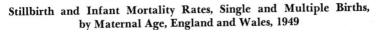

FIGURE 4.9

Stillbirth and Infant Mortality Rates, Single and Multiple Births, by Maternal Age, England and Wales, 1949

(Stillbirth rates per 1,000 live births and stillbirths; other rates per 1,000 live births)

the white rate, a nonwhite girl in this age bracket was about three and one-half times as likely to be having a second child, six and one-half times as likely to be having a third child, and more than 11 times as likely to be having a fourth child before she was 20 than was a white girl in the same range.

Such a differential has two implications. One is that childbearing is more often rapidly repeated among nonwhites, with all the hazards to both the mother and the child attendant upon births too closely spaced. Lilienfeld and Pasamanick (1956) found that the combination of youth and high parity in the mother was associated with a dramatically increased risk of mental deficiency in the child. The combination of a birth order of three with a maternal age of less than 20 years was associated with a risk of mental deficiency considerably higher than that found in any other age-parity group. The second implication of multiparity in a woman under 20 is that she

99

has begun childbearing earlier than a primipara of the same age; and though the rates of reproductive failure tend to be high for the whole group of women under 20, they are highest, as Figure 4.7 shows, for those under 15 years of age—an age group containing a much higher percentage of nonwhite girls, of out-of-wedlock pregnancies, and of girls from the lowest socioeconomic classes.

Stine *et al.* (1964), for example, found that over 20% of the births to 16-year-old Negro girls in Baltimore in 1961 were second or subsequent pregnancies, a finding similar to that of Aznar and Bennett (1961) on 1,080 white and Negro patients aged 12–16. The 1967 Vital Statistics data, as we have seen, show births to girls aged 10–14 to be almost fourteen times as common among nonwhite as among white girls. Thus part of the conflict between the apparent physiologic benefits of early childbearing and the high rates of prematurity and infant loss associated with it may arise from the practice of lumping together as "under 20" a large number of mothers who are not only considerably younger than 18—an age below which requirements for maternal growth may, as Baird *et al.* (1958) suggest, compete with fetal growth—but even younger than 16, an age which some authors (e.g., Harris, 1922; Marchetti and Menaker, 1950) have concluded is "obstetrically optimum" if socially inadvisable. Among these youngest women, illegitimacy rates are high, toxemia and difficult labor are more frequent than among women in their twenties, and most investigators have found excessively high rates of prematurity and perinatal loss (Aznar and Bennett, 1961; Marchetti and Menaker, 1950; Donnelly *et al.*, 1961, 1964; Hassan and Falls, 1964).

Thus the greater risk associated with youth among poor minority group mothers as compared to their more privileged contemporaries would appear to relate in part to their poorer general health and physique; to their much earlier initiation of childbearing; to their tendency to young multiparity; and, when they are single, to the social and personal stresses attaching to their marital status. Among these women, "a first pregnancy is often a sudden complication of early maturity rather than a planned undertaking." But, as Baird *et al.* (1958) conclude, there is no implication that the disadvantaged woman would be significantly more physiologically efficient as a mother if she were to postpone childbearing—as do many middle-class women—into her middle or late twenties. Her biological youth is one of her advantages; to delay her first pregnancy past the age of 20 would merely be to impose on an already less competent maternal organism "the progressive deterioration of physiological efficiency" that accompanies advancing age.

We have seen in this chapter, then, that poor women, and especially nonwhite women, so time their pregnancies—whether by design or, as is more likely, by inadvertence—that they appear in excessive numbers in age and parity groups in which childbearing is risky. We have also seen, however, that at every age and at each parity disadvantaged women are at greater risk of reproductive casualty than those who are better off, a fact which has suggested that for these women other biological risk factors interact with their suboptimal reproductive pattern to help produce an excessive level of morbidity and mortality in childbearing. In the chapters that follow we will continue to explore some of these other factors.

CHAPTER FIVE

The Consequences of
Poor Growth

If one has seen a plant or animal only in one environment, all one knows about its genetic constitution is what it can do in that environment and not what it may do or not do in any other.

ISABELLA LEITCH

We can say that stature is inherited; it is more accurate to say that the stature depends upon heredity as well as environment. Each heredity responds to each environment by producing a certain stature.

DUNN AND DOBZHANSKY

F O R M O S T poor women poverty is not a sudden circumstance of adulthood but a lifelong condition. Explanations for their poor performance in childbearing must be sought, as Illsley has written (Baird and Illsley, 1953), "in the influences which have determined the mother's outlook and physique from an early age, and not merely in the events of pregnancy itself." In seeking out the variables which mediate between depressed social status and poor reproductive performance, we have considered in the last chapter the effect on pregnancy outcome of a woman's pattern of childbearing. We turn now to a consideration of the relationship between a woman's size, as a record of her growth, and her reproductive performance, for it seems evident that the competencies of women as childbearers are influenced, long before they have begun to reproduce, by the environments in which they have grown into reproducers.

One measure of the adequacy of any environment is the extent to which it facilitates growth. What we will argue here is that stunting of poor women, reflected in their short stature, is one of the mechanisms through which poverty may be contributing to high rates of reproductive failure. In other words, poor women are at risk in childbearing when they are short, and they are often short because they are poor. But before we examine the relation of childbearing to height, we wish to consider the somewhat broader notion that height is a variable related to social condition and that shortness of stature, especially among those who are poor, may be a consequence of their exposure to influences which have stunted growth.

There is little question of the existence of a general relationship between height and social condition. On the international level there is incontrovertible evidence that groups of people from poor and underdeveloped nations are, on the average, smaller than are those from the more developed countries. Figure 5.1, for example, compares the growth curves of boys from Ethiopia, Jordan, Thailand, and Vietnam with those of a group of middle-class children from the U.S. (Jackson, 1964). It is clear from the parallelism of the lines beyond the age of about 4 that these children from underdeveloped countries, who at 16 are still so far behind their more affluent contemporaries, will end up as relatively small adults. Even though ethnic factors complicate interpretation, such data clearly document what many Americans who have visited Asia, Africa, or Latin America have experienced at first hand, namely, that in relation to such populations they are outsized. In countries like Sweden and Germany, on the other hand, where there is a generally high and universally adequate standard of living, average heights for unselected populations probably equal or exceed average heights in the U.S. (Bakwin and McLaughlin, 1964).

But significant differences in height are not only found across national boundaries between populations which are, after all, ethnically as well as economically disparate. Even in the industrialized countries—since the benefits of industrialization have been unequally disposed—height differences are associated with varying social circumstances. In Britain, which has a long history of anthropometric concern, height differences have been found for decades between different segments of the population, with mean heights tending to decline regularly with declining social class.

Jackson, 1964

AVERAGE HEIGHTS AND WEIGHTS

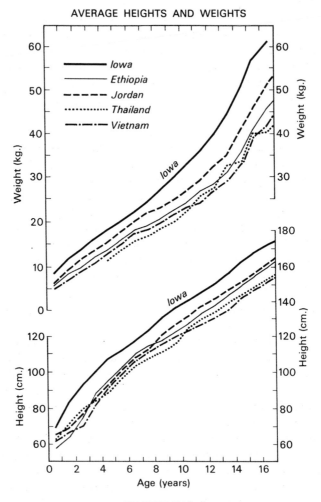

FIGURE 5.1

**Growth of Boys in Ethiopia, Jordan, Thailand, and Vietnam
Compared with Iowa Norms**

Orr, in his classic study of British diet and health *Food, Health, and Income* (1936), brought together early anthropometric studies showing that, in 1883, boys of the professional class were 5.8 inches taller on the average than boys of the same age from the artisan classes, who in turn were 2.6 inches taller than lower-class boys. Compiling available measurements for the period 1926 to 1935, Orr showed that even though average heights for all classes had risen in 50 years, the differences between them had not been markedly

Orr, 1936

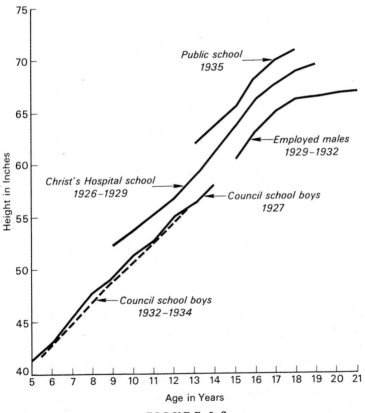

FIGURE 5.2

Height of Boys and Young Men by Social Group, 1926–1935

reduced (Figure 5.2). Two years after Orr's study, the general relationship between height and social class was once more confirmed on several groups of pregnant women whose diets were studied by McCance, Widdowson, and Verdon-Roe (1938). Lower-class women were found to be shorter and heavier than higher-class women, with heights for the whole group tending to rise regularly with income. Figure 5.3, from a study almost three decades later, depicts the

Illsley, 1956

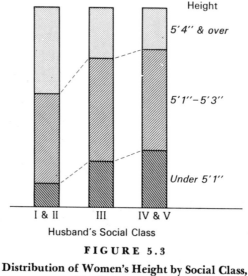

FIGURE 5.3

Distribution of Women's Height by Social Class, Aberdeen, 1950–1953

(Married city primiparae)

social class distribution of short, medium, and tall individuals in another group of pregnant women (Illsley, 1956). Almost half of the women from the two highest classes were 5 feet 4 inches or taller, but only 20% of the lowest-class women had attained such a height.

Although it can thus be easily demonstrated that persistent differences in average height exist between different nations, and within nations between different social groups, it has long seemed likely that such group differences in stature were for the most part hereditary, and that shortness in a given race or in a given social group was either a primary "racial" characteristic or the consequence of some process of genetic segregation.

Where populations may differ in genetic height potential, differences in stature obviously cannot be assumed to arise solely out of differences in life condition; rather, different mean sizes in groups of children or adults could be reflecting genetic differences, environmental differences, or, most commonly, an interaction between the two. Now if shortness does indeed arise predominantly from "short" genes, two things should follow. First, short people should continue to be short under whatever dietary and environmental circumstances they are raised; and second, shortness should not be excessively associated with other pathologic indicators of poor growth. As we shall see, neither of these propositions is true. On the contrary, the offspring of groups which are genetically homogeneous turn out to differ greatly in ultimate size according to the environments in which they grow to maturity—an effect which can be examined by observing the relationship of growth to environment within gene pools and by analyzing the effects of changed environment upon given ethnic groups when they move to countries in which standards of living and health are elevated. We shall see, moreover, that pathologies associated with poor conditions for growth are excessively prevalent among groups of short individuals or among economically deprived groups in which short stature is endemic.

That children of immigrants stood taller than their immigrant parents was long a part of American folklore. But it was Franz Boas who in 1910 first documented as fact the observation that changing environmental circumstances in one generation were followed by changing height in the next. Boas' classic study, *Changes in the Bodily Form of Descendants of Immigrants,* authorized by Congress to assess the impact of the American environment on our immigrant population, produced what was called at the time a "major discovery in anthropological science." Boas found, within a single racial stock, changes both in children's heights and in their head shapes which were directly related to the length of time their parents had resided in this country. Boas compared the heights of Jewish immigrant children born abroad, those born within 10 years of their parents' arrival in this country, and those born to mothers with 10 or more years' residence. Compared with the average stature of all the children at a given age, children born in Europe were consistently shorter than the mean; those born at least 10 years after their parents' arrival here were consistently taller than the mean; and falling between the two groups, clustered around the mean, were the heights of children whose mothers had arrived here less than 10 years before those children's births.

Recently, H. Bouterline Young on one coast and Gruelich on the other demonstrated that the process of New World growth enhancement was still going on. Young (1962) looked at the children of Sicilians who had either stayed in Sicily, moved to Rome, or moved to Boston, and found that the descendants of the Boston group were taller than the descendants of the Rome group who, in their turn, were taller than the children of parents who had never left Sicily, the greater heights of the Rome and Boston groups apparently reflecting the effects of an improved standard of living.

Gruelich, 1958

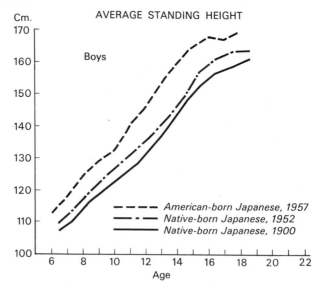

FIGURE 5.4

Height of American-born Japanese Boys Compared with That of Boys in Japan, 1900 and 1952

Gruelich, 1958

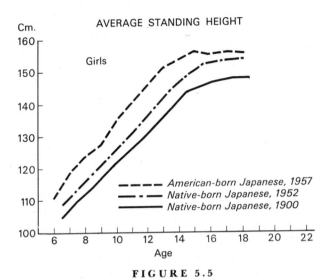

FIGURE 5.5

**Height of American-born Japanese Girls Compared with That of
Girls in Japan, 1900 and 1952**

On the West Coast, Gruelich (1958) discovered the same process
to be at work among the descendants of another group of immigrants, the Nisei, or American-born Japanese, in California. He
found that the stature of the Nisei boys in 1957 exceeded that of
native-born Japanese "by an amount greater than the increase
which has taken place in the average stature of the boys of Japan
since the beginning of the present century," and that the Nisei girls
enjoyed almost as great a superiority over their native-born counterparts. Figures 5.4 and 5.5 show the disadvantage in height of the
Japanese-born compared to the American-born children, a difference which Gruelich attributed to the "less adequate diet and other
environmental conditions which are not so conducive to optimal
growth as those existing in this country."

Gruelich concluded that his findings indicated "the need for
caution in interpreting . . . relatively retarded growth and devel-

opment . . . in less favored parts of the world as the expression of some basic genetic difference. . . ." It is quite probable, in other words, that even national differences in stature, which until recently have been assumed to be genetically determined, may at least in part reflect differences in national growth environments. This is not to argue, of course, that there are no inherited height limits which may vary from group to group (and which may already have been reached among the most affluent groups in the developed countries—Bakwin *et al.*, 1964), but rather that we shall remain unsure of what they may be until environmental opportunities for growth have been equalized. It is no doubt right, Boyne and Leitch (1954) have written, "that the maximum height to which any individual can attain is fixed by type, stock, or heredity, but it is equally sure that over the last 100 years a very high proportion [of individuals] were debarred by disease and deformity from coming near to their potential upper limit."

It is invariably difficult to sort out the genetic and environmental variables in human populations. But Hiernaux (1964), studying boys of two different tribes in rural Rwanda, was apparently able to achieve a degree of separation between them and thus to demonstrate quite clearly the growth-enhancing effects of improved environment. Using cross-sectional data, Hiernaux found that among the Rwanda Tutsi, both boys and girls were taller at all ages than their counterparts among the Hutu tribe. Though they lived in a similar environment and had a similar, perhaps even better, diet, the Tutsi also had a much lower weight-to-stature ratio, that is, they were consistently thinner as well as taller than the Hutu. Data were also available, however, on a second group of Hutu children, born and reared in the copper-mine camps of the Katanga, where hygiene, food, and medical care were better than among the agricultural Hutu of Rwanda. The data in Table 5.1 show the effect of the improved mine-camp environment "acting on a similar gene pool." Even in the improved environment the mine-camp Hutu were still somewhat shorter than the Tutsi, but they were considerably taller and heavier at any given age, as well as heavier for any given stature, than their rural fellow-tribesmen. Thus although the Hutu seem to be genetically shorter than the Tutsi, the findings suggest that both groups were probably stunted in the rural

TABLE 5.1

Mean Stature and Weight of Tutsi and Hutu Boys in Rwanda, and of Hutu Boys Born and Reared in U.M.H.K. Mine Camps

| | TUTSI | | | RWANDA HUTU | | | U.M.H.K. HUTU | |
Age (in years)	N	Stature (cm)	Weight (Kg)	N	Stature (cm)	Weight (Kg)	N	Stature (cm)	Weight (Kg)
6.5	34	115.23	18.65	61	111:36	18.17	53	113.92	20.22
7.5	39	119.93	20.60	60	115.89	19.46	53	118.02	22.55
8.5	52	123.72	21.41	65	119.88	21.21	60	123.63	24.43
9.5	56	128.92	23.36	63	122.94	22.30	23	125.52	25.36
10.5	48	135.81	26.52	59	128.83	25.17	12	131.72	28.67
11.5	64	139.69	28.56	61	133.11	27.13	8	135.01	30.65
12.5	62	142.66	30.26	61	136.97	29.20 ⎫			
13.5	63	149.14	33.82	53	141.90	31.86 ⎬ 10	144.06	37.01
14.5	56	149.93	33.88	46	143.61	33.47 ⎭			
15.5	56	155.45	38.01	43	149.08	36.34			
16.5	35	162.41	42.75	26	154.68	41.51			
17.5	25	166.14	48.47	21	155.91	44.06			

Hiernaux, 1964

environment by the effects of bad sanitation, poor diet, and inadequate medical care.

Although these examples of height increase following imigration of a segment of a gene pool to an improved environment provide some of the most dramatic evidence we have of the effects of growth opportunity on the size of human populations, height changes can also be observed within stay-at-home groups which have benefited from national economic advances. In Japan itself, for example, where the growth of children was badly set back by the war, children at every age level had surpassed prewar heights by 1957 (Insull and Kenzaburo, 1968). In the decade between 1950 and 1960 the increase in stature of Japanese children was reportedly as great as that observed in other countries in three or four decades (Mitchell, 1962), and had apparently occurred in response to the improved standard of living that attended Japan's dramatic economic resurgence. Mitchell (1964) has pointed out that in 22 Japanese orphanages children whose diets were not improved during the same period did not share in the general growth advancement and had average heights at each age level which were consistently below the national mean.

It is probable that the apparently decreasing size of the gap between the heights of the different social classes in Britain is itself clear evidence of a significant improvement in the growth environment of the lower classes which has allowed them to start catching up to the already well-grown upper classes. There is some controversy about the extent to which the apparent secular increase in size of various populations is merely a reflection of accelerated growth and earlier maturation rather than a real change in the height of adults, but it seems clear that among some populations the mean heights have increased over time. In 1883, as we have seen, the difference in height between the highest and the lowest classes in Britain was more than 8 inches. In 1961, Tanner estimated that the mean difference in height between offspring of families in the professional and managerial classes and those of unskilled laboring-class families was somewhere between 1½ and 2 inches.

Acheson and Fowler (1964) observed this "catching up" process in action, so to speak, by examining the relationships between economic status and heights of succeeding generations in two groups of men, women, and children. In one group—families of London professional men—both parent and child generations had grown up in relative prosperity; in the other group—families of Welsh coal miners—prosperity had come only during the adulthood of the parent generation. If changed economic status was indeed the source of increased height in succeeding generations, they argued, then there should be greater differences between fathers and their children in the Welsh group than in the London group. And there were. Although the professionals were taller than the coal miners at all ages, the between-generation height differences were significantly greater for the Welsh coal miners, apparently as a direct consequence of their greater improvement in economic status. The result was that in mean height the younger generation of coal miners was closer to the young of the professional families than each group of fathers had been to the other.

If shortness of stature in the lower classes was simply genetic, social forces in Britain would act to increase rather than decrease social-class differences in height. For as Illsley has shown in Aberdeen, and as Schreider has recently confirmed on data from the British Perinatal Mortality Survey (Illsley, 1955; Schreider, 1964), a woman's height decidedly affects her chances of moving up or down the social scale at marriage. Women who are taller than the average for their class tend to marry "up," and those who are shorter tend to marry "down," a process that would serve to reinforce any linkage between "short" genes and low social status.

As it happens, Illsley found that marrying "up," like achieving a height greater than average for one's class, tended to occur in conjunction with a whole constellation of advantageous background factors. Women who married "up" were not only taller and healthier but came from smaller families, were less likely to have left school by the age of 14, were more likely to be of above-average intelligence, and were more likely to have taken skilled jobs than were women in the same class who married "down" or who did not change class at marriage (Baird and Illsley, 1953). What is suggested, of course, is that a lower-class girl is likely to be tall for her class if she has had a better than average upbringing.

There is growing body of evidence, then, that among groups who are endemically short, increase in stature follows an improvement in economic status, and that the shortness of such groups under their original environmental conditions arises not from"short genes" but from social and environmental inadequacies. Further evidence that this is the case comes from studies showing shortness to be associated with various abnormal features of growth and development. Figure 5.6 shows the distribution of women of poor physique and poor health by social class among the same group of Aberdeen mothers whose height distribution was charted in Figure 5.3. Fifty percent of the women in the lowest classes were graded as having very poor physiques and being in very poor health, but less than one-fourth of the women in the highest classes were so graded. Using a much larger sample, 4,312 Aberdeen women having first babies, Thomson and Billewicz (1963) were able to show that, regardless of class, physical grade and height were strongly related. As Table 5.2 shows, though 42% of the women whose health was judged "very good" and 29% of those in "good" health were tall, the

Illsley, 1956

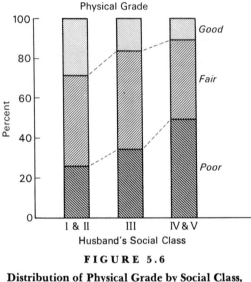

FIGURE 5.6

**Distribution of Physical Grade by Social Class,
Aberdeen, 1950–1953**

(Married city primiparae)

percentage of tall women declined to 18% among those in fair condition and to 13% among those in poor or very poor condition. On the opposite end of the height scale, the percentage of short women went from 10% among those in very good condition to 48% among those in poor or very poor condition.

Poor growth is further associated not merely with generally poor physique, but also with certain specific features of growth distortion. Leitch (1951) has reminded us that in man development proceeds from the head and chest region forward and backward, and that the hindquarters mature last. "If the rate of growth is sufficiently slowed, the adult is not only small but underdeveloped, with normal or nearly normal size head, moderately retarded trunk, and relatively short legs." Not unexpectedly, then, it is in the pelvis and the legs that other indicators of poor growth can be found among groups of short people.

TABLE 5.2

Height in Relation to Health and Physique, Aberdeen

(4,312 primiparae)

	Health and Physique			
	Very Good	*Good*	*Fair*	*Poor, Very Poor*
Number of subjects	707	2,088	1,294	223
Percentage tall (5 feet 4 inches or more)	42	29	18	13
Percentage short (under 5 feet 1 inch)	10	20	30	48

Thomson and Billewicz, 1963

With the development of x-ray pelvimetry in the 1930s an attempt was made to establish classifications of "normal" pelvic shapes, but an understanding of the sources of variance in pelvic configuration was hampered by the conviction that the shape of the pelvis was genetically determined. In 1939, however, Gruelich, Thoms, and Twaddle observed that the rounded or long oval pelvis, which appeared to be functionally superior for childbearing, was found predominantly among economically well-off, well-grown student nurses as well as among young children. Seventy-three percent of a group of student nurses, compared with 37.3% of a group of economically less privileged clinic patients, had such functionally superior pelvises. The fact that the clinic patients tended to be much shorter than the nurses, and that among both groups the women with the round and long oval pelvises were always tallest, suggested to Gruelich and his colleagues that differences in nutritional status between patients and nurses might account for the variance in both height and pelvic shape.

Subsequently, Bernard (1952), following up the lead, examined the distribution of pelvic types in two groups of women at extremes of height: one group consisted of 100 women over 5 feet 5 inches; the other group consisted of 100 women under 5 feet. Through x-ray pelvimetry on this group of 200 Aberdeen primiparae, Bernard was able to show that a flattening of the pelvic brim, an abnormality suggesting inadequate growth, occurred considerably more frequently among women under 5 feet tall than among those over 5 feet 5 inches. Thirty-four of the 100 short women examined had a flattened pelvis, compared to only seven of the taller women, though, as Bernard observed, "the shape should be equally distributed if it were 'normal,' " and not an aftermath of defective growth. Bernard found further that when the 200 women were examined for general physical condition, 76% of the tall women, compared with 19% of the small women, were graded superior (Grade I) and, as Figure

Bernard, 1952

	Tall Women			Small Women	
	Grade I	Grade II		Grade I	Grade II
Round	88.2%		Normal Pelvic Shapes	73.6%	
		83.3%			63.0%
Narrow	6.6%			0.0%	
		4.2%			0.0%
Flat	5.2%		Abnormal Pelvic Shapes	26.4%	
		12.5%			35.8%
Scutiform	0.0%	0.0%		0.0%	
					1.2%
Number of Cases	76 (100%)	24 (100%)		19 (100%)	81 (100%)

FIGURE 5.7

Pelvic Type Incidence by Physique

5.7 shows, within each height group those women judged physically inferior (Grade II) showed a larger proportion of abnormal pelvic shapes.

Another indicator of unfulfilled growth potential, Leitch (1951) has pointed out, may be short legs; long legs—hailed in romantic literature and popular taste—may thus be the biologic as well as the aesthetic ideal. The relation between diet and leg length was demonstrated on a large scale in Britain in the Carnegie U. K. Dietary and Clinical Survey (1937–1939). In that survey, as Leitch (1951) and

Thomson and Duncan (1954) have all pointed out, leg length was found to be a better predictor of family expenditures on food than was height or weight. There are even fewer data on leg length than there are on height differences among different social classes. But Mitchell has pointed out that by 1959 the sitting height of Japanese children was already equal to the American norm; that Japanese children were, therefore, shorter on the average than American children only because of their short legs; and that experimental improvement of the protein quality of the diets of Japanese children increased their leg growth more than it increased their trunk growth (1962).

It is quite clear, then, that although individuals and racial groups may vary in height potential, short stature in groups which have been exposed to less than optimal conditions for growth is evidence of some degree of stunting; and that having had, or not having had, opportunities for optimum growth is one of the factors which differentiates between women of different social classes.

Since height within any population appears to be a record of antecedent opportunities for growth, we can now consider whether women's poor growth, as reflected in short stature, does indeed affect their reproductive performance. The relationships between height, growth, and reproductive performance have been examined extensively only in Aberdeen, Scotland, where Sir John Boyd Orr inspired an early interest in the effects of diet and environment on growth. More than 20 years ago, Dugald Baird observed that the reproductive performance of "tall and healthy" women was on the whole much better than that of their "small and unhealthy" counterparts, and that short stature was more than five times as common among a group of lower-class women delivering at Aberdeen Maternity Hospital than among a group of upper-class women delivering at a private nursing home (Baird, 1947). Following up the lead provided by these observations, Baird went on to analyze the reproductive performances of 3,600 mothers delivering first babies in Aberdeen. He found that for women of all ages having a first child, fetal mortality rates were 26/1,000 for women more than 5 feet 4 inches tall and almost twice that, 50/1,000, for women who were under 5 feet 1 inch. The highest standard of reproductive performance was found among a group of tall women under 25 years of age who came from social classes I and II. Among these 171 women there were no cesarean sections, only 1 stillbirth, and no neonatal deaths (Baird, 1949). On further investigation it turned out that short stature was associated not only with stillbirth and difficulties in delivery, but also with the incidence of births under 5½ pounds. Among 2,133 Aberdeen women having first babies, Baird and Illsley (1953) found that the incidence of prematurity was 5.6% for those 5 feet 4 inches and over, 7.8% for those 5 feet 1 inch to 5 feet 3 inches, and 11.7% for those under 5 feet 1 inch.

When Thomson examined a later series of 26,589 Aberdeen births covering a 10-year period, he found that the association between decreasing stature and increasing rates of prematurity, delivery complications, and perinatal death persisted for each parity and for age groups within parities (1959). Moreover, despite the tendency for smaller women to produce smaller babies, and, as a group, to be younger and thus more biologically efficient, they were much more likely than taller women to experience delivery complications. Finding that the relationship between height and perinatal death persisted for deaths due to causes other than birth trauma, Thomson concluded that "it is evident that whatever the nature of the delivery, the fetus of a short woman has lower vitality and is less likely to be well-grown and to survive than that of a tall woman."

From the data already presented it could be argued that short stature may only appear to be associated with increased reproductive risk as a consequence of its strong relationship to social class, and that it is in fact not the mother's history as a grower but rather her lower-class status which has put her at risk as a reproducer. Such an argument is easily dealt with, however, for the association between height, general physique, and reproductive performance exists for each social class. Table 5.3 shows that for both prematurity and perinatal loss there is no tendency for height to "matter" less, as Thomson has put it, in any social class. There is a double gradient of reproductive casualty—prematurity, and perinatal mortality rates increasing in each social class as height declines, and increasing within each height group as social class declines, so that rates of prematurity and perinatal loss are lowest among the tall and well-off and highest among the poor and short. Thomson and his colleagues also found that for any given height women judged to be

TABLE 5.3

Perinatal Mortality and Prematurity Rates by Height and Social Class, Aberdeen, 1948–1957

(Primigravidae)

Height		I, II	III	IV, V	All Classes
Tall	Perinatal mortality	14.5	25.5	35.0	24.6
(64 inches and over)	Prematurity	(3.8)	(4.8)	(6.7)	(4.9)
Medium	Perinatal mortality	22.2	33.4	36.8	32.8
(63 inches to 61 inches)	Prematurity	(5.6)	(7.3)	(9.7)	(7.7)
Short	Perinatal mortality	35.5	36.5	55.0	42.1
(< 61 inches)	Prematurity	(8.6)	(11.3)	(14.3)	(12.1)

Baird, 1964

in good physical condition had a lower incidence of prematurity, cesarean section, and perinatal death than those whose physical condition was assessed as poor or very poor.

Though there has been no investigation of the relevant variables in other communities comparable in thoroughness to the Aberdeen studies, the relationships between social class, stature, and perinatal mortality found in Aberdeen have recently been confirmed on a national sample of women in Britain. Data from the Perinatal Mortality Survey of 1958 showed that heights of women followed the same regional distribution as did perinatal deaths: women were tallest in the South, shorter in the central zone, and shortest in the North, and in each region the proportion of tall women declined from the professional class to the unskilled laboring class. The 30% of the women in the total sample who were 65 inches or more in height had a perinatal mortality rate 21% below the national average; on the other hand, the 22% of women in the sample who were less than 5 feet 2 inches had a perinatal mortality rate 14% above the national average (NCHS, PHS 1000, 3:12, 1968).

Thomson and Billewicz (1963) have published data from Hong Kong which show a similar relationship between height and three indicators of reproductive casualty—prematurity, cesarean section, and perinatal death—for Chinese women in their first pregnancies; and Baird (1964), using data on all births in a western Nigerian village, has also shown a clear relationship between premature birth (under 2,500 grams) and maternal height. Low birth weight babies were born to 10.4% of the tall women and 17.9% of the short women. Moreover, the 239 tall women had no cesarean sections and only one perinatal death, but the 150 short women required 6 cesarean sections and experienced 14 perinatal deaths. Other scattered findings have been cited by Illsley (1967).

Up to now we have said nothing about height, social status, and reproductive performance in the U. S. The reason, quite simply, is that there are virtually no data available. The relationship between growth environment and complications of pregnancy and birth has as yet not been seriously investigated in this country. To the extent that it has been, the Aberdeen findings were confirmed. Yerushalmy (1967), in a preliminary report on a large study, reported finding an incidence of births under 2,500 grams of 6.7% among short mothers, 5.1% among mothers of medium height, and 3.5% among tall mothers. And Donnelly et al. (1964), studying births in North Carolina University Hospital, found both a differential distribution of height by social class and an association between prematurity and maternal size in every class. In class I (the most advantaged whites), just over half (52%) of the women were less than 5 feet 5 inches. In class IV (the least advantaged nonwhites), 70% of the women were under 5 feet 5 inches. Moreover, the proportion of shorter women increased consistently from class I to class IV, and within each class the incidence of prematurity was higher for women who were less than 5 feet 3 inches tall.

Among the factors complicating both research and data interpretation in the U. S., however, is the fact that ethnicity is confounded with social class in this country, and the social classes are neither so well defined nor so stable as is the case in Britain. It is quite likely that the picture that emerges from the Aberdeen data of, at most, a gradual shift, generation to generation, from one social class to another in response to intraclass environmental variations, is most valid in a society with a traditional and relatively structured social system. Although it may be harder than it ever was before to move from rags to riches in the United States, interclass movement is still relatively free here, dramatic changes in economic status do take place, and a shift from the unskilled manual laboring class to professional status within one generation is not only not unheard of but is rather the model of achievement against which successive groups of "disadvantaged" peoples have measured their progress.

The greatest disparity between the childhood growth environment of a given generation of mothers and their immediate economic situation at the time of childbearing is likely to be found among groups in which upward movement has been most recent and most rapid. Thus the professional man and his wife in this country are less likely than their counterparts in Britain to have come from an environment closely similar to that implied by their present status. Such facts help to explain why, among traditionally disadvantaged minority populations in our own country, risk rates may remain high even among those who in the present generation may have attained adequate or superior economic status.

Moreover, just as social class is a more unstable variable in the United States than in Britain, just so is our racial and ethnic diversity a factor exerting a number of unexamined effects on size. Stature in adulthood thus becomes a measure of environmental adequacy easier to accept than to apply in this country. In Donnelly's study, the most advantaged nonwhite group contained more short women and had higher rates of prematurity at any maternal stature than the least advantaged white group. Such a finding could be interpreted as supporting our earlier assumption that prior conditions of growth have handicapped even the more privileged among the present generation of Negroes, or it could be assumed to demonstrate merely that under all environmental conditions Negroes are shorter than whites.

Since the issue of size in relation to race will be dealt with more fully in a subsequent chapter, it need only be pointed out here that there is no good evidence at present that U. S. whites and U. S. nonwhites differ significantly in mean height if present and past socioeconomic status are taken into account (e.g., Ohlson *et al.*, 1956). There is also no good evidence that they do *not* differ under such circumstances; that is, the possibility of genetically determined differences in height potential cannot be ruled out. Neither relationship can be demonstrated, however, until growth environments have been equalized.

Meanwhile it seems clear that women whose growth environments have been poor are at greater risk in childbearing than are those whose opportunities for growth and development have been adequate. If we can document, then, as we shall in a subsequent chapter, that there are significant differences in the growth environments of the poor and the not-poor in this country, then the Aberdeen and the Donnelly data require us to assume that poor growth must be another of the variables through which depressed class or minority status produces an excess of reproductive failure among the poor, especially among the nonwhite poor women in this country.

In the next two chapters we will be considering some of the circumstances which affect women when they are pregnant, in order to examine the extent to which a woman's risk on entering pregnancy is multiplied if she must bring it to term under substandard conditions. We will take up first a rather substantial body of literature on the relationship between pregnancy diet and pregnancy outcome, a topic which, as will become evident, is part of the complex of factors related to the issue of growth with which we have been here concerned.

CHAPTER SIX

Pregnancy and Food

Perfect health may be defined as a state of well-being such that the possessor carries no stigmata to which a nutritional origin can be assigned, and in whom no improvement in health can be effected by change of diet. In other words, optimum nutrition in an adult implies and postulates optimum nutrition of that person as a child, that child as a foetus, and that foetus of its mother.

MCCANCE, WIDDOWSON, AND VERDON-ROE

THERE is no scientific basis for the popular notion that the woman who has conceived a child is in some sense "eating for two," but it is a fact that a pregnant woman bears within her body another organism which for nine months is dependent on her for its sustenance.

The effect of women's nutritional status on their reproductive performance, which we shall be examining in this chapter, is a topic which we have, without really acknowledging it, already begun to explore. For in using growth as a variable to be considered in relation to childbearing, we have taken an archaeologist's look at nutritional status, reading in a woman's height a partial record of her prior health and nutrition—the most significant of the environmental variables affecting growth. Though, as we have seen, too little attention has been paid by investigators to lifetime nutritional status in relation to pregnancy outcome, the effect of diet *during* pregnancy on its outcome has been extensively studied.

There are at least two reasons for this focus on the effects of contemporaneous rather than lifetime diet. The first is common sense. The idea has long been widespread that good nutrition is especially important for the pregnant woman whose body nourishes the fetus, and alteration of diet in response to pregnancy, or in anticipation of pregnancy, is common even among primitive peoples (Mead and Newton, 1967). The second reason for the attention given to diet during pregnancy is scientific-historical; i.e., having to do with the juxtaposition in time of a series of events in the laboratory and in the field, which argued for the view that alterations in the diet of a pregnant woman could affect pregnancy outcome. Since these historic events still constitute some of the most telling evidence on the subject, it will be worth reviewing them briefly.

The scientific study of nutrition was still young when Mellanby (1933), acknowledging that "direct and accurate knowledge of this subject in human beings is meagre," asserted that nutrition was undoubtedly the "most important of all environmental factors in childbearing." It was Mellanby's conviction that the high incidence of ill-health among poor mothers during pregnancy, and their high perinatal mortality rates, could be reduced by improving the quality of the diet during pregnancy. Both Mellanby's attitudes and his experiments—e.g., utilizing the reputed "anti-infective" powers of vitamin A to reduce postpartum morbidity—were characteristic of his time, conditioned by the fact that so many of the vitamins had been and were even then being discovered in dramatic association with heretofore mysterious and widespread diseases. Thus the natural tendency of investigators at the time was to see vitamins and other nutrients as therapeutic and prophylactic specifics.

The idea that such a view of nutrition might also be applicable to anomalies of pregnancy gained support from a long series of animal studies beginning with those of Hale (e.g., 1935; 1937) on vitamin A in the 1930s. This work, as carried forward in the investigations of Warkany in the 1940s (e.g., Warkany and Nelson, 1942; Warkany, 1944, 1948), demonstrated conclusively that pregnant animals maintained on rations deficient in certain dietary ingredients produced offspring suffering from varying types and degrees of malformation. From these studies it appeared that a diet adequate to maintain maternal life and reproductive capacity could, in certain cases, be inadequate to sustain the normal development of the fetus; that the fetus was thus not a perfect parasite and, for at least some features of growth and differentiation, could have requirements different from those of the maternal host.

PREGNANCY AND FOOD

At about the same time that the first animal experiments were being reported, Orr (1936) and subsequently McCance, Widdowson, and Verdon-Roe (1938) demonstrated that within the British population the well-known social-class gradient in reproductive risk was paralleled by a similar gradient in quality and quantity of dietary intake, with the poor generally and poor pregnant women specifically taking diets that were "in all respects inadequate for perfect health." The growing conviction that serious damage in the offspring might arise from these demonstrably poor diets gave rise in England to some large-scale supplementation efforts involving thousands of pregnant women (Balfour, 1944; People's League of Health, 1946) and on this continent to two small but important studies: a food supplementation study by Ebbs, Tisdall, and Scott in Toronto (1941) involving 90 pregnant women, and a dietary survey by Burke and her associates in Boston comparing spontaneous dietary intake and pregnancy outcome in 216 women (Burke *et al.*, 1943*a, b, c*).

Almost all the human studies conducted before World War II were scientifically faulty; the large and largely uncontrolled supplementation studies were considerably more humane than scientific, and the smaller studies suffered from being based on samples which were too small or unrepresentative to provide statistically convincing data. But for the most part they showed positive results. Burke's findings led her to conclude that differences in spontaneous dietary intake among pregnant women were reflected both in differences in the mother's health during pregnancy and in the size and quality of the infant she produced; the supplementation studies lent support to the idea that both the pregnant woman and her child benefited from improved nutrition during pregnancy. Knowledge of the results from these studies thus helped to engender a widespread if sometimes uncritical enthusiasm for the potentially beneficial effects on child-bearers and their progeny of a program of dietary improvement during pregnancy.

Perhaps the most fortunate outcome of the resultant enthusiasm for "optimum nutrition" was the conscious and successful effort made by the British wartime government to upgrade the diet of its people—in particular, the diets of children and pregnant women. Thus was set up what amounted to an informal "feeding experiment" on a national scale not normally feasible. It was of great interest that during the 5 years of war, from 1940 to 1945, the stillbirth rate in England and Wales underwent an accelerated decline, falling from 38 per 1,000 births to 28 per 1,000 births.

Duncan, Baird, and Thomson (1952) have argued convincingly that the dietary improvement and the abrupt fall in stillbirths as well as a significant but lesser decrease in neonatal deaths were clearly related. Thomson (1959a) has argued further that the reduction was convincing as a "nutritional effect" since "it was achieved in the context of a society where most of the conditions of living other than the nutritional were deteriorating." Not only was routine antenatal practice and obstetrical care limited by the siphoning-off of so many doctors into the armed services, but the greatest reduction in deaths during those years was among those very cases least affected by level of care, in which death was attributed to "ill-defined or unknown causes" and appeared to be related to low fetal vitality.

Further "wartime" evidence as to the importance of diet in pregnancy came from a similar though smaller-scale feeding experiment on the continent. In 1939, Dr. K. Utheim Toverud set up a health station in the Sagene district of Oslo to serve pregnant and nursing mothers and their babies (Toverud, 1950). Though the war made it progressively more difficult to get certain "protective" foods, the use of supplementary and synthetic sources assured every supervised woman of an adequate intake of all essential nutrients. Despite food restrictions, which became increasingly severe toward the end of the war, the prematurity rate among 728 women supervised at the station never went above the 1943 high of 3.4% and averaged 2.2% for the period 1939 to 1944. Among unsupervised mothers the prematurity rate was 6.3% in 1943, and the average for the period was 4.6%. In addition, the stillbirth rate of 14.2/1,000 for all women attending the health station was half that of the women in the surrounding districts.

Even while the British and Norwegian feeding experiments were in progress, some hopefully never-to-be-repeated "natural" experiments in starvation were taking place elsewhere on the continent. Reported after the war, the childbearing experiences of various populations of women under conditions of famine provided evidence of how severe deprivation could negatively affect the product of conception—just as the British and Norwegian data suggested that dietary improvement could affect it positively.

Smith (1947) studied infants born in Rotterdam and The Hague during the period between the autumn of 1944, when the Dutch rose against the German invaders, and the German collapse in the spring of 1945. As a consequence of German reprisals against the rebellious population, it was a period of severe and universal hunger (Berger *et al.*, 1947). Smith found that infants born during this period of deprivation were shorter and lighter (by 240 grams) than those born either before or after the famine winter. However, those babies who were 5- to 6-month fetuses when the hunger period began appeared to have been reduced in weight as much as those who had spent a full 9 months in the uterus of a malnourished mother. From this Smith concluded that reduced maternal food intake had its major effect on fetal weight beginning about the sixth month of gestation.

Published simultaneously, Antonov's report (1947) on pregnancy and birth in Leningrad, during the 18-month German siege of that city, agreed with Smith's finding that weight was reduced in infants of starving mothers. In addition, Antonov showed that prolonged deprivation could interrupt pregnancy and finally prevent conception altogether. During a 6-month period which began 4 months after the start of the siege there was an enormous increase in prematurity in Leningrad—as judged by length and weight at birth—with 41.2% of all babies born during this period being shorter than 47 cm., and fully 49.1% weighing under 2,500 grams. The babies were also of very low vitality: 30.8% of the prematures and 9% of the full-term babies died shortly after birth. In the next 6-month period, both the prematurity and the birth rates plummeted. Close to 400 babies were born between January and June of 1942; less than 80 between July and December.

Available information suggested that the lower prematurity rate among women who had managed to conceive during a period when amenorrhea was widespread was a consequence of their being better-fed than the majority, being employed in food industries or working in professional or manual occupations which had food priorities. It was Antonov's conclusion from his own data that although the fetus might behave for the most part like a parasite, "the condition of the host, the mother's body, is of great consequence to the fetus, and that severe quantitative and qualitative hunger of the mother decidedly affects the development of the fetus and the vitality of the newborn child."

After the war, Dean (1951) confirmed the Smith and Antonov results with a careful analysis of a series of 22,000 consecutive births at the Landesfrauenklinik, Wuppertal, Germany, during the years 1937–1948. He found once again that food deprivation produced small infants, and that maximal deprivation produced maximal size reduction, average weights and lengths at birth being lowest in 1945, the year of the greatest food shortages. But it also became apparent that the babies in his series were not so much early (i.e., truly premature) as they were undersized, the small reduction in the average duration of gestation being insufficient to account for the degree of weight reduction observed. Thus Dean's data appeared to demonstrate once more that severe hunger could act to reduce the growth of the infant in the womb.

As a whole, the prewar and wartime experiences supported— indeed, promoted—the view that the quality and quantity of the mother's diet during pregnancy bore a significant relationship to the course and outcome of that pregnancy. By the end of the war it appeared likely that the filling in of the details of the indicated relationships would require little more than the replication, under more carefully controlled conditions, of certain aspects of the studies already reported. Thus, the approaches taken to the investigation of the problem after the war were in essence those already utilized: surveys which attempted to relate differences in dietary intake during pregnancy (sometimes in conjunction with clinical or biochemical evaluations of nutritional status) to differences in course and outcome; supplementation studies designed to examine whether alterations in the course of pregnancy and birth would result from nutritional improvement; "natural" studies looking at reproductive performance under conditions of severe dietary stress; and studies of animals on variously restricted diets.

Among these methods the dietary survey was the least expensive to conduct in human mothers-to-be, and an impressive number of such studies were carried out in a variety of settings (e.g., Sontag and Wines, 1947; Dieckmann *et al.*, 1951*a*, 1951*b*; Speert, Graff, and Graff, 1951; Berry and Wiehl, 1952; Darby *et al.*, 1953*a*, 1953*b*; McGanity *et al.*, 1954*a*, 1954*b*; Woodhill *et al.*, 1955; Jeans, Smith, and Stearns, 1955; Thomson, 1958, 1959*a*).

No purpose would be served here by a detailed consideration of each of these studies. Suffice it to say that by using selectively the data which they produced, it would be equally possible to demonstrate either that diet does or that it does not affect the course and outcome of pregnancy. Consequently the results, taken as a whole, have tended to produce somewhat more confusion on the question of whether or not nutrition is important during pregnancy than appeared to exist right after the war. Although some of this confusion may be attributable to poor data—for "the snags and pitfalls that beset the path of those who attempt to make accurate estimates of what people eat are countless" (Hytten and Leitch, 1964)—even those studies which were the most carefully carried out have produced apparently conflicting results. Sontag and Wines (1947), for example, using a detailed dietary survey method developed by Burke were unable to replicate Burke's finding that higher maternal protein intake was reflected in the increased size of the infant. Woodhill *et al.* (1955), however, also using Burke's method on an Australian population, confirmed the relationship of infant size to protein intake.

Even more puzzling, perhaps, were the results of two of the largest and most carefully conducted studies: the Vanderbilt Study of Maternal and Infant Nutrition, involving 2,129 delivered pregnancies at Vanderbilt Hospital in Nashville, Tennessee (Darby *et al.*, 1953*a*, 1953*b*; McGanity *et al.*, 1954*a*, 1954*b*), and a study by Thomson of a socially stratified group of 489 Aberdeen women in their first pregnancies (Thomson, 1958, 1959*a*). The findings in both studies were largely negative, with a complex relationship demonstrated between dietary intake during pregnancy and any of the measures of reproductive performance considered. Hence the dilemma which Thomson pointed out at the time of his study: "On the one hand a belief which seems generally reasonable and is backed by much circumstantial and historical evidence that mothers can more efficiently undertake the physiological burden of pregnancy and lactation if they are well fed, and, on the other hand, the apparent failure of survey methods to provide a convincing confirmation of this belief."

The addition of clinical and biochemical measures of nutritional status to some of these dietary surveys contributed little to the elucidation of relationships between nutrition and reproduction, largely because no straightforward and regular relationship was demonstrated for most nutrients between level of dietary intake and level present in the body as measurable by biochemical methods currently available; nor were there clear-cut relationships between biochemically measurable "nutritional status" and most clinical signs of malnutrition (e.g., Dieckmann et al., 1944; Speert, Graff, and Graff, 1951; McGanity, 1954). As regards these "clinical signs" themselves—minor abnormalities of the skin, eyes, gums, and so on, which Tompkins (1941, 1948) had concluded could be used to measure nutritional status—they, too, proved difficult to evaluate. The authors of the only major postwar study which attempted to utilize them were forced to conclude that examiner differences were the single most important variable in determining whether or not "subclinical deficiency" was noted in a particular woman. Indeed, where the diagnosis of obesity was concerned, it "actually seemed to correlate inversely with the weight of the individual examiner" (Darby et al., 1953b).

Results from the major supplementation studies conducted since the war have been equally inconclusive. In an intriguing and never-replicated study, Harrell et al. (1956) supplemented the diets of pregnant white and Negro women in an attempt to influence the intellectual level of their children. Tompkins, Wiehl, and their associates (Wiehl et al., 1955, Tompkins et al., 1955a, 1955b; Kasius et al., 1955; Randall et al., 1955) supplemented the diets of pregnant white and Negro women in an attempt to improve their pregnancy performance and the quality of their infants. Harrell found some apparent correlation between supplementation and children's IQ level at 3 and 4 years for the Negro group, but not for the white group, among whom supplements were less reliably utilized. However, the results of the study are difficult to interpret.

The Tompkins group (Kasius et al., 1955) found that supplementing mothers had no effect on the physiologic condition of their infants "at birth or upon their growth during the first 3 months of life," but the incidence of prematurity and toxemia appeared to have been reduced by supplementation for mothers at some ages and parities. Unfortunately for the interpretation of the results, women in this study who were uncooperative about taking the supplements were put into the control group—so that it is difficult to separate out the effects of supplementation from correlates of cooperativeness—a variable which does seem to relate to a better reproductive outcome (Dieckmann, 1951a; Thomson, 1958).

Thus the overall results of both the survey and the supplementation studies conducted since the mid-1940s have been at best confused, and at worst negative. The assumption that a direct relationship between diet in pregnancy and pregnancy course and outcome could be demonstrated conclusively has not yet materialized; and, as Thomson has pointed out, "continuing uncertainty may lead those responsible for the public health to consider, in defiance of the lessons of history, that nutrition in pregnancy is unimportant and may be neglected." Now it is possible to argue that the negative findings of these studies may in some cases be a consequence of their having focused on the wrong outcome. It is clear from the wartime experiences as well as from the animal studies that poor diet may exert a negative influence on the fetus even when pregnancy course and maternal health are unaffected, so that the specific focus of many of these investigations (on pregnancy rather than on its product) may account for their apparent lack of findings.

Some support for this view comes from a study by Dieckmann and his collaborators in Chicago (1951a, 1951b). These investigators, having conducted an impeccable survey of the nutrition of mothers, looked at their babies. Because the mothers in the group were carefully supervised and required to keep weighed-diet records, the group retained in the study was a highly selected one. Of more than 1,100 patients who met the entry criteria, only 602 remained in the study; and of those eliminated, 461 were dropped solely for keeping insufficient records. The general superiority of the group was reflected in its strikingly low rate of prematurity: 3.3% of the women had premature infants, compared with the usual hospital prevalence of 6.3%. Yet even within such a highly selected group, Dieckmann found significant differences in the quality of the infants produced as a factor of the level of protein in their mothers' diets. A protein supplement supplied to women already taking relatively high protein diets effectively exaggerated the differences between the good and the poor diets, so that in the final sample about 12% of the women were taking on the average less than 55 grams of protein a day, while over 20% were taking more than 85 grams per day. As the figures in Table 6.1 show, increasing maternal protein intake was accompanied by a steady rise in the percentage of excellent babies.

TABLE 6.1

Correlation of Mothers' Average Protein Intake
and Condition of Babies *

Level of Protein Intake (grams)	Pediatric Rating			
	Number Poor to Good	Number Excellent	Total	Percent Excellent
Less than 55	18	10	28	35.71
55 to 70	52	37	89	41.57
70 to 85	46	81	127	63.78
Over 85	19	54	70	72.86

* $p = 0.5701$ $\chi^2_{\frac{2}{3}} = 23.4$
$q = 0.4299$ $P = $ approximately 1×10^{-4}
$pq = 0.2451$

Dieckmann *et al.*, 1951*a*

Dieckmann's study thus suggests that failure to look at the right variable may be one explanation for the apparent lack of results in many of the studies. Most of the studies have assumed, perhaps wrongly, that the prevalence of prematurity and other abnormalities of pregnancy and delivery would be affected by diet during pregnancy, whereas it may be that except under conditions of famine and war, differences in infant functioning will be the only measurable consequences of different levels of dietary intake during pregnancy.

Another source for the confusion of results, however, is the failure of virtually all of these studies to take into account the complex relationships between diet, maternal health, and pregnancy outcome. The consequences of a given diet for pregnancy are determined by the general health, size, and nutritional status of the mother. For example, poorly grown and malnourished women may well profit from supplementation in pregnancy, although no discernible effect may accompany such intervention among well-grown women whose health and nutritional status are relatively good on entering pregnancy. The need to understand this complex of relationships warrants a substantial consideration of several methodological issues, including the crucial problem of population selection in diet studies, for if these are not understood, then we are in danger of failing to recognize the scope of the problem and of reaching the conclusion Thomson feared: namely, that nutrition is unimportant in pregnancy.

Let us first consider the much-neglected question of starting points. It is perfectly clear, though it has seldom been overtly acknowledged, that all diet-survey studies which concern themselves with the relationship of mother's diet *statim* to her pregnancy are really looking at one feature of an interaction among at least three factors: present diet, diet immediately prior to pregnancy, and past nutritional history. So far as preconceptional diet is concerned, it is obvious that if the diet taken during pregnancy (with or without supplementation) has a biochemical rather than a magical effect, then it must matter whether the woman begins gestation in a condition of nutritional adequacy, especially since the extra demands of pregnancy make deficiencies during that period more likely.

Although there are no studies which distinguish in a useful way between nutritional status prior to and diet during pregnancy, it is interesting that Dieckmann found a marked correlation between protein intake in early pregnancy (i.e., diet on entering the study) and abortion. No abortions took place among 106 women who during the first trimester were ingesting over 85 grams of protein a day, while 6 abortions occurred among 68 women who were ingesting less than 55 grams of protein per day—a rate of 8.8% (Table 6.2). There are also data on weight gain which tend to confirm the independent impact of prepregnancy and pregnancy dietary status on outcome. A number of researchers have found that there is a relationship between prematurity and too low a weight gain during

TABLE 6.2

Correlation of Early Protein Intake and the Incidence of Abortions *

Early Protein Intake (grams)	Normal Deliveries	Abortions	Total	Percent Abortions
Less than 55	68	6	74	8.11
55 to 70	171	7	178	3.93
70 to 85	235	3	238	1.26
Over 85	106	0	106	0.00
Total	580	16	596	

$$* \quad p = 0.0268 \qquad \chi^2_3 = 14.2$$
$$q = 0.9732 \qquad P = \text{approximately } 0.002$$
$$pq = 0.0261$$

Dieckmann et al., 1951a

pregnancy (e.g., Berry and Wiehl, 1952; McGanity et al., 1954b; Thomson and Billewicz, 1957).

Tompkins and his colleagues, however, found that a low preconceptional weight also predisposed the mother to a premature birth, whatever her gain during pregnancy, and that a low pregravid weight interacting with a low weight gain during pregnancy produced an even more strikingly increased risk of prematurity (Tompkins, Mitchell, and Wiehl, 1955). An essentially similar pattern, characterized by overweight before pregnancy, with or without high weight gain during pregnancy, identified mothers excessively subject to toxemia (Tompkins and Wiehl, 1955). Thus they concluded that the nutritional status of the mother as evidenced by her weight prior to pregnancy and her gain during the first and second trimesters may be critical in setting a pattern which will determine the outcome of that pregnancy.*

But whatever the specific effects on outcome of diet prior to or

---

* Underweight probably always reflects either illness or undernutrition or both, but overweight, especially among the poor, is not per se evidence of overnutrition. On the contrary, malnutrition-induced obesity as a consequence of very poor high-starch, low-protein diets is often endemic in communities where hunger is chronic (Mermann, 1967; Hunger, USA, 1968).

during pregnancy, the results of the surveys we have considered, including Dieckmann's, are all heavily contaminated, if not actually overwhelmed, by the long-range effects of nutritional status on growth and reproductive efficiency. Nutritional status and diet are not the same thing. "Diet," as Tompkins and Wiehl (1951) have written, "aids in the support of nutrition but is *not* nutrition and in pregnancy usually becomes secondary in importance to the many other conditions which can influence individual nutrition." The quantity and nature of the food ingested may tell us little about the quantity digested, absorbed, or utilized. Moreover, even with equivalent food utilization, nutritional status will vary from one woman to another, depending on the presence or absence of a variety of stressors such as disease (Birch and Cravioto, 1968), extremes of temperature (Mills, 1945, 1949), excessive energy expenditure, and even psychological stress (Macy, 1950; Scrimshaw, 1950; Widdowson, 1951). This is why height as a *record* of chronic nutritional status is such a useful variable. Given the different physical circumstances associated with lives of poverty or relative affluence, most of the nutritionally relevant correlates of socioeconomic status other than diet itself will tend to operate synergistically to exaggerate rather than to reduce differences in chronic nutritional status between social groups and thus to produce different rates of growth and different ultimate growth achievements.

In general, therefore, stature may be used among groups "as a statistic which reflects dietary habits during growth; and since food habits acquired during growth tend to persist, adult stature also tends to reflect nutritional status" (Thomson and Billewicz, 1963). Any randomly chosen study group containing women from a range of social and economic strata, however, is likely to include not only well-grown women on good diets and poorly grown women on inadequate diets, but also some well-grown women on poor diets and, especially in the case of the upwardly mobile groups in our own country, at least a few of the newly middle-class, poorly grown women who are currently taking diets adequate to their needs in response to a significant improvement in their economic status. If nutrition during pregnancy had no effect at all on outcome, one would expect to find that in such a group all the poorly grown women would have a higher incidence of reproductive failure than the well-grown women, whatever the nature of their present diet. But if a woman's diet during pregnancy does have an effect, the uncontrolled interaction of these nutritional variables might be expected to produce a confusion of results similar to that with which the available studies confront us.

In theory, carefully controlled supplementation studies should offer a way out of the confusion. Given a population of women of equivalent antecedent nutritional status, controlled supplementation of their diets should provide a technique for separating out the effects of nutrition during the course of pregnancy and nutrition at any other time.

It is unfortunate that most of the supplementation studies have failed to take starting points into account in even the most immediate sense of determining which nutrients might be lacking in the self-selected diets.* Only Ebbs, Tisdall, and Scott (1941) in their early work in Toronto actually determined which women were on poor diets and then provided them with appropriate food. By contrast, Harrell *et al.* (1956) supplemented women *from whom they were unable to get useful dietary data* with various combinations of vitamins; and Tompkins and Wiehl used a "vitamin-free" protein supplement, a polyvitamin capsule, or both, without first determining whether the specific nutrients given were undersupplied in the self-selected diets. Indeed, the women in the study were on pre-supplementation diets containing 73–75 grams of protein per day, an amount which, though not overgenerous, is by no means deficient.

Nutritional requirements in pregnancy are not yet firmly established, but it is quite clear that in pregnancy as during the rest of life, the metabolic requirements for various nutrients are inter-related. An increase in carbohydrates, for example, appears to increase the need for thiamine, and an artificial excess of thiamine can create severe relative deficiencies of the other B-vitamins, and so on. Where nutrients are derived from "natural" sources—i.e., food—diets containing adequate amounts of protein are usually also adequate in other nutrients, so that nutrient balances will tend to be main-

---

* Dieckmann's study was not really a supplementation study. Rather, it examined the effects of different lifetime levels of protein intake. The supplement, *given only to women on adequate starting diets,* merely served to assure the continued adequacy of their diets during pregnancy.

tained (e.g., Jeans, Smith, and Stearns, 1952). However, high levels of supplementation with one or another artificially isolated nutrient or combination of nutrients may, under certain circumstances, produce or intensify a condition of malnutrition. This fact may help to explain the Tompkins and Wiehl finding that although supplementation with protein and vitamins reduced prematurity among young women of low parity, similar supplementation among women over 30 or over parity two was associated with the highest rate of prematurity of any group, including the controls. It is possible that under circumstances where prior nutritional demands have been high, body reserves may not be available to compensate for a supplement-induced nutritional imbalance.

We have thus considered two methodological difficulties which may have contributed to the confusing results produced by the studies examining the relation between diet in pregnancy and pregnancy outcome. The first is a failure either to consider adequately or to control for interactions among the remotely historical, the immediately antecedent, and the current nutritional status of pregnant women. The second is the tendency to supplement women in whom no specific dietary inadequacies have been demonstrated and in whom, therefore, no improvement in reproductive performance based on supplementation can reasonably be expected. But the methodological consideration overriding both of these is that of sample selection. The women included in the largest and best controlled studies are simply not the women who are at greatest potential reproductive risk for dietary reasons. These are the very poor—women who, as we will see in the next chapter, may never be seen by a doctor between one delivery and the next or who, if they book for prenatal care at all, book too late to be included in dietary surveys. They are the women who not infrequently fail to deliver at the hospital where they have sought care, whose outcome of pregnancy is unknown, and who are therefore dropped from any study in which pregnancy outcome is being related to diet during pregnancy.

And since the women with whom we are most concerned *characteristically* come to obstetrical notice far too late to be included in any detailed dietary survey, the lower-class women who do turn up in time to be included are likely to be in a variety of ways quite unrepresentative of the disadvantaged group. Crump *et al.* (1959), for example, studying prenatal nutrition in relation to prenatal care in a group of pregnant Negro women in Nashville, had to omit as noncomparable the nutrition records of 61 women who had had no prenatal care, since their "prenatal" nutrition scores could not be obtained until after delivery. Even when these women were eliminated and only those women who sought care were considered, Crump found that there was a trend for women who sought the earliest care to have the highest nutrition scores.

In the large Vanderbilt study, the highest-risk population—the nonwhites—were missing entirely. In addition, the 2,046 women studied were not merely white, but they were apparently privileged white, a fact suggested by their prematurity rate of 6.7% for the period 1945–1950, which was lower than the 1950 national rate of 7.2% for whites as a whole. Moreover, their diets, which contained an average of more than 70 grams of protein per day, were far superior to the 47-gram-a-day diet which Hinson and Ferguson (1951) had found in the same year among a group of indigent white women studied at the New Orleans Charity Hospital.

One consequence of this inadvertent selection is that often there is no great difference between diets of the most- and the least-privileged women studied. In Thomson's careful study of Aberdeen women (1958), for example, the mean protein intake varied from 71.2 grams in the lowest class to 79 grams in the highest class. In so narrow a range the likelihood of finding any significant association is remote on statistical grounds alone. Furthermore, there is no good evidence that a continuous gradient of reproductive risk attaches to different levels of diet. Rather, it may well be that there is a minimum intake, in life as in pregnancy, above which most women will function adequately, and that only at the poorest levels of intake will nutritional effects be significant. The effects of diets at this low level of reproductive outcome have never been explored at all, either in this country or in Britain, for those very studies which have produced the most reliable and convincing data have fallen victim to their own methodological requirements for an accurate dietary survey and have completely excluded the very women for whom the study would be pertinent. Whenever efforts have been made to examine the effects of the poorest diets, such efforts have usually been thwarted by the greater tendency of the very women who take such diets to produce incomplete or inaccurate records. Back before World War II, when some of the most optimistic diet studies were being carried out, Bibb (1941) attempted to explore the hypothesized relationship between low blood protein and toxemia in low-income patients in Philadelphia, but found his effort to conduct a dietary survey frustrated by the fact that "few [patients] returned the diet sheets in any form that was good enough for analysis by the dietician." Fifteen years later, Harrell *et al.* (1956) complained that their desire to get a diet history from each woman in their study "was frustrated by the demonstrated tendency to gross fabrication in the Norfolk group, and by the extraordinary individual reticence of the Kentucky mountain folk." Thomson (1958), who deliberately included women of all social classes in his careful nutritional survey, found that there was a striking social-class variation in the ability to produce a reliable dietary record and, even more critically, that women who kept the best records had the best reproductive experience. Of the women in social class A, the wives of white-collar workers, 92.7% kept usable diet records. But only 75.3% of the women in class B, wives of skilled manual laborers, did so; and among the wives of semi-skilled and unskilled manual laborers, class C, only 60.8% kept accurate and usable records.

Subjects in any social class who produced reliable dietary data turned out to be on the average slightly older, *taller*, healthier, and more intelligent than the average of the original samples, suggesting that those who responded were already a select group with lower risk of reproductive failure. "Analysis of the clinical data showed that in Social Group C, the reliable subjects experienced less prematurity and perinatal mortality than the doubtful and no-data subjects. Such clinical differences were much less evident in groups A and B" (Thomson, 1958). In short, dietary records available among the lowest-class women were available from those who— being taller, healthier, more intelligent, more reliable, and more likely to have a favorable reproductive performance—were also more likely to have been brought up on and to continue to eat a diet better than the average for their class.

In one form or another the social-class differential in cooperativeness, in educational level, in sophistication about the requirements of research, in duration of prenatal care, and in a variety of other factors relevant to the production of a reliable dietary record has so far thwarted attempts to make a careful, convincing, and at the same time pertinent study of the relationships between poverty, poor diet, and pregnancy outcome. Consequently we have no studies examining the effects on reproductive performance of *very* poor pregnancy diets. Much the same is the case so far as lifetime diets are concerned; and the Aberdeen finding, that there is a marked relationship between stunting and poor reproductive performance, is probably the best present evidence we have tying poor nutritional status in a lower-class population to lowered competence in child-bearing. However, our assumption that very poor diets, during pregnancy or during life, would, if studied, prove incompatible with the progress of a normal pregnancy and birth also gains support from two other sources: first, from some recent animal studies and, second, from cross-cultural data from areas where malnutrition has been prevalent.

As we have previously noted, the early animal studies had demonstrated the general proposition that the fetus could be damaged by maternal nutritional deficiencies which were not sufficient to prevent reproduction altogether. These deficient animals were, however, often difficult to keep alive, difficult to get pregnant, and difficult to bring to term. It appeared that in nature such pregnancies would be quickly aborted and that, as Warkany (1948) wrote, "the birth of mature offspring with congenital defects represents a relatively high degree of reproductive performance" in a spectrum of failure running from "sterility of the mothers to debility of the young." As it has turned out, however, the extent to which the fetus is an efficient parasite depends on the nutrient involved. Nelson (1957) and others have demonstrated that with deficiencies of certain nutrients, such as folic acid, mothers can be kept in apparent health with their pregnancies apparently proceeding normally, while the young are rendered either abnormal or totally lifeless, depending on the timing and the duration of the deficiency.

So long as the presumptive effects of nutritional deprivation were limited to the production of specific physical defects, however, the relevance of such findings to the problems of more generalized handicap in human offspring appeared limited. Compared with children who appear to be "minimally" damaged, relatively few viable children are brought to birth with the kinds of gross physical deformities which experimental vitamin deficiencies tend to produce in animals. It was Whiteley, O'Dell, and Hogan (1951) who showed that "normal-appearing" rat pups born to mothers on a folic-acid-deficient diet suffered from what appeared to be a functional deterioration of the nervous system capable of depressing their performance on a maze test. Since this study involved an artificial and selective restriction, it is still perhaps less relevant to human deficiency than the more recent studies with animals which have involved generalized undernutrition or protein malnutrition.

Chow and his co-workers (Chow and Lee, 1964; Chow, 1964), for example, have demonstrated that a reduction of as little as 25% in the dietary intake of rat mothers, without any reduction in the quality of their diet, affected both the number of pups produced and their survival. Moreover, though the pups themselves were fed *ad libitum* from weaning, they were still reduced in size at 1 year of age compared with pups from normally fed mothers. Subsequently Hsueh, Agustin, and Chow (1967) found that the growth of rat pups was also reduced when their mothers were fed a diet in which quantity was normal, but protein quality was poor.

In other studies the Chow group continued the undernutrition of the mother into the nursing period and produced pups with abnormal metabolic rates and abnormal neuromotor development (Chow *et al.*, 1968; Simonson *et al.*, 1967, 1968). Caldwell and Churchill (1967) fed female rats a protein-deficient diet during the second half of pregnancy. The pups of these mothers weighed less at birth and at weaning and had a higher preweaning mortality rate than the pups of rats fed a normal diet during pregnancy. Moreover, at 30–35 days of age the control rats learned a maze faster and with fewer errors than did the low-protein rats and were superior on an avoidance conditioning task. Zamenhof *et al.* (1968) maintained female rats on a low-protein diet for one month before mating and throughout the entire period of gestation and found that the brains of the young born to these low-protein mothers contained less DNA (indicating fewer cells) and less protein. Evaluated at three months of age the low-protein animals responded abnormally to environmental stimuli and showed abnormalities of gait.

Platt and his colleagues (1964), working with dogs, found that bitches fed on a low-protein diet produced pups whose mortality rate by 6 weeks of age was 50% with survivors showing clinical and neurological abnormalities.

And in a series of experiments perhaps the most relevant to the human experience (where deprivation tends to be chronic), Cowley and Griesel (1959, 1962, 1963, 1964, 1966) raised successive generations of rats on a diet lacking about 25% of the protein normal for a rat diet. Mothers gestated and nursed the pups on the deficient diet; their female offspring, maintained to adulthood on the same diet, produced a second generation; *their* daughters a third. By the second generation the low-protein pups showed generally slowed development as well as learning abnormalities; and when, in the third generation, a group of females rehabilitated on a normal diet mated and produced young, their pups still showed retardation as the result of the intergenerational deprivation.

Such data, though highly suggestive, cannot be transferred directly to humans, of course—if for no other reason than the fact that, as Smith (1962) has observed, prenatal growth in man is "extremely sluggish" by comparison with other animals. No amount of prenatal deprivation is likely to limit human fetal growth "either quantitatively or qualitatively nearly as much as a laboratory experiment can affect fetuses of other animals."

Fortunately we are not solely dependent on the animal studies for evidence that diets restricted either chronically or even during pregnancy alone may be associated with a depression in the quality of the offspring. Smith (1947), it will be recalled, found birth weights reduced among the infants in Holland where mothers had been exposed only briefly to diets estimated to contain at their lowest point 34 grams of protein and 1,145 calories. (Similar diets, as we will show, appear to be chronic among some of the poor in this country.) Hiernaux found evidence of the persistence of such a famine effect when he studied growth patterns in two genetically different tribes in Rwanda (see Chapter Five). Comparing successive age-classes of Tutsi and Hutu he found that the 14-year-old boys of both groups, born during the time of the last severe famine in Rwanda, showed a retardation in both height and weight, with the 14-year-old Tutsi boys having "approximately the same mean weight and stature as the 13-year-old class born when the famine was over."

Since growth in all age classes was apparently already depressed by a poor environment, Hiernaux concluded that famine around birth, acting "through poorer intrauterine nutrition and poorer maternal lactation," was capable of producing growth retardation even in a population already growing at a less than optimal rate.

So far as lifetime diet is concerned, a number of investigators have found very low birth weights among infants from groups in Africa and Asia on markedly deficient diets (e.g., Hollingsworth, 1960; Timmer, 1961; Achar and Yankauer, 1962; Udani, 1963; also see Hytten and Leitch, 1964).

Among South Indian women on diets containing 1,408 calories and 38 grams of protein, Venkatachalam found a 29.3% incidence of birth weights under 2,500 grams. The small size of these infants and others from populations where adults tend to be short has often been thought to reflect the small body size of the mothers. However, it is of interest that Venkatachalam (1962) found a statistically significant increase in mean birth weight among one group of these women who were kept in the hospital on bed rest and an adequate diet for no more than 4 weeks before delivery.

Thus on one hand we have a series of inconclusive and confusing studies, which have failed for a variety of methodological reasons to provide us with any convincing evidence on the relationships between diet and pregnancy outcome, and others which are methodologically sound but have failed to consider such a relationship among those very poor women most likely to be at nutritional risk. On the other hand, we have a convincing body of animal and cross-cultural data which suggest that diet does indeed affect the outcome of pregnancy. Such a configuration would seem to provide us with a compelling reason for concerning ourselves with the diets of poor women, not only because the quality of their diets during pregnancy may be contributing to their high rate of reproductive casualty, but, even more critically perhaps, because women do not begin eating badly when they conceive. That is, poor pregnancy diets are likely to be found in women with poor lifetime diets, and poor lifetime diets are associated with poor growth and poor reproductive performance.

The data we have been considering give us sufficient cause for concern that we are inevitably led to ask about the quality of diets among poor childbearing women in this country. When we do so, we find once again that there are surprisingly few data. Until recently, when some observers have asserted that many families were actually starving (Testimony, Nutrition and Human Needs—Parts 1 *et seq.*, 1968, 1969), the question of how the poor were eating appeared to have been of scant interest to any but the poor themselves. The consequence of this long neglect is that we have little hard information on their recent nutritional status. Jean Mayer, in "Nutritional Status of American Negroes," written in 1965, found the shortage of published data "striking" and for information was forced to rely on interviews and correspondence with "qualified nutritionists and dieticians from various sections of the country." A similar "striking" lack of data has long existed where the nutrition of poor whites is concerned. The fact is, however, that we do have some published data, and though a number of the studies are old, they are in several ways especially useful to our purposes. They tell us, first of all, what the mothers (and in some cases the grandmothers) of the current generation of childbearers were themselves eating when they bore their children; and second, they document the persistence of low levels of nutrition, of unchanging low levels of nutrition, over more than a decade—a topic of particular interest in the light of animal studies showing the intergenerational effects of poor diets (e.g., Cowley and Griesel, 1966).

More than a quarter of a century ago, Whitsitt (1941) found that the diets of antenatal clinic patients in Kent County, Maryland, consisted mainly of "hog meat," white bread, potatoes, corn syrup, cabbage, and dried beans, and were strikingly deficient in milk, butter, eggs, green vegetables, and fruit. Among women on such diets, 19 out of 62 examined in 1940 had contracted pelvises, and over 70% of such patients seen at a monthly prenatal clinic over a 2-year period were anemic. Five years later in Louisiana, Moore and her co-workers took diet histories from a rather select group of white and Negro women receiving antenatal care from clinics or private physicians and found that Negro women had both a lower caloric intake (1,546 compared to 2,041 for the white women) and poorer quality diets. Forty percent of the white women had diets rated excellent or good, but none of the Negro diets was excellent and only

13% were good. Forty-nine percent of the Negro women had poor and very poor dietary ratings, 36% of them meeting *none* of the dietary recommendations of the Food and Nutrition Board of the National Research Council. And in the case of certain nutrients, an even larger percentage was deficient—65% of the Negro women, for example, had poor or very poor ascorbic acid intakes, compared with 36% of the whites (Moore *et al.*, 1947).

The special poverty of the Negro diet is also documented elsewhere. Ferguson and Keaton (1950) have described their findings from a 1-day diet survey of a group of 372 Negro and 30 white pregnant women in southern Mississippi during the same period. On the day prior to the survey, 46% of the women had had no milk, 39% had had no lean meat, 57% had had no eggs, and 90% had had no other proteins. Twelve percent had had no fruits *or* vegetables, and 33% had had only one serving of one or the other (often greens which had been cooked "all day"). Sixty-one percent of the women had a protein intake below 60 grams per day (recommended, 85 grams), and 16% had no animal protein at all. These were women who had sought prenatal care and who had, in some cases, improved their diets (or their dietary reporting?) as a result of prior clinic attendance.

The most revealing studies, however, are a series which allows us to examine the protein intake of groups of patients in the New Orleans Charity Hospital at intervals over a 10-year period. In the early 1940s Arnell *et al.* (1945) found that 24% of a group of Negro patients and 14% of a group of white patients examined in the prenatal clinics of the hospital had a protein intake of less than 42.5 grams, i.e., less than half the amount of protein recommended by the Food and Nutrition Board of the NRC, with the Negro patients having an average intake of 49 grams. Several years later, Hinson and Ferguson took diet histories on 85 Negro and 15 white women in the prenatal clinics of the same hospital (1951). The results are shown in Figure 6.1, where 92% of the diets of Negro women and 74% of the diets of the white women ranked "poor" or "very poor." On the day before the survey, 45% of the women had had no milk, 31% no meat, 66% no eggs, and 28% no fruit or vegetable. Protein intake averaged 46 grams for the whole group, 44 grams for the Negro women, and 47 grams for the white.

Hinson and Ferguson, 1951

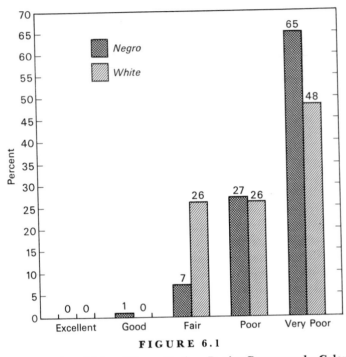

FIGURE 6.1

Distribution of Mean Dietary Ratings During Pregnancy by Color

Subsequently, Ferguson and Hinson, examining protein intake among 209 women at the same clinic (1953), found a mean (and a median) intake of 45 grams. Thirty-eight percent of the women had less than 40 grams of protein a day, and 22% less than 30. "A point not to be overlooked," they wrote, "is that this dietary protein record is not simply a record of the protein eaten during a particular pregnancy, but represents the more far-reaching fact that this is the amount of protein eaten almost daily for a lifetime." And, as they observed ruefully, looking back over the Charity Hospital studies, "the protein intake of the Charity Hospital women does not appear to be improving."

Such were the diets of the mothers of today's mothers. Do such diets persist? Mayer, in his 1965 survey, concluded that among Negroes, at least, they did. For Southern rural Negroes, he found, a monotonous limited diet low in "protective elements" still appeared to be the rule—a diet the inadequacy of which is exaggerated for Southern urban Negroes, since in the city those who formerly did so can no longer grow their own vegetables. "Consumption of fresh vegetables is low and consumption of citrus fruits is negligible. Milk consumption is substantially lower than in white families. . . . This is for a large part a reflection of lower income; but even at equal income milk consumption may be lower for Negro families." Although their calorie requirements are usually met, such families are often deficient in almost every nutrient.

In the North, Mayer observes, "even as approximate a description of the nutritional status of the Negro population is impossible to arrive at" on the basis of recent evidence. But case studies show that like the Southern urban Negroes, or like the Puerto Ricans who move to Northern cities from their island, Negroes in-migrant to the urban slums tend to eliminate from their diets those items of fresh produce which they formerly grew or which were otherwise easily available—and come to subsist on a limited diet made up of those familiar items of their traditional diet to which they have convenient access. Only recently Jerome (1968) examined meal patterns among a group of Negro women in Milwaukee who had come from Southern, largely rural, backgrounds. She found that although the names of the meals and the times of their serving were modified to suit the demands of new occupational schedules, traditional food items and ways of preparing them tended to be retained in the urban environment. It is little realized, Mayer has commented, to what extent the Southern Negro, migrant to the North, clings to old eating habits, spending disproportionate amounts of his already limited income to obtain familiar foods. "It can be fairly stated that in general the state of nutrition of Negroes is inferior to that of the whites in the same geographic area; in some cases it is vastly inferior."

Delgado *et al.* (1961), studying Negro migrant agricultural workers, made a detailed analysis entitled "Eating Patterns Among Migrant Families" in Palm Beach County, Florida. Analyzing the diets of 35 families, the investigators found that 97% were deficient in vitamin C, 86% were deficient in calcium, 80% were deficient in riboflavin, 58% were deficient in thiamine, and well over 60% had inadequate intakes of vitamin A and iron, according to National Research Council standards. Furthermore, only 40% of the families obtained sufficient protein and only 20% obtained sufficient calories, a shortage which would tend to diminish further the adequacy of the diets, since the utilization of protein and calories are interdependent, a too low intake of one reducing the dietary value of the other (Fryer, Miller, and Payne, 1961; Platt, Heard, and Stewart, 1964).

The diets which produced these deficiencies were remarkably poor. Only 43% of the families met daily meat requirements, three families (8%) had recommended amounts of eggs, and none met the recommended allowances for milk or for green or yellow vegetables. Twenty-two of them (63%) ate *no* green or yellow vegetables, and the other 37% ate less than half the recommended amounts. As Table 6.3 shows, only in such food categories as dry beans, fats and oils, and flour and cereals did a substantial majority of the families meet recommended standards. Women in these families were drawn

TABLE 6.3

Percentage of Families Meeting U.S. Department
of Agriculture Allowances

| Food Group | Total | *Fraction of Allowances Met* | | | |
		$\frac{3}{4}$	$\frac{1}{2}$–$\frac{3}{4}$	Below $\frac{1}{2}$	None
Milk	0	0	3	97	0
Green and yellow vegetables	0	0	0	37	63
Citrus fruits and tomatoes	2	8	8	48	34
Potatoes and sweet potatoes	5	5	8	14	68
Other fruits and vegetables	2	12	6	60	20
Meats, poultry, fish	43	38	8	11	0
Dry beans	94	2	2	0	2
Eggs	8	2	14	74	2
Flour and cereals	80	15	0	5	0
Fats and oils	88	8	2	2	0
Sugar and preserves	66	23	5	3	3

Delgado *et al.*, 1961

from the same group among whom Browning and Northcutt (see p. 90) found a high proportion (49%) of pregnancies less than 2 years apart. Findings such as these led Mayer to conclude that Negro migrant agricultural workers have the "highest proportion of malnourished individuals of any group in the country."

There are those who would argue that the cause of such diets as these, both past and present, is not poverty but ignorance (New York Times, June 17, 1968). It is questionable whether such an argument really matters if our concern is with the extent of risk in a hungry population. But the fact is that the reasons why some families are eating so badly in a society with an abundant and often enriched food supply are largely uninvestigated. Aldrich (1965) has observed that "man's choice of food is influenced by a whole host of factors, including cultural background, habits, taste preferences, susceptibility to advertising, family finances, religious beliefs, economic situations, and many others. . . . We need to know much more about why individuals, ethnic groups, and even nations eat as they do." For the poor, however, there seems little doubt that the answer lies in three broad areas: tradition, information, and money.

As the New Orleans Charity Hospital studies show, traditional diets which have persisted for generations tend to continue to persist *in the absence of significant economic improvement;* even lower animals, which have less complex reasons for their food choices than man, will stick to a starvation diet once the preference for it has been established. Young and Chaplin (1945) found long ago that although protein-starved rats would normally tend to select casein over sucrose, establishment of a sugar preference prior to protein starvation would lead them to persist in selecting sugar in spite of a steadily increasing need for casein. "New habits tend to form," they concluded, "in agreement with metabolic needs, but established habits persist as independent regulators of food selection" (Young, 1967).

Among verbal animals, habits are compounded by misinformation. The eating of clay and starch, for example, apparently a causative factor in serious iron-deficiency anemia, may have grown out of the habit of eating dirt to kill hunger in slave times, but it is currently viewed by Negroes who practice it as having a variety of healthful effects, especially during pregnancy (Ferguson and Keaton,

1950*a;* Edwards *et al.,* 1959; Payton *et al.,* 1960; New York Times, July 24, 1967; Keith *et al.,* 1968). Cornely *et al.* (1963) analyzed nutritional beliefs among a low-income urban population and found that a high percentage of their informants, both white and Negro, were poorly informed nutritionally and that the Negroes were somewhat more poorly informed than the whites. Not only did they subscribe to a number of potentially damaging food myths ("People with too much acid in their blood should not eat citrus fruits"), but when they were asked what foods they thought were good for them, only 33% of both races listed meat, and the milk group was listed by less than 30% of whites and less than 25% of Negroes.

But the potency of habit, folklore, and downright ignorance as a source of poor diet must not be overrated so as to obscure the fact that ability to pay for a good diet may well be the more critical factor. It is important not to attribute to habit what can more parsimoniously be chalked up to economic circumstance and conditions of life. The ubiquitous problem of the poor family is a shortage of money. When funds are low, food expenditures inevitably account for a disproportionately large fraction of the family income—often the only reducible one in the face of fixed monthly costs for housing, transportation, and other essentials. Economy, as the poor have always known, must often begin as well as end at the table because there is little else to scrimp on.

Among the 35 migrant worker families studied by Delgado *et al.* (1961), all but 9 had 7 or more members living in one or two rooms with average weekly earnings from $36 to $43. "From $18 to $22 per week, about half their weekly earnings, was spent for food by the 18 families which had from 7 to 9 members each. According to Department of Agriculture standards, from $35 to $47 would be required to feed families of this size a low-cost adequate diet."

Even when adequate purchasing power according to Department of Agriculture standards is available, the ability to feed a family well under such stringent circumstances demands bulk food purchasing, careful planning of meals, and inventive food preparation, requirements which neither the physical nor the emotional exigencies of their lives permit many poor women to fulfill. Moreover, there are circumstances under which it is irrelevant to speak of economizing at all. In many parts of the South, Negro tenant-farmer families, their usefulness eliminated by technology, subsist on a barter economy and seldom see money at all. For these moneyless families, often classified by their local governments as ineligible for welfare, there is presumably government surplus food—if their communities are willing to pay to distribute it. But living solely on surplus foods is only a partial and piecemeal nutritional solution. The commodity distribution program was never planned to produce a balanced diet, and the food items supplied in a given community would not necessarily allow for a balanced diet even if they were fully utilized, which apparently they are not. The commodity distribution programs have been characterized not only by a lack of concern for nutritional requirements, but also by indifference to the realities of the recipients' transportation and storage facilities. Where distribution is (as it is often) on a once-a-month basis, problems are created by the sheer bulk of food which must be picked up, brought home, and kept palatable for an extended period. To such objective obstacles to obtaining and storing surplus foods must be added the difficulties, in poor families, of utilizing them.

Two recent investigations have shown that where women have a low level of education, poorly equipped kitchens, and little practice in following recipes or trying new dishes, large quantities of unfamiliar foods of limited intrinsic interest will simply not be utilized, not even by a hungry family (Neff, 1964; Pontzer *et al.*, 1963). Things can and do get even worse, of course, where people have no money and commodities are not distributed at all. Under such circumstances people simply starve.

It is quite clear that although differences in food habits and beliefs are important, poverty is the basic factor which, compounded by ignorance, keeps poor women badly fed. Grant and Groom (1959) found a direct relationship between protein intake—specifically the intake of the more complete (and expensive) animal proteins—and economic level among a group of Negroes in the Charleston area of South Carolina in the summer of 1956. The average adult in all classes obtained roughly similar amounts of vegetable protein; but the amount of animal protein taken per day went from 12 grams in the lowest class to 53 grams in the highest class, so that total mean protein intake for the respective groups was 50 in the one case and 90 in the other.

Moreover, cultural differences in type of diet appear to lose their significance relatively quickly when adequate funds are available. More than 20 years ago Milam and Darby (1945) surveyed 160 white and 40 Negro families of various economic groups in Alamance County, North Carolina, during the relatively prosperous war years of 1943–1944. Though the families were rural, mills in the area provided work for at least one individual in most households. The investigators found the families, both white and Negro, eating equally varied and wholesome diets containing adequate amounts of milk, eggs, peas, beans, butter, fruits (including citrus fruits), and an excess of lean over fat meat. The diets of most of the families studied were adequate in all nutrients and were "in striking contrast to the fat pork, grits, and molasses monotony so often said to characterize southern rural diets." The high quality of the diets, the authors concluded, "is in keeping with the assumption that a people eats a good diet when it can be afforded."

Where good diets cannot be afforded, however, whole families eat poor ones throughout their lives. Women growing up in such families are at nutritional risk during growth; and in maturity—feeding their own families as they were fed—they continue at nutritional risk. In the light of such a process it is doubtful whether the effects of diet during pregnancy can be considered apart from the effects of diet and other conditions throughout life. It is, of course, possible that risk for poorly grown women can be reduced by dietary improvement during pregnancy, but for some of them such intervention may well be too late. Where there is "permanent physical damage reproductive performance may also be permanently impaired, so that there may be a less effective response to improvements in diet during pregnancy" (Duncan, Baird, and Thomson, 1952).

Certainly it is clear from even the limited data we have that the most significant diet-related improvement in reproductive performance will occur when we have seen to it that all women, and all children before them, are adequately nourished throughout their lives. However, it is important to remind ourselves of the level of nutrition with which we may be dealing. In the group of pregnant women studied by Ferguson and Hinson (1953) in New Orleans, 38% had less than 40 grams of protein on an average day, and 22% were probably consistently taking less than 30 grams a day. The Negro women studied by Moore (Moore *et al.*, 1947) in Louisiana were on diets whose caloric value was 1,546. Among South Indian women on similar lifetime diets (1,408 calories, 38 grams of protein) Venkatachalam (1962) found a 29.3% incidence of birth weights under 2,500 grams, and it was among just such women that mean birth weights were increased after a month of rest and improved diet. These considerations, taken together with the positive results of the early supplementation studies and the wartime experiences in England and Norway, appear to suggest that improving the pregnancy diets of the women who are at present the most badly fed may reduce unfavorable reproductive outcomes. Certainly such an improvement can do no harm.

Suboptimal diet during pregnancy is thus added to a lifetime of poor feeding as another of the potential risks for reproductive casualty to which her poverty exposes the poor woman. What effect does the quality and quantity of care which she receives during pregnancy have on these accumulated risks? It is to this question that we now turn.

CHAPTER SEVEN

Medical Care and Reproduction

All known human societies pattern the behavior of human beings involved in
the process of reproduction.

MEAD AND NEWTON

Some women go to a physician only in cases of obvious emergency; others do not
go even then. . . . It is perfectly possible for a woman to have 12 children,
cervical cancer, and TB and to have no agency aware of her existence.

SHERI E. TEPPER

CHILDBEARING is a normal function for women. That it
is not a routine one is emphasized by the fact that in most societies
women who are reproducing, or of an age to reproduce, are subject
to a variety of special practices intended to insure the health and
well-being of both mother and infant. In most modern cultures it
is considered appropriate—and beneficial to the coming generation
—that childbearers be provided not only with specialized medical
supervision during pregnancy, but also with some sort of consultative
and supervisory care from puberty to the menopause. In the United
States such care is only a theoretical ideal. In practice there are some
women who get sustained professional attention during their reproductive years, and others who do not. Before we examine either
this fact or its implications for children, however, we need to consider for a moment the rationale which underlies this ideal of obstetrical care.

From the data we have reviewed in Chapter Five, it is clear that
a serious concern with the well-being of potential mothers should
begin even before their own births so that they would be assured of

life conditions which foster optimal growth and development. Medical care specifically directed toward the reproductive process is properly seen as beginning in early adulthood, before conception. At this time a physician can provide birth control and family planning information and can caution a young woman seeking to become pregnant about such postconceptional hazards as drugs and x-rays which are sometimes administered unknowingly before a pregnancy has been confirmed.

A preconceptional physical examination permits the identification and treatment of preexisting conditions—nutritional, structural, or medical—which might interfere with the normal course of a pregnancy. After conception, during a regular schedule of prenatal visits, a woman cared for either privately or in a clinic will have her weight watched, her diet and work status monitored, and her needs for rest and reassurance considered. Where conditions such as anemia and diabetes or tuberculosis and other infections are treatable, they will be treated. Manageable conditions such as Rh incompatibility, pretoxemia, and heart disease will be early identified and appropriately managed with resultant reduction in risk to the mother and the fetus. Abnormal pregnancies will be terminated and difficult ones eased. As the end of pregnancy approaches, the physician, prepared by his knowledge of the woman's general health status and her probable eccentricities as a childbearer, can anticipate difficulties at delivery, induce labor for appropriate complications before term, and perform operative deliveries in a planned rather than in an emergency fashion. Delivery will normally take place in a hospital setting in which are available both the staff and the facilities to deal with any postpartum emergencies. In this environment such hazards as asphyxia, jaundice, and other metabolic, anatomic, and respiratory problems common in newborns can be dealt with swiftly and with minimum risk of consequent damage. Thus the application of contemporary obstetrical knowledge and skill in a setting designed to optimize its impact can reduce the risks attendant upon labor, delivery, and the postpartum period for both the mother and the child.

It is evident from this descriptive summary that the principal function of obstetrical care is protective: sustained supervision serves to forestall preventable abnormalities of the reproductive process and to minimize the effects of those which are not preventable. This being the case, it naturally follows that the absence of such care does not have equally negative consequences for every woman and her infant. Although care is desirable for all women the greatest risk attends its absence among those who, for reasons we have already discussed, are most subject to having disordered pregnancies and damaged babies. Illsley (1967), reviewing available data on the demography of pregnancy, has concluded that "on purely obstetric grounds certain groups of the population should receive the highest available levels of maternity care. These are primigravidae . . . grand multiparae, women with a poor obstetric history, young mothers with rapidly recurring pregnancies, women of short stature and poor physique and health, mothers having illegitimate pregnancies, and the socially underprivileged. . . ." As we shall see, in the U. S. it is precisely these women who are least likely to get sustained high-quality care.

In a speech made in 1967, Dr. William Stewart, United States Surgeon General, noted that by current estimates from one-third to one-half of all women delivered at city hospitals in the major cities of this country have had no prenatal care at all. What this means is that a very large percentage of pregnant lower-class women come to medical notice for the first time when they are in labor. Lesser (1964), bringing together data from various cities, has pointed out that the percentage of women delivering babies without prenatal care ranged from 23% in Atlanta, to 33% in Dallas, to 41% in New York's Bedford-Stuyvesant area, and to 45% of those delivering at D. C. General Hospital in the nation's capital. Moreover, the situation appears to be growing worse, not better. According to reports from the U. S. Children's Bureau, the proportion of pregnant women in the lower classes who receive prenatal care is decreasing by about 2% a year (Conference on Prenatal Clinic Care in New York City, 1963).

Women who are totally without care are, moreover, only a part of the problem. Many of the rest get only token amounts of care. Hartmann and Sayles (1965) found that 43% of 1,380 medically indigent patients delivered at Minneapolis General in 1962 had either no prenatal care at all or, at most, one visit to the clinic; and of those who did attend prenatal clinics, 71% came for the first time in the third trimester of pregnancy. In Chicago, a special study of health care for the poverty population estimated that 85% of all the obstetric patients (19,000 a year) at Cook County Hospital had received inadequate or no prenatal care (Chicago Board of Health, 1965). And in New York City the Hospital Commissioner has estimated that of all the mothers delivered in 14 municipal hospitals, three-fourths of the primigravidae do not seek care until the 20th week of pregnancy or later; and the majority of the multigravidae seek care some time after the 24th week of pregnancy (Gollance, 1966).

These figures of course refer only to women who have delivered in large city hospitals. As is well known, in many urban areas an influx of the poor and an outflux of the middle class have combined to create simultaneously an excessive demand on existing services and a declining tax base with which to finance them. For example, Tayback and Wallace (1962) have shown that in Baltimore, between 1950 and 1960, during a time when the total city population showed a slight loss, there was a 39% increase in the number of public assistance clients, a 56% increase in the number of nonwhite live births, and a 133% increase in the number of women registered at prenatal clinics.

It is doubtful, however, that poor women receive much more care outside the cities. One reason why even rough estimates of care are hard to come by for rural women is that many of them are delivered in small, often unaccredited, hospitals; in fact, in many parts of the South large numbers of them are delivered outside of hospitals altogether, by midwives (Anderson and Lesser, 1966). There is every reason to assume that prenatal care is poor among such women, as it doubtless is among isolated Appalachian whites, many of whom are dependent for medical care on nurses or midwives (Erickson, 1966), among large numbers of reservation Indians, or among women in the various migrant streams. Northcutt et al. (1963) studied a group of migrant and nonmigrant Negro women of similar economic status in Belle Glade, Florida, in an area where there was a health center available; and where most women were hospital delivered because midwifery was not practiced. Although most of the women in both groups had made at least one visit to a physician or clinic, more than 30% of them had made their first visit after the sixth month of pregnancy and less than one-fifth had made an initial visit during the first trimester.

Failure to get antenatal care is not confined to a single social or economic group; in all classes and ethnic groups some women will get and others will fail to get adequate antenatal supervision. Yet even in communities where the overall level of care is relatively good, there appears to be a persistent differential in duration of care related to both socioeconomic status and educational level. In Baltimore only 10% of the total city deliveries in 1964 were to women who had received no prenatal care; but when the records were examined by economic status, 40% of the lower-income groups were found to have had either inadequate or no prenatal care (Sundberg, 1966). When Yankauer et al. (1958) studied a large sample of New York State women, 95% of whom were getting prenatal care from private physicians, they found that even in this medically privileged group the time of the first prenatal visit varied with social class. Eighty-one percent of the women in the three highest classes sought care in the first trimester of pregnancy, but only 73% of those in class IV, and 61% of those in the lowest class (V) sought care so early. Schonfield et al. (1962) found that the level of the mother's education as well as the source of care (two factors closely related to socioeconomic status) also affected the time of first attendance for prenatal care; those with least education and those seeking clinic care tended to come later than those who had more education or who had prenatal care from a private physician. Once again the group was a relatively privileged one in which only 1% of the sample had no prenatal care at all.

The disadvantage associated with low income is exaggerated by minority status. Baumgartner (1965) found that in 1960 40% of nonwhite mothers had late or no prenatal care in New York City compared with only 15% of white mothers—a figure similar to that found by Buetow (1961) in Baltimore in 1958, where 43.5% of all Negro mothers delivering at one hospital (which accounted for almost 40% of Negro births in the city) were without any prenatal care at all. Data from the Obstetrical Statistical Cooperative covering maternity discharges from 18 hospitals across the country show that in 1962, 31.2% of more than 15,000 nonwhite patients attended the prenatal clinic for the first time on or after the 28th week of pregnancy, compared with only 11.1% of the white patients; and that 30.2% of the nonwhite compared with only 10.5% of the white patients had three or fewer visits.

The disadvantage of minority status extends to another group: the unwed mothers. Table 7.1, drawn from Pakter's study of illegitimate maternities in New York City (1961), illustrates quite clearly that (1) Puerto Rican and nonwhite mothers tend to have less prenatal care than whites, and (2) among all groups the extent of antenatal care is reduced in out-of-wedlock pregnancy.

TABLE 7.1

Obstetric Care in Different Ethnic Groups

	White		Puerto Rican		Nonwhite	
	Married	*Unmarried*	*Married*	*Unmarried*	*Married*	*Unmarried*
Private services	85.8	17.3	—	—	—	—
Ward services	12.2	81.0	90.4	97.5	82.1	97.4
Prenatal care in first six months	87.2	36.7	60.4	43.5	61.7	42.9

Birch, 1968

Many have asked, and tried to answer, the question of why such differences in care exist. Over two decades ago Eastman (1947) irascibly argued that it was possible to define the "general characteristics, as a class, of those patients who habitually neglect to seek medical attention though it is known to be available. . . . They are in the main the shiftless and improvident of our populace . . . [whose] habits of living in general are doubtless just as ill-managed as their habits in relation to prenatal care." The politer current version of this explanation is that the failure of poor women to seek care reflects a different (i.e., "ignorant") cultural attitude among the impoverished about medical care in general. "Non-utilization or minimal utilization of public and quasi-public health facilities is considered to be the result of residents not being aware of the value of preventive medicine, since most aspects of their lives are run on an emergency basis, taking care of a condition only when severe pain is experienced" (Chicago Board of Health, 1965).

But Cornely and Bigman (1961), who investigated attitudes toward health among poor families in Washington, D.C., found that the difference lay not so much in attitude as in practice. They asked a group of white and Negro low-income families what measures one should take to stay in good health. Although the whites were of slightly higher economic and social status than the Negroes, only 11% of the whites, compared with 38% of the Negroes, mentioned seeing a doctor for general preventive care. Asked specifically whether health checkups were important, 81% of the whites and 94% of the Negroes agreed that they were. Yet despite both groups' expressed belief in preventive care, a third of the Negroes and half of the whites had never had a physical checkup.

In Boston, Donabedian and Rosenfeld (1961) found much the same discrepancy between word and deed among pregnant women. Women of little education and low income, they discovered, differed from better-educated, higher-income women less in their awareness of the need for care than in their behavior. The researchers found that 70% of the women who were living on incomes of less than $2,000 a year believed that prenatal care should be initiated during the first trimester of pregnancy, but only 40.3% had sought care that early. Of women living on family incomes of $7,000 or over, however, 97.9% thought that care should begin in the first trimester of pregnancy, and 97.8% had so begun it. Educational level also affected the tendency to equate word with deed. Almost 25% of the women with 11 years of school or less did not seek prenatal care as early as they believed they should, compared to only 6.8% of those with more than 12 years of education.

Thus although ignorance of the need for preventive care may account for some of the differences in the amount of care received by different social and ethnic groups, it is clearly not the only factor nor probably even the most important one. It is likely that the degree to which women utilize available prenatal care cannot really be understood without taking into account the type of care facility to which a woman's social, ethnic, and economic status gives her access. In other words, how much money a woman has and the kind of care that it enables her to buy are probably the most critical variables affecting her tendency to get or not to get care. Donabedian and Rosenfeld found, for example, that although the discrepancy between opinion and performance as to the appropriate time to begin prenatal care disappeared at the income level of $5,000 a year, it was not until the income level reached $7,000 or over that most women were judged to be receiving adequate amounts of care.

The average middle-class or upper-class woman, who can pay for private care, is followed through pregnancy and delivery by her own physician, whom she sees by appointment in his office. For the poor woman, on the other hand, antenatal care is clinic care which may represent a very different kind of predelivery experience. Theoretically, at least, a large percentage of even the poorest women have access to care through antenatal clinics (often sponsored by local health departments) in which services are offered according to financial need, for a nominal fee or no fee at all. However, Monahan and Spencer (1966) concluded that even in clinics financial factors remained among the significant "Deterrents to Prenatal Care." In some communities, they noted, women who could not afford private care were nevertheless often ineligible for clinic care on the basis of income. "Knowing that under the law the county hospital has to accept them if they come to delivery as emergencies, many of the women make no other arrangements for care." Even where prenatal clinics make no direct charge, they are not free for poor women unless they are within walking distance of patients' homes. Carfare alone represents an unmanageable expense for some families; and if clinics hold only weekday sessions, women who work must lose, in addition, at least part of a day's pay if they attend. Among the poor, where a choice must often be made, health, as Jeffers (1964) has observed, does not have the same priority as other more immediate demands on the purse.

For the impoverished woman who overcomes such practical obstacles, the experiences she may have in utilizing prenatal clinics are likely to be of such a nature as to discourage her attendance. "For one thing, as one visits hospitals one gets the impression that the outpatient service is the stepchild of the obstetric service. . . . Prenatal clinics are, in the main, overcrowded and understaffed, have too few physicians in attendance, and often lack adequate obstetric supervision. It is not uncommon to find no attending physician present for guidance and consultation." Unfortunately nothing much appears to have been changed in the years since Baumgartner and Pakter wrote those words (1956). In the Chicago study of health services in poverty areas, when residents themselves were asked what they perceived as their problems, they cited among the major difficulties a lack of facilities, inadequate clinic space resulting in long waits, and discourteous service. "Many expectant mothers wait until their sixth or seventh month before seeking prenatal care," one agency director observed, "and when they finally do arrive at the clinics they are usually treated poorly and are 'talked down to' for not coming earlier. Consequently, many persons who learn of such treatment are reluctant to make use of the facilities."

The qualitative impact of such conditions is summed up in the report of a highly trained nurse-observer sent around by the Maternity Center Association of New York to do a spot-check of antepartum clinics in seven voluntary and five municipal hospitals in that city (Conference on Prenatal Clinic Care in New York City, 1963). In her report, Miss Keane concluded that antepartum clinics actually discouraged early attendance through procedures ranging from inconsiderate scheduling to outright refusal to permit early registration. Three of 12 clinics had registration only when the clinic was *not* in session; none had clinic sessions during evening or weekend hours for working women; and two of the clinics did not permit registration before the 20th week. In one of these the applicants waiting to register were told to go home "if you haven't felt your baby move." Perhaps even more critical in the long run was the fact that for an individual woman who did manage to register, coming for antepartum care was almost inevitably a dreary, exhausting, time-consuming, and often meaningless activity—if indeed it was not actually frightening and humiliating. Long waits were standard where appointments for all patients were made at the same hour (in 9 clinics); and combined with overcrowded waiting rooms, inadequate seating, inadequate toilet facilities, and inadequate or absent food facilities, delays of 3 to 4 hours produced not only boredom but active discomfort.

A woman coming to register might be briefly involved with 6 to 9 people, each of whom applied some procedure (weighing and measuring, taking urine or blood specimens, taking medical history, obtaining signed releases for inoculations, and so on) but none of whom was likely to explain the meaning of the entire experience. In half the clinics the initial interviews involving personal questions on marital and financial status were conducted within the hearing of other patients. When, after the completion of preliminary procedures, the woman was prepared for what might be her first pelvic examination, she would be helped to undress, drape and position herself on the table, often wordlessly, by an assistant whom she was seeing for the first time. "Throughout the examination conversation between patient and doctor or patient and chaperone is minimal. . . . Only once was any woman observed being encouraged to ask questions or express her own concerns. No one in any clinic at any time was observed to introduce himself or herself to the patient." On revisits "the amount of time spent with the doctor, nurse, nutritionist or social worker in potentially meaningful activity for the patient is very small compared to the waiting time between these activities." Clocking the time spent with the doctor in 8 of the clinics, the observer found that for normal patients it ranged from 38 seconds to a maximum of 3 minutes 40 seconds.

It is not unreasonable to infer from such reports that so long as clinic care is provided reluctantly, patronizingly, inconsiderately, impersonally, and at inconvenient times and locations, poor women will continue to seek an inadequate amount of prenatal attention. Somewhat improved conditions and a good experience during a previous pregnancy can serve to change the pattern. The Maternity Center Association observer reports one case of a woman who willingly spent sixty cents in carfare, lied about her address in order to be eligible, and traveled 3 hours in order to come regularly to a clinic in which she had previously had a satisfactory pregnancy experience. Less anecdotally, Illsley (1956) has pointed out that, in Britain, making prenatal care equally and freely accessible to all and educating women in its importance has tended markedly to reduce if not entirely to eliminate social-class differences in the extent to which and the time at which women register for care during pregnancy.

But it would be self-deluding to assume that equalizing the quality and availability of care would automatically result in its equal utilization by all segments of the population. Particularly in the lower social class groups, women of greatest reproductive risk—those of high parity and those pregnant but unmarried—appear to be most resistant to such change. The data obtained by Illsley (1956), who has subjected this issue to a detailed analysis in Britain, have indicated (Figure 7.1) that in 6,200 births occurring in Aberdeen, dura-

Illsley, 1956

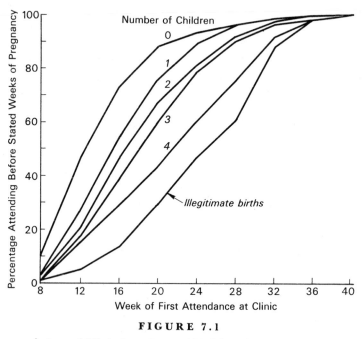

FIGURE 7.1

Antenatal Clinic Attendance of Multigravidae by Number of Living Children and Marital Status, Aberdeen

(6,200 births)

tion of care tended to be shortest "for women with four or more children and women bearing an illegitimate child"; and that heavy overrepresentation of these two groups among the lower classes accounted for their reduced duration of prenatal care. The delay in attendance associated with illegitimacy, Illsley concluded, was probably inevitable "in a society where it is conventional for conception to occur within wedlock."

Some of these same factors and some additional ones as well appear to affect economic, educational, and ethnic differences in prenatal care in this country. Here as in Britain, the woman who is unmarried and pregnant is overrepresented among those who get little or no prenatal care (e.g., Oppenheimer, 1961; Pakter, 1961a). And Schonfield et al. (1962) and Donabedian and Rosenfeld (1961) found that higher parity among the women they studied was also associated with a marked decline in the tendency to seek care early in pregnancy, although they disagreed on whether this effect persisted despite increasing education. Anderson and Lesser (1966) have noted that, for a mother with preschool children, getting to a prenatal clinic is a problem not merely because of the cost but because it is difficult either to find someone to sit with the children at home or, if they are brought along, to keep them under control on bus or subway and during the long waits at the clinic.

But high parity in association with low social class may also interact with another factor: the nature of the available care. The Maternity Center Association observer found one patient who had come to the same hospital clinic for five of her children and had never yet managed to deliver a baby at that hospital. "They'll tell you to come regularly so that they can have a complete record of your pregnancy for the doctor who delivers you," she told the observer. "Each time they have no beds, and I get taken to another hospital, so what good does the record do them? The last one and this one, I got wise and didn't bother coming back until the last month for a final checkup." Although the persistence of the woman and the repetitiousness of her experience are probably unique, the fragmentation of care implied by the anecdote is not infrequent, and such experiences probably account for some of the decline in attendance associated with high parity.

Some years ago, Yankauer and his associates (1953) compared two groups of lower-class women, one which had and one which did not have adequate prenatal care, to find out which characteristics distinguished between them. Both groups were ward patients, and both "possessed characteristics known to be associated with the economically underprivileged in our society." Both groups occupied the worst census tracts in Rochester, New York, both were residentially unstable and contained a high proportion of Negroes and a high proportion of day laborers relative to the population as a whole. On the basis of the study Yankauer concluded that the principal characteristics which differentiated the no-care group were their greater youth and higher fertility (age-for-age), their greater welfare dependency (36% *vs.* 10%), and the higher percentage of out-of-wedlock births. Women with such characteristics were less likely than others of their socioeconomic status to seek the admittedly more "impersonal, inconvenient and time-consuming" clinic care which was available. Such a finding suggests that the failure of large numbers of poor women to get care is the result of an interaction between certain characteristics in the women themselves and certain characteristics of the care to which they have access.

The marked differences in quality and quantity of care obtained by different economic and ethnic groups during the prenatal period appear at first glance to be somewhat diminished at delivery. Physician-attended births (all but a tiny minority of them in hospitals) have been the standard for over 97% of the women in the United States for more than a decade. Nationally the percentage of births outside of hospitals attended by midwives or other unspecified personnel has been less than 2% since 1963 (NCHS, Vital Statistics of the U. S., 1965). But, as is the case with other health statistics, these national totals tend to obscure the actual experiences of the socially disadvantaged and especially of the nonwhite disadvantaged segments of the population. If birth data are distributed in accordance with economic level, the one-third of the states which have the lowest per capita income turn out to have a rate of midwife-assisted deliveries 6 times that of the states in the upper third for per capita income (Hunt, 1966). When data are distributed regionally, they show that deliveries conducted with semiprofessional assistance are overwhelmingly concentrated in the South. The implication is clear, given our knowledge of the ethnic makeup of the populations characteristically defined by these geographic and economic attributes, that it is predominantly the poor nonwhite women who are delivering their babies with suboptimal assistance.

The facts confirm the implication. For more than a decade 99% of white deliveries in the United States have been physician-attended. Thus in 1965 there were no midwife-attended deliveries among whites in 30 states, and in 15 other states such deliveries accounted for less than half of 1% of all births reported. Only in

Texas, with its large Mexican-American minority, was there any significant proportion (3.3%) of deliveries which were not medically attended among populations classified as white. In the same year, however, more than 10% of nonwhite women still delivered their children outside of hospitals, and more than 7% of them did so with no physician in attendance. Table 7.2 makes explicit the extent to which nonwhite women

TABLE 7.2

**Incidence of Births Outside of Hospitals
in Selected States, Nonwhite, 1965**

	Percentage Born Outside Hospitals
Alabama	35.3
Arkansas	29.5
Mississippi	43.0
Georgia	25.8
South Carolina	26.7

NCHS, Vital Statistics of the U.S., 1965

in a number of Southern states still bear their babies outside of hospitals. The percentage of unhospitalized births in 1965 ranged from a high of 43% in Mississippi to a low of 26.7% in South Carolina. Although a proportion of the nonhospital births in each of these states is attended by a physician, the percentage of home deliveries attended by midwives in 1965 ranged from just under 20% in Georgia and South Carolina to more than 37% in Mississippi.

It must be emphasized that the same women who are not receiving prenatal care, and who are in many cases not even medically attended at delivery, are those who are also not receiving adequate care before, after, or between pregnancies (Slatin, 1967). Even among the relatively privileged and well supervised group of women studied by Yankauer et al. (1958) in upstate New York, 26% of the lowest-class mothers had received no postnatal checkup some 3 months after the birth of their babies. As Eliot (1956) has pointed out, "continuity of medical care does not exist [for the poor mother]. She may be seen by more than one physician during a single pregnancy and be delivered by still another. Between pregnancies she may not be seen at all by either physician or nurse." One of the clearest evidences of this neglect is the degree to which poor women are both ill-informed and ill-prepared to plan, space, and limit their pregnancies. That they want such information and preparation is beyond dispute. Browning and Parks (1964), surveying the childbearing aspirations of a group of public health maternity patients in Florida, found that 70% of the Negro women and 20% of the white women did not want more children. Of those who did want another child, more than 90% wanted to wait for at least 2 years after the present birth. Darity (1963) found that among a group of low-income mothers attending a birth control clinic in Charlotte, North Carolina, the desired family size was 1 or 2 children, though the average number of children already produced was 4.8—and the women's mean age was only 29.

On questioning a socially stratified sample of Negro women in New Orleans, Beasley et al. (1966) found that it was the least educated women who were most likely to have exceeded the family size that they wanted. Though only 34.2% of the women with 8 or fewer years of school had wanted 4 or more children at the time they married or first became pregnant, 68.4% of these women already had that many children—and most had many potential childbearing years ahead of them. Among the entire sample there was widespread ignorance of the basic physiology of conception and birth; but most thought that couples should be able to plan the number of children they wanted, and 94% thought that family planning services should be available to the medically indigent. However, no family planning facility readily available to the poor existed in Louisiana until 1966. Indeed, until August 1965, the operative interpretation of the Louisiana Criminal Code made it a felony in that state to distribute birth control information of any kind (Beasley and Harter, 1967).

The disbursement of family planning information, like the provision of prenatal care, has been widely hindered by lack of funds. Hutcheson and Wright (1968) have estimated that in Georgia there are 174,000 indigent women between the ages of 18 and 39 in need of family planning services. However, available funds provided only 8% of them with such services in 1968. But the provision of birth control services has been further hampered by law, custom, religion, and superstition. In New York, one of the more advanced states, a law passed *in 1881* restricted public health programs from a general dissemination of birth control information—*until 1960*. And it was not until 1965 that the New York State Board of Welfare made provision for the dispensing of family planning services to women, married or unmarried, who were heads of households.

Statistics show that the number of state health departments offering any family planning information in their maternal health programs has grown from 7 in 1959 to 32 in 1965 (Eliot, 1966), but Jaffe (1967) has pointed out that many of these programs are minimal, operating in one or two counties. This observation is confirmed by Corsa's calculation (1966) that by mid-1965 less than 20% of the local health departments in the United States were actually providing *any* family planning services for their clientele.

The gap between the need and desire for family planning among the poor, and the availability of services to this end, has been underscored by Alonzo Yerby (1967) in his evaluation of New York City's experience with tax-supported family planning services. In total, New York City's municipal and voluntary hospitals system, the Department of Health, and other institutional family planning agencies are capable of serving only about half of the indigent female population in the city. Though such services are expanding, Yerby observes, their growth is delayed by a lack of funds, by political and religious obstacles, and by what he sees as a value judgment by society which would deny to the poor the right to enjoy a normal sexual relationship without fear of pregnancy. Planned Parenthood, in its 1966 annual report, observed that there were still only 12 states which permitted welfare workers to *initiate* birth control discussions with their clients. It is little wonder that Wilbur Cohen (1966), commenting on family planning as "one aspect of freedom to choose," suggested that restrictive state regulations often hinder progress in this field.

Moreover, federal support is by no means munificent. Specific budgetary estimates and appropriations requests vary from month to month, but Langer, writing in *Science* in 1967, pointed out that birth control programs on the federal level were off to a very slow start. Despite the fact that Senate and administrative experts estimated that a modest beginning in a realistic program would require at least $100 million over a 5-year period, less than $15 million had been made available. Planned Parenthood (Five Million Women, 1967) has estimated that of the projected 5.3 million medically indigent women who need publicly financed family planning services, 7 out of 8 are as yet unserved.

Thus far we have summarized some of the differences in health care which exist between the poor and the not-so-poor woman during their childbearing years, and have speculated on some of the probable reasons why such differences exist. Even from this brief look it is evident that the poor woman, especially if she is nonwhite, often conceives and bears her children with a minimum of professional advice or attention. Conceiving more children than women who are more affluent, she carries conceptuses which she does not abort through unsupervised pregnancies to routinely managed or even unmanaged births. But does it matter? This is not an outrageous question, for we are not asking whether it matters in a humanitarian sense, but whether it matters in terms of the larger argument—namely, that what happens to the mother and to her child before and during birth may affect the child's later development. In other words, do inadequacies in the advice and care a mother receives preconceptionally, prenatally, at delivery, and in the interpregnancy period really place the children who are the products of that mother's pregnancies at increased risk?

It is surprisingly difficult to prove that they do. It is simple enough, of course, to demonstrate that patients without prenatal care have much higher rates of prematurity, complications of delivery, prenatal, neonatal, and maternal death than do women who receive continuing care at relatively good levels during their reproductive years. For example, Hunt (1966) has reported on a study in which 30 New York City Health Districts were ranked according to the proportion of maternity cases on "ward" or general service. In the 10 districts which had the lowest proportion of maternity cases on general service, only 11% of the mothers had no prenatal care and the prematurity rate was 7%—lower than that for the city as a whole. In the 10 districts which had the highest proportion of "ward" cases, however, more than three times as many mothers (38%) had late or no prenatal care and the rate of prematurity was almost twice as high, 13%. Pakter et al. (1961b) found that mothers with no care who delivered on ward service in New York City had a prematurity rate (24.1%) three and one-half times that of those on private service who had received early care (6.9%). Oppenheimer (1961) found that the rate of neonatal deaths at city hospitals in Washington, D.C., was 23.7/1,000 for those with prenatal care, and 41.6/1,000 for those without. In Minneapolis, Hartmann and Sayles (1965) found that mothers having no prenatal care experienced fetal deaths at a rate of 4%, more than 5 times as high as the 0.7% fetal death rate for mothers having one or more visits to the prenatal clinic. Moreover, Buetow (1961) found that a marked increase in neonatal mortality among nonwhites at a Baltimore hospital—from 27 deaths per 1,000 in 1950 to 36 per 1,000 in 1958—was associated with a significant increase in the proportion of nonwhites who had had no prenatal care, the percentage of women without care having increased from 38% in 1956 to 43.5% in 1958. Such examples can be multiplied almost endlessly.

The question is, How are such associations to be interpreted? Abramowicz and Kass (1966), observing, as we have, that the highest rates of prematurity occurred in the New York Health Districts which had the lowest percentage of antepartum care, pointed out that the "meaning of the association, if it exists at all, is lost in the fact that lack of prenatal care is most characteristic of the same groups already identified as having a high risk of prematurity: the poor, the Negroes, women in underdeveloped areas, young primiparas, and grand multiparas." Thus the question of "which causes what, remains totally mysterious." The same multiplicity of associations exists not alone for prematurity but for all faulty reproductive outcomes; and the interpretation of these associations is further complicated by the fact that the very women who are already at risk as a consequence of their social and biological attributes and who have had little or no prenatal care are, to a statistically overwhelming degree, the same women who seek clinic rather than private care and who are in urban areas delivered on the ward services of large public hospitals. Thus "in a large heterogeneous urban complex," as Illsley has written (1967), "the division into voluntary, proprietary, municipal, teaching and non-teaching institutions is cross-cut by neighborhood and ethnic groups such that Catholic, Protestant, and Jewish groups, white, Negro, and Puerto Rican groups or different class and residential groups may dominate particular hospitals or types of care." It thus becomes virtually impossible to assess the effects of adequate or inadequate care on an epidemiologic basis since "social groups, obstetric risks, and types of care vary simultaneously."

There is, however, another way in which we can assess the potential negative contribution of defective care to pregnancy outcome. Acknowledging first that poor women have less of all kinds of care and more of all kinds of complications, we can then ask whether at least some of these complications could be treated or prevented if care were improved. If we ask such a question, that is, whether adequate and continuing care could improve the reproductive chances of the women who are presently most at risk, the answer would unquestionably have to be "yes." Indeed, there is some evidence that a well-organized comprehensive program of health care can improve the reproductive performance of both poor women and those who are relatively better situated.

Shapiro (1960) compared prematurity and perinatal mortality rates for members of the Health Insurance Plan of Greater New York with those of various city populations and found that the record of the insured patients, 72% of whom were delivered by obstetric-gynecology diplomates, was markedly better than that of city women as a group. Since there were obvious differences between these populations in social composition and type of care, however, he then went on to compare HIP outcomes with outcomes of only those city women delivered by private doctors. He found that prematurity rates wei lower in the insured group than in the city group served by private physicians for both white and nonwhite women. Perinatal mortality rates were also significantly lower among the insured patients than among private city births; and where perinatal loss could be examined by occupational groups, the better record of the health-plan women persisted at every occupational level.

Considering the large number of risk conditions which may be affected by adequate and continuing care, such an improved performance is not surprising. For example, it is clear from the data we have presented in Chapter Four that an excessive risk of poor outcome is associated with a reproductive pattern in which childbearing is begun too early, repeated too rapidly, and continued too long. Reducing family size among poor women and improving pregnancy spacing would thus have undoubted positive effects on the pregnancies which such women do undertake. What is now clear is that if prepregnancy and intrapartum care, including family planning help, were made available to poor women, they would act to reduce family size and increase the time between pregnancies (Hill and Jaffe, 1966; Benjamin, 1966). Planned Parenthood has reported birthrate declines of from 22% to 36% among low income U. S. populations in areas where intensive family planning programs have been introduced (When More Is Less, 1969).

Adequate care at birth can affect a number of other hazards. Such causes of perinatal death and morbidity as birth trauma, asphyxia, infection, and jaundice may be markedly affected by the ways in which they are managed around the time of delivery, so that, as Baird suggested (1960), rates of death around birth may indicate more about the quality of obstetric care than do prematurity rates which probably more fully reflect the basic health and prior growth of the mother. Moreover, although certain complications are remediable by appropriate management at term, such conditions are more effectively dealt with when anticipated as complications than when encountered as unexpected emergencies. Thus continuing care during pregnancy becomes the precondition for the least risk during delivery just as it is the precondition for lowered risk during pregnancy itself.

The positive effects of care during pregnancy on at least some complications are unquestionable. The earlier in pregnancy such conditions as anemia, drug addiction, diabetes, TB, hypertension, heart disease, and RH incompatibility are diagnosed and brought under expert management, the more likely it is that their potentially adverse effects can be mitigated. The importance of continuing supervision for preeclampsia and toxemia are well established (Hamlin, 1952). And while hazards associated with high levels of disease in the community (e.g., Hill et al., 1958; Siegel et al., 1960; Pineda et al., 1968) are irremediable by medical care in pregnancy, the risk associated with some infections can apparently be reduced by their treatment during pregnancy. Tuberculosis, for one, has already been mentioned. In addition, several investigators have found that the asymptomatic bacteriuria of pregnancy is associated with a higher incidence of premature birth, that such subclinical infection is more common in ward than in private patients (and even higher in indigent Negro patients—Turck et al., 1962), and that treatment reduces the level of prematurity among infected women (Kass, 1960; Henderson et al., 1962; Abramowicz and Kass, 1966). Clearly, one obvious benefit of care during pregnancy is that it permits a doctor to identify pathologic or potentially pathologic conditions early.

In an even broader sense comprehensive care allows a doctor to keep under continual supervision what Clifford has called "high risk pregnancies," not only those in which there is an existing pathologic condition, but also those in which the woman's prior reproductive history (NOVS, Loeb, 1958; Shapiro et al., 1965), her age, her parity, and her physical and nutritional status indicate the likelihood of difficulties in the current pregnancy. Seeking to define the epidemiological profile of the high-risk mother among hospital patients delivered in Miami, Florida, Griswold and Cavanaugh (1966) observed that the high-risk woman was one who, among other things, was Negro, short, with a weight gain of less than 16 pounds in pregnancy and a hemoglobin level of under 11 grams percent at labor. To these features of the profile may be added grand multiparity and pregnancy among those (especially adolescents) who are unmarried. Women with these characteristics tend to have few if any prenatal visits, yet early detection of such "high-risk pregnancies," Clifford (1964) maintains, is the *sine qua non* of reducing rates of prematurity and associated perinatal loss.

Even if such women were to have careful and continuing supervision, however, it is perfectly clear from Shapiro's data on HIP patients in New York that such care would not eliminate in a single generation the higher rates of morbidity and mortality among poor or nonwhite women. In his study (Shapiro et al., 1960), a social-class gradient in reproductive outcome persisted among the insured women receiving regular care, infant mortality rates increasing with declining social class among both whites and Negroes. And the special handicap of minority status was still evident in the fact that even with supervision the wives of nonwhite professionals lost more infants than did the wives of the poorest whites. Prematurity rates were also higher among nonwhites, the rate of 9.4% for health-plan nonwhites being more than one and one-half times the 6% rate of insured whites.

That even excellent care cannot fully compensate for a lifetime of poor health and poor growth should not lead us to discount the need for care. Even as we seek to improve the reproductive efficiency of future generations by improving their life conditions, we should simultaneously provide the present generation of mothers with the optimum level of care. We have earlier pointed out that when fertility control has been made available to poor women they have tended to alter their reproductive patterns in such a way as to reduce their own risk. If we add to the benefits which can derive from reducing family size and improving pregnancy spacing for women in poverty, the beneficial effects of health education and continuing supervision of their general health and nutritional status, there can be little doubt that adequate care for mothers can make a difference in the quality of their children.

In the preceding chapters we have focused on reproduction and on the characteristics of mothers which may affect the condition of their infants in the womb and at birth. It is evident that the factors which have been discussed, and others which we have mentioned only in passing, tend to occur together as characteristic features of lower-class life and are found to an exaggerated degree in the nonwhite segment of the population. The poor woman having a baby may be at risk because of her age, her nutritional status, her probable poor growth, her excessive exposure to infection in the community which she inhabits, her poor housing, and her inadequate medical supervision, as well as because of complex interactions between these and other potentially adverse influences (e.g., if she is unwed, she is likely to have even poorer housing and less medical care—Pakter et al., 1961a). If in seeking causes for reproductive failure we are unable to give them statistical independence from one another this means only that as scientists we may never decide which of them, if any, is the most significant causative factor. Therefore as humanitarians we may have no choice but to effect a general improvement in the quality of mothers' lives, generation unto generation, if we are to prevent the damage to children that may arise out of conditions preceding their own births.

But birth is only a dramatic event in the long-term development of a child. Propelled from the womb to the world, he comes for the first time into direct contact with his mother's surroundings. If her environment is a good one which fosters and supports him, there is a chance he may compensate for a poor start. If on the other hand his life after birth is one that piles risk on injury, his prospects are bleak. It is to the prospects of children in their postnatal lives that we now turn.

CHAPTER EIGHT

Nutrition, Growth, and Development

My mother groan'd! my father wept,
Into the dangerous world I leapt
Helpless, naked, piping loud . . .
        WILLIAM BLAKE

WE HAVE been considering up to this point the evidence that poor infants, and especially poor nonwhite infants, are excessively exposed to conditions of biological risk for survival and, when they survive, for normal development, as a result of circumstances which affect the reproductive competence and behavior of their mothers. Since babies do not spring full-grown from mothers' brows, however, it is clear that the physical threats to which children are exposed by poverty are not limited to adverse events preceding their own infancies. Although a human is a being somewhat less fetal at birth than such fellow creatures as the opossum or the white rat, he enters the world quite helpless and naked, indeed, destined for a period of almost total dependency far longer—both absolutely and in proportion to his full span of years—than that to which even his closest primate relatives are subject. Therefore the human infant, whether or not he is healthy at birth, is extraordinarily vulnerable to the beneficence or hostility of his environment after birth; and since he will probably live postnatally in an environment like that of his mother before he was born, the effects of his life condition on his health and development will tend to be continuous and cumulative.

Thus the infant conceived and brought to birth by a well-grown and healthy woman is likely to be raised in a fostering environment. The poor child, on the other hand, before he reaches school age, will have been subjected to 5 or 6 years of the same life conditions which handicapped his mother as a reproducer. Born prematurely or otherwise vulnerable—a not unlikely fate for such a child—he may be in double jeopardy in postnatal life, excessively subject to damage in an excessively pitiless environment. In this and in the following chapters, then, we turn to a consideration of life after birth and the effect of its quality on the development of children.

Health in a human being can be defined in two ways: negatively, as the absence of disease, or positively, as a state in which growth and function are optimal. Of the factors in a child's postnatal environment which affect his resistance to disease and his growth and functioning, the most important is probably nutrition. Our awareness of conditions of life among mothers who are poor would lead us to expect to find high rates of illness and a prevalence of poor nutrition among the infants of these mothers. We shall be looking at these indicators of health in the following chapters. Before we do so, however, we wish to examine the nature of the relationships between disease, growth, nutrition, and mental development.

We can begin our examination with the well-established fact that there is an intimate association between poor nutrition and disease. Deficiency diseases like scurvy, pellagra, rickets, beri-beri, and kwashiorkor and such clinical signals of deficiency as dermatitis, depigmentation, and night blindness are the most direct and dramatic evidences we have of the effect of diet on health. Some of the cause-and-effect relationships of these conditions have been empirically recognized for centuries—as in the recognition that citrus fruits prevented scurvy; and some, like the link between protein lack and kwashiorkor, have only recently been elucidated. The more complex relationship between nutrition and infectious disease was also acknowledged in a general way centuries before it was understood. The Bible itself defines a path leading from famine to pestilence, from malnutrition to disease. Subsequent scientific exploration of that path, however, has shown it to lead not in one but in two directions. Scrimshaw, Taylor, and Gordon (1968) have pointed out that the characteristic relationship between malnutrition and illness is actually a synergistic interaction in which nutritional deficiency contributes to an increase in the frequency and severity of infection, and infection in turn exacerbates malnutrition.

The exaggerated vulnerability of the malnourished body to infection apparently arises from the adverse effect of malnutrition on various of the body's mechanisms of defense. Olarte et al. demonstrated in 1956 that malnourished children had a markedly reduced ability to develop an immune reaction to infectious agents; and more recently the study of Kumate (1964) has suggested that levels of complement and of circulating gamma globulins, the major mechanisms of resistance to infection, are significantly reduced when children are malnourished. Not unexpectedly, then, surveys in areas of chronic malnutrition have demonstrated that malnourished children experience higher rates of infection (Gordon et al., 1964) and more frequent complications (Vega et al., 1964) than those who are well nourished, as well as higher rates of mortality from types of infections which would not normally be fatal (Scrimshaw, 1965).

But not only does poor nutritional status promote infection; infection in its turn depresses an already poor nutritional status. In countries where there is a high prevalence of severe malnutrition, clinically expressed by the syndromes of marasmus and kwashiorkor, these illnesses usually occur in children who have histories of repeated infectious illnesses accompanying persistent undernutrition or malnutrition. Already in a marginal nutritional state, such children are thrown over the brink by the occurrence of an infectious illness; and not infrequently they develop a degree of malnutrition which, if untreated, can result in death (Brock and Autret, 1952; Autret and Behar, 1954).

The strongly unfavorable effects of infectious illness on nitrogen balance, and thus on protein requirements, is well established (Wilson, Bressani, and Scrimshaw, 1961). Co Tui (1953) has pointed out that during severe illness as much as 135 grams of body protein may be destroyed in a single day; and even if (though it is unlikely under conditions of deprivation) dietary intake compensates for the loss, reduced synthesis often appears to prevent the child from restoring his nitrogen balance at least during the acute phases of the illness.

Infectious illnesses in general tend to reduce the blood levels of vitamins A and C and to increase the rate of loss of vitamins through urinary excretion. Febrile illnesses produce a rise in caloric requirements; and infections in the gastrointestinal tract may directly interfere with the synthesis of certain of the B-vitamins.

Moreover, it is not only the illnesses themselves but also their treatment that may affect nutritional status. Drugs used in therapy may act on the intestinal flora of the child, at the least reducing the normal ratio of the bacterium E. coli to other varieties of microorganism in the gut and thereby modifying the autogenous production of B-vitamins and other substances which are marginally, if at all, present in the extrinsic diet. In whole sections of Latin America, for example, neomycin is used in the treatment of infectious diarrhea in infants (De la Torre, 1963). A recent study in South Africa using a patient who had an isolated loop of gut showed that the administration of various antibiotics, particularly neomycin, resulted in a very substantial reduction in the absorption of amino acids and the production of various B-vitamin fractions (Orten *et al.,* 1962).

Among poor and undereducated populations there is often a further social effect of illness on nutritional status when, out of ignorance, or poverty, or both, parents withhold from the child who is ill precisely those foods which he most needs if he is to maintain his nutritional status and recover from the illness. Not infrequently they interpret diarrhea as "worms" and administer purgatives which further deplete his nutritional reserves.

Thus a child's nutritional state may not only modify his body's reaction to infection, but the presence of infectious disease can in turn result in increased nutritional stresses. Since much of the discussion which follows will deal with the effects of nutritional status on various phases of development, it must be kept in mind that in children a state of malnutrition is often the product of an interaction. Thus in discussing malnutrition we are not talking only about diet; we are talking about a physical condition which may have been brought on by poor diet, or disease, or a combination of both.

If disease is the absence of health, adequate growth is, in children, its positive reflection. We have earlier indicated (see Chapter Five) that adult height in any population is a product of the environment in which the growth has taken place, as well as of the genetic potential of the population. Among children, however, *rate* of growth appears to be relatively independent of ultimate size so that when life circumstances are favorable, growth curves from widely disparate human populations show great similarity. As Jackson (1964) has written, "one cannot help being impressed with the consistency and predictability of growth in length of normal infants."

On the other hand, where environmental conditions are not favorable, growth among children falters. A large body of evidence accumulated over the last few decades on impoverished peoples from Africa, Asia, Latin America, and other parts of the world shows that growth rates among children in these groups are depressed far below those of children from more affluent segments of their populations. In Figures 8.1 and 8.2 (Rao *et al.*, 1958) the growth curves of more than 4,500 children in South India are compared with those

Rao *et al.*, 1958

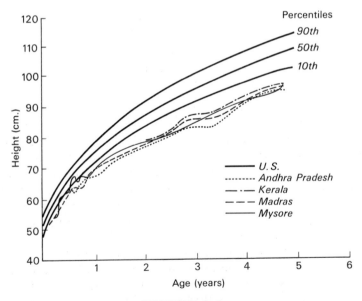

FIGURE 8.1

Average Height of South Indian Children Compared with Observations from the United States

Rao *et al.*, 1958

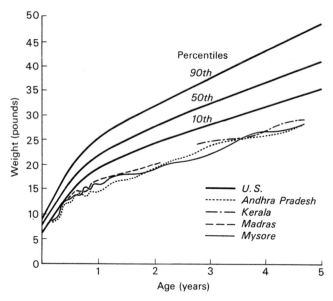

FIGURE 8.2

Average Weight of South Indian Children Compared with Observations from the United States

of a representative United States sample (Watson and Lowrey, 1959). The growth retardation of the Indian children is extreme, their average heights and weights falling below the third percentile of the U. S. sample. More recently Jackson has examined the results of a number of such studies from different cultures and found, as Figure 8.3 shows, that similar patterns of growth retardation occur in disparate geographic areas, all of which are characterized by substandard environmental conditions.

In all these communities, growth rates, which appear to be relatively normal at birth and in the first 6 months of life, begin to be depressed after 6 months, and become increasingly so during the second and third year of life. We have seen earlier that growth which has been so depressed may return to a normal acceleration rate by late childhood, but that the earlier losses are never fully recouped, and

Jackson, 1964

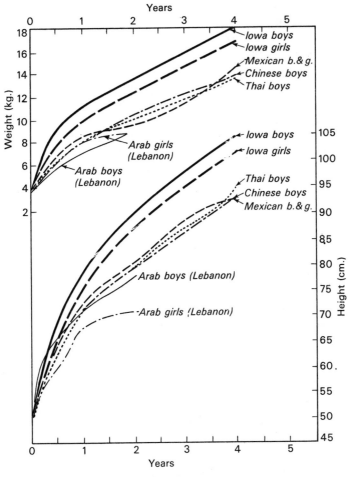

FIGURE 8.3

Growth of Preschool Children in Lebanon, Thailand, Mexico, and China Compared with Iowa Norms

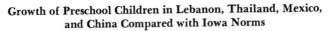

that children who have been exposed to such a growth depression—smaller at adolescence than their normally growing contemporaries—are ultimately smaller as adults.

Although other adverse environmental factors may contribute to abnormal growth rates (e.g., McGregor, Billewicz, and Thompson, 1961; Baker, 1969), a large body of data collected over the last few decades indicates strongly that depressed nutritional status is probably the single most important factor in producing stunted growth. In Uganda, Dean and his colleagues (1960), studying children who have been rehabilitated from severe malnutrition, have shown that in such children body length continues to be reduced after recovery, and skeletal development retarded, in comparison with that of normal children of the same age and ethnic group. In Venezuela Barrera-Moncada (1963) has followed children who have recovered from episodes of severe malnutrition and found, over periods as long as 10 years, that such children remain retarded in their growth. Moreover, the effects of nutritional inadequacy on growth are not limited to cases of severe clinical malnutrition. Ramos-Galvan, working in Mexico (1964), has found abnormal ratios of body proportions in school children living under conditions conducive to malnutrition; and we have earlier (see Chapter Five) presented data from Britain and Japan showing that leg length in children as well as mean height appear to be responsive to the relative adequacy of the available diet.

Over the past 10 to 15 years, as the effects of nutritional deprivation on physical growth have become more widely recognized (György, 1960), concern has increased that malnutrition might not only be limiting skeletal growth but might also be exerting deleterious effects on the central nervous system (Chandra, 1964; Coursin, 1965), and thus be functioning to depress the adaptive and intellectual capacities of children who have been at nutritional risk in infancy (Eichenwald and Fry, 1969). A number of observations contributed to this concern. One was the finding of various investigators that children who were stunted also exhibited a diminished head circumference (Dean, 1960; Ambrosius, 1961; Graham, 1966, 1967). If the size of the head could be assumed to reflect the size of the brain, then diminution in head size would suggest a reduction in brain size as a consequence of malnutrition. As Graham has pointed out, head growth is very rapid in infancy. At birth man has achieved some 63% of his adult head circumference in contrast to 30% of his adult height. And by the age of 3, when the individual has achieved little more than half his adult height, head growth is 90% completed.

Following up children who had been malnourished at various ages, Graham (1967) concluded that those malnourished in their youngest years had the poorest prognosis for full recovery in growth and particularly for full recovery in head size. His data in Figure 8.4

Graham, 1966

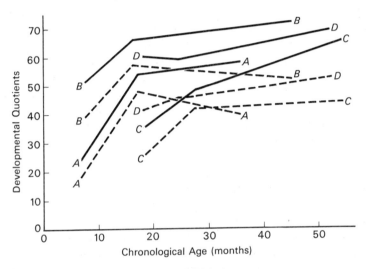

FIGURE 8.4

Evolution of Developmental Quotients for Height and Head Circumference During Recovery from Malnutrition

The solid lines correspond to height and the broken lines to head circumference. Lines *A* are the mean of 14 infants under 12 months of age on admission with height quotients of less than 40 percent, and lines *B*, of 14 infants under 12 months of age with height quotients of 40 percent or more. Lines *C* are the mean of 13 children 12 months of age or more on admission with height quotients under 50 percent, and lines *D*, of 12 children 12 or more months of age with height quotients of 50 percent or more.

show differences in the degree of recovery of head circumference in infants who have experienced varying degrees of malnutrition at different age levels. "Because of very slow growth in head size after the first year of life," Graham pointed out, "it is possible . . . that

. . . the capacity for make-up growth is quite limited after the age of one year. . . . When near starvation occurs during a significant part of the first year, failure to grow in length and head size is so striking that even under the best of circumstances significant permanent deficits occur."

The behavior of malnourished children at the time they come to notice for their condition has also given rise to concern as to their subsequent mental development. From the time of Correa's (1908) first descriptions of severe malnutrition in young children it has been clear that one characteristic feature of the clinical syndromes of nutritional stress was psychological disturbance. There is agreement in the reports from workers in many different countries that the single most common behavioral finding in malnourished children is apathy accompanied by irritability. Children severely ill from any cause seem to lose all the child's normal curiosity and desire for exploration, but so marked is this condition of unresponsiveness in malnutrition that renewal of interest in the environment has become in many clinical centers one of the most reliable signs of a child's improving nutritional status (Trowell, Davies, and Dean, 1954; Gomez et al., 1954; Valenzuela et al., 1959; DeSilva, 1964). "Once a child can be persuaded to smile he is well on the way to recovery" (Clark, 1951).

It can be argued that apathy and irritability may be responses to hospitalization or to other factors in the environment as well as products of the child's depressed nutritional status. But whatever the specific factors which cause the behaviors, there is no question that the child's ability to respond appropriately to significant stimuli in his environment is reduced during the period of chronic malnutrition; and that continued malnutrition is accompanied by progressive behavioral regression.

As evident and as troubling as are these head size and personality changes among malnourished children, both are questionable as signs that there has been permanent retardation in the development of either the nervous system or the intellect. So far as head size is concerned, there is no certainty that it is a reliable indicator of brain size or capacity. As for the markedly unresponsive behavior of malnourished children, it appears to be confined to the time they are clinically ill. Once severely malnourished children have recovered, relatively normal responsiveness is regained; but the degree to which prior unresponsiveness leaves permanent effects on subsequent development is not fully determined. Hence the most potent source of concern as to the mental effects of malnutrition is a more direct one, specifically, the widespread observation that children who have been exposed to the risk of malnutrition or who are stunted are over-represented among groups who experience school failure. This observation more than any other has provoked a series of studies designed to clarify the relationships between early malnutrition and subsequent mental performance.

Given the nature of the personality changes which accompany acute malnutrition, it is not surprising that children with severe clinical illness arising from protein calorie malnutrition should show depressed levels of intellectual functioning (Geber and Dean, 1956; Gomez et al., 1954; Robles et al., 1959; Barrera-Moncada, 1963). But these are acutely sick children. More significant sources of concern are the extent to which developmental lags appear to persist after recovery, and the degree to which similarly reduced intellectual functioning accompanies less severe but chronic nutritional deprivation. Cravioto and Robles (1965), following the developmental course of 20 children recovering from malnutrition in the Children's Hospital in Mexico City, found that although most of the children appeared to "recover" mentally as their physical status improved, those who were youngest on being admitted did not. The children's level of development was assessed on the Gesell Developmental Tests on admission and at 2-week intervals thereafter for the entire period of hospitalization. Because children were at different ages when admitted, data were available on 6 infants admitted below 6 months of age, 9 children admitted between 15 and 29 months, and 5 children who were between 37 and 42 months of age on admission. Scores were depressed, on admission, in all fields of behavior; but in most patients, as clinical recovery took place, the gap between the child's performance and that expected for his age progressively diminished—though at varying rates of speed. Figures 8.5 and 8.6 compare the adaptive and language behavior scores of the 15–29-month age group with the theoretic normal scores for children of the same age. Though scores for language behavior improved much more slowly than adaptive behavior scores, the slopes of the lines suggest that the remaining deficit in both areas may disappear with time. For the 37–42-month age group, recovery in all areas tested was even more rapid. However, among those children younger than 6 months of age on admittance, "the increment in mental age . . . was equal to the number of months expended in the hospital. . . . In other words, in the youngest group the initial deficit remained constant throughout the observation period which in some cases extended up to six and a half months." Figures 8.7 and 8.8, which compare the scores in adaptive and language behavior for this group with the theoretic normal indicate that there was no tendency for the lines to converge, and that the gap tended instead to widen over time. The authors concluded that "the persistence of low scores

Cravioto and Robles, 1965

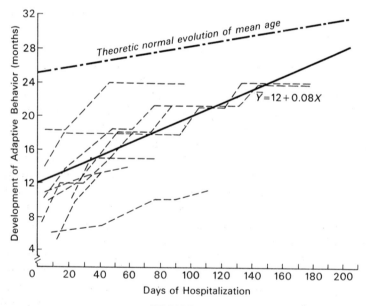

FIGURE 8.5

Relation Between Days of Hospitalization and Improvement in Adaptive Functioning in Children of Different Ages Recovering from Advanced Malnutrition

(*Children 15–29 months of age*)

Cravioto and Robles, 1965

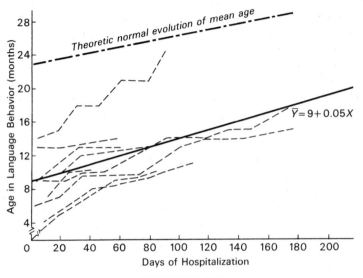

FIGURE 8.6

Relation Between Days of Hospitalization and Language Behavior in Children of Different Ages Recovering from Advanced Malnutrition

(Children 15–29 months of age)

of performance in adaptive behavior during rehabilitation . . . seems to indicate a probable loss in intellectual potential."

In another report on the later development of previously malnourished children, Cabak and Najdanvic (1965) found lowered IQ scores among a group of 36 Yugoslav children originally admitted to a hospital for malnutrition when they were between 4 and 24 months of age. When the children were reexamined at ages 7–14 and their IQs compared with those of Serbian children generally, their IQs were found to be significantly depressed. The mean IQ was 88, a score lower even than the mean of 93 for the lowest socioeconomic group in the standard sample, and fully half the children scored below a "limit of normal intelligence" above which 79% of the children in the standardization group are found.

Brockman (1966) found that children hospitalized for kwashiorkor performed significantly less well on a spontaneous sorting task than adequately nourished children of similar social class, and that the scores showed no improvement when children were retested after treatment. And Champakam *et al.* (1968) tested Indian children who had been treated for kwashiorkor on a test of intersensory integration developed by Birch and Lefford (see below) and compared their scores with those of controls matched for such variables as age, sex, and caste. The scores of the children who had been ill with kwashiorkor were markedly retarded compared with those of their better-nourished controls.

Such studies as these would appear to suggest that some retardation in mental development persists after recovery among children who have been seriously ill as a consequence of malnutrition. It is of somewhat broader significance, however, that similar findings have been reported among children who were less acutely malnourished, or among whom malnutrition can only be inferred from reduction in stature. Pek Hien Liang *et al.* (1967) have reported on

Cravioto and Robles, 1965

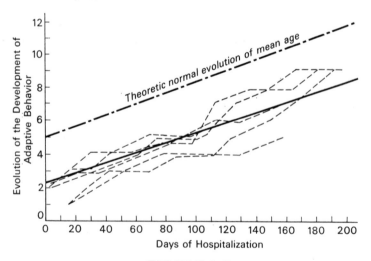

FIGURE 8.7

Relation Between Days of Hospitalization and Improvement in Adaptive Functioning in Children Under Six Months of Age Recovering from Advanced Malnutrition

Cravioto and Robles, 1965

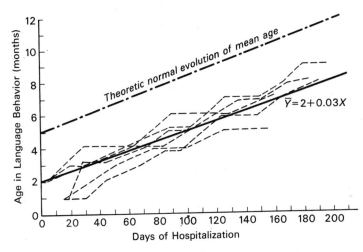

FIGURE 8.8

Relation Between Days of Hospitalization and Language Behavior in
Children Under Six Months of Age Recovering from
Advanced Malnutrition

107 Indonesian children between 5 and 12 years of age from lower
socioeconomic groups, 46 of whom had been classified as malnourished, and in some cases also as vitamin A deficient, during a
previous investigation into nutritional status in the area. Children
were tested on the WISC and the Goodenough drawing test. When
scores were compared according to height and present clinical status,
there was a clear advantage for the better-grown and better-nourished
children. But the largest differences were found when the children's
scores were grouped according to prior nutritional status. Children
who had been both malnourished and vitamin A deficient 6 years
earlier had scores on both tests significantly lower than those of the
group which was adequately nourished in infancy.

Stoch and Smythe (1963) have used a semilongitudinal method to
follow the physical and mental development of two groups of South
African Negro children, one judged as being grossly underweight
due to malnutrition and the other as adequately nourished. Parents

of both groups belonged to the lowest economic stratum of unskilled laborers with minimum incomes and had similarly low IQs. The children were weighed, and their height and head size measured when they entered the study. If they were under 2 (18 out of 21 in each group) they were initially assessed for development on the Gesell. The others were assessed on the Merrill-Palmer. The intellectual assessments were repeated at 6–12-month intervals throughout the period: on the Merrill-Palmer between 2 and 6 years, and, when the children were over 6, on a South African modification of the 1916 Stanford Revision of the Binet-Simon scale. Physical measurements were also repeated.

As a group the malnourished children had lower IQs, were shorter, lighter, and had smaller heads than the well-nourished group, and these differences persisted throughout the period of up to 7 years during which the children were followed. At the time of final testing, a statistically significant difference of 22.62 points in IQ was found between the two groups, and a more recent follow-up (Stoch, 1968) has shown that these differences were sustained in adolescence. Unfortunately, interpretation of these findings is made difficult, not only because there were rather large differences between the families in rate of employment, income, quality of housing, and other possibly significant variables, but because the adequately nourished children were well-fed precisely because they attended an all-day nursery school where they received adequate meals and a vitamin supplement. Consequently the undernourished children not only were deprived of food, but were also deprived of nursery school experience.

In these studies of the later intellectual status of children who have been malnourished in infancy, early malnutrition was assessed directly. Since stunted growth is evidence of poor nutrition, relatively short stature in older children has also been used, in areas where malnutrition is prevalent, as an indicator of their prior nutritional stress. Ramos-Galvan (1960), in the course of a series of cross-sectional and longitudinal studies, has constructed provisional tables of weight and height for age of normal Mexican children. When the heights of rural Mexican children affected with mild-to-moderate protein-calorie malnutrition were expressed as a percentage of this provisional standard and related to the children's performance on a locally

adapted Terman-Merrill test, a positive correlation was found between the children's heights and their intellectual performance. The
finding that mental age was better associated with height age than
with chronological age among these children strongly suggests a
concurrent deceleration of somatic and mental growth (Cravioto,
1964). There are also reports from various populations showing that
depressions in height and weight among low-income children are
accompanied by depressions in motor and adaptive scores (Robles
et al., 1959; Ramirez, 1960; Ramos-Galvan et al., 1960; Espinosa-
Gaona, 1961).

Cravioto, DeLicardie, and Birch (1966) used height to assess the
extent of prior exposure to malnutrition among children living in
a Guatemalan village. A group of 146 children, representing the
shortest and the tallest quartiles of all children aged 6 to 11 living
in the village, were tested on a measure of intersensory integration
which Birch and Lefford had previously demonstrated was capable
of measuring development of integration among the sense systems
of touch, vision, and kinesthesis. The test required a child to make
judgments of similarity or difference about eight geometric forms
presented as a series of stimulus pairs in two different sensory modes.
The sensory modalities involved were the visual, the kinesthetic,
and the haptic, i.e., the sensory input derived from active manual
exploration of a test form. The cross-modal judgments required
were the visual kinesthetic, the visual haptic, and the haptic kinesthetic.

In evaluating the results, two types of error were distinguished:
errors of nonequivalence in which identical forms were judged as
different by the child, and errors of equivalence in which nonidenti-
cal forms were judged as being the same. For both types of error the
visual haptic proved easiest, as had been the case among middle-
class American children on whom the test had previously been used,
and the integration of visual and kinesthetic information proved the
most difficult. An examination of the scores showed that over the
whole age span, and for each combination of senses, differences in
ability between the taller and the shorter children were evident. All
the data clearly indicated "the lag in development of intersensory
competence that was present in the shorter children." No such
height-related differences in ability were found among 120 tall and

short children drawn from an urban private-school population in which nutritional stress was not a factor contributing to differences in height. Thus, as the study makes clear, a difference in height among children who had been exposed to nutritional risk was associated with a difference in intersensory integrative ability in such a manner that, on the average, reduced stature was reflected in reduced competence; differences in height among children not exposed to nutritional risk appeared to have no such negative implications.

Taken all together, these data increase our suspicion that children who have been acutely or chronically malnourished are retarded in their mental development compared with children who have not experienced malnutrition. The data cannot be interpreted, however, as demonstrating conclusively that malnutrition directly affects either nervous system development or intellectual growth. Unfortunately for the firm conclusions of both the scientist and the citizen, malnutrition in man does not occur in isolation from other important biologic and social circumstances. One does not find a high prevalence of malnutrition in families which are well-to-do, well integrated, and well situated, nor, indeed, in nations so endowed, except when particular social circumstances within these nations result in the inequitable distribution of resources. Rather, the greatest aggregates of malnourished children are to be found among the poor. Thus not only are malnutrition and disease almost inevitably found in populations where children begin postnatal life already having been exposed to excessive prenatal and perinatal risks, but undernutrition and high levels of infection in the postnatal period are almost always found among children who are likely to be simultaneously exposed to multiple biological, social, economic, cultural, and familial hazards for optimal physical growth and optimal mental development.

To acknowledge the coincidence of malnutrition with poverty and its other attendant hazards is to recognize that at least two other kinds of factors need to be controlled before the relationship between malnutrition in childhood and later mental or intellectual dysfunction can be confidently defined. The first set of factors are the biologic background characteristics that tend to be associated with poverty, and the second are conditions of the familial environment which may in themselves contribute to the poor development of intellect.

It has often been argued, usually with more conviction than evidence, that low social status is associated with hereditary intellectual inferiority—that the poor, drawing on an inferior gene pool, produce an inordinately large number of children who are intellectually defective by inheritance. Although evidence for the existence of such a pool of inferiority is at best sparse and inferential, its presence has been postulated sufficiently often, and with sufficient force, to warrant serious concern. If a high rate of familial retardation exists among the poor, and if one consequence of this retardation is a social incompetence which increases the likelihood of malnutrition, one could be confronted with a body of data showing mental backwardness to be significantly associated with nutritional inadequacy. Under such circumstances no cause-and-effect relationship could be assumed, since in reality both the malnutrition and the retardation could be reflecting familial and inheritable features of intellectual incompetence. To deal seriously with this issue, in even a partial way, requires a body of information on sibships in which some of the members are significantly affected by malnutrition and others either only mildly affected or not at all. Studying such sibships one could begin to tease out the effects that could, with safety, be attributed to malnutrition rather than to the facts of family origin. The genetic problem, therefore, requires for its solution the control of the confusing factor of malnutrition.

Yet another type of intergenerational influence needs to be considered. It is clear that malnourished children are frequently the offspring of mothers who as children were themselves malnourished, and exposed also to a variety of other conditions which increase perinatal risk. Therefore we must recognize that children who suffer from malnutrition are likely to be the same children who were at earlier risk of perinatal damage. To deal with this likelihood it is essential to have a body of longitudinal data on the prenatal status, the deliveries, and the neonatal characteristics of children who later come to be at nutritional risk. By identifying children with equivalent circumstances in the perinatal and neonatal periods, and by comparing them in terms of the degree, type, and timing of their nutritional deprivation, one can begin to disassociate background reproductive factors which may contribute to intellectual impairment from contemporary factors, such as lack of food, which affect the development and growth of the child.

From even so brief a consideration of the factors complicating interpretation, it is clear that we cannot at present come to an unequivocal conclusion about the long-range effects of children's malnutrition on their intellectual competence. It would be unfortunate, however, if our awareness of the complexity of the problem ended by clouding our thinking rather than by illuminating our studies. No human organism exists without a social environment containing a culture and a background of explicit experiences, as well as a breast, a bottle, and a bowl of porridge. Recognizing this, our task is not to ignore the complexity by substituting one prejudicial interpretation of outcomes for another, but rather to examine the manner in which, within given cultures, multiple factors interact with one another to affect an individual's capacity to grow and to profit from his experiences.

One of the ways in which we as scientists have traditionally tried to tease out various aspects of a complex situation, which resists dissection in the natural human environment, is to remove the problem to the laboratory and to translate it into definable subproblems capable of being investigated in detail. In this translation we often make use of animal models. There are, of course, many benefits to be derived from the use of animals. We cannot in good conscience experimentally deprive children of food; and, if they are in want, humanitarian considerations dictate that they be immediately fed.

Few such constrictions apply to the use of animals. Populations of animals can be genetically regimented, uniformly handled, deprived of food deliberately, and re-fed at will; and though the price of such convenience is probably always the sacrifice of some relevance to the human condition, such studies permit us to separate out for close inspection the significant aspects of the questions which concern us. By means of such studies we can begin to consider whether the association between malnutrition and poor mental growth is merely an inadvertent consequence of their common association with a set of disadvantageous antecedents, or whether the poor nutritional status of children may itself cause or contribute to intellectual depression and learning incompetence.

NUTRITION, GROWTH, AND DEVELOPMENT

We are going to be considering in some detail, therefore, a large body of data which explores, largely through animal models, the relationships between malnutrition, growth, and mental development. We will structure our examination around three general questions. First, what is the effect of nutritional deprivation at various periods of infancy on the growth and maturation of the bodies and brains of young animals? Second, what is the effect of nutritional stress on the physiology of the brain? And finally, what is the effect of nutritional deprivation on behavior and learning in animals? In each of these areas there are, in addition to the systematic animal data, varying amounts of often less systematic human data; as we consider each of the questions the human findings will be interspersed where relevant.

Although it has been clear for decades (e.g., Jackson *et al.*, 1920; Jackson, 1925) that extreme experimental malnutrition in animals, depending on the time at which it is introduced, causes some reduction in the size of both the animal and his brain in adulthood, it has been known for an equally long time that the brain has a favored position nutritionally and that starvation is relatively sparing of it. Results from early experiments were not consistent on these points because they sometimes failed to take into account species differences in the timing of brain growth in relation to time of nutritional stress, as well as the rapidity with which the brain grows to completion in some species before and after parturition. As the experiments to be reviewed will make clear, it is the appropriate timing of the nutritional deprivation that is critical in demonstrating both the extent and the permanence of its effect on brain and body size.

In Figure 8.9 (Davison and Dobbing, 1966) the curves of brain growth for different species in relation to time of birth are plotted to show the differences in the points of time at which maximum increases in brain weight occur in various animals and in man. It is clear that the period of maximum growth, which in man occurs from the sixth month of gestation to the end of the first half-year after birth, occurs somewhat later for dogs and still later for rats (also for rabbits and mice) in whom the largest weight increments occur during the 3 weeks after birth. Once begun, however, development is rapid; a rat's brain achieves 80% of its adult weight by the end of the fourth week of postnatal life.

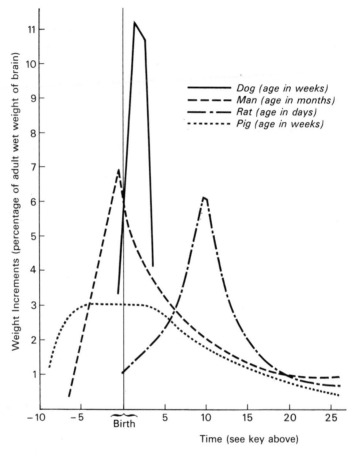

FIGURE 8.9

The Timing of Brain Growth in Different Species
in Relation to Birth

Curves of the rate of brain growth in different species are expressed as weight increments (percentage of adult wet weight of brain) per unit period of time. Donaldson (1911) proposed that the growth characteristics of rat brain become comparable with those in man if account were taken of their 30-fold difference in life span. This concept has been extended to dogs and pigs. Brain-weight data are taken from the following sources: man (Spector, 1956); rat (Dobbing, unpublished); dog (Himwich and Petersen, 1959); pig (Dickerson and Dobbing, unpublished). The assumption that brain development is in any way related to life span is, of course, quite arbitrary. The diagram shows the species variation in the timing of the brain-growth spurt. The earlier part of each growth spurt mainly represents cell division and increase of cell size (Dickerson and Dobbing, unpublished); this period overlaps with one of subsequent lipid accumulation representing myelination.

Davison and Dobbing have proposed that in any species this period of rapid development may represent a vulnerable period during which brain growth may be interfered with by undernutrition. In terms of such a hypothesis, the brain of a 10-day-old rat and that of a 7-month human fetus, whether *in utero* or prematurely born, would both be entering periods of maximum vulnerability to nutritional deprivation since both are on the eve of a period of rapid growth. The human brain, in fact, which is adding weight at birth at the rate of 1 to 2 mg. per minute (Cravioto *et al.*, 1966) continues to grow rapidly for some months after birth, going from 25% to 70% of its adult weight between birth and 1 year of age, after which growth begins to taper off. By the age of 4 the human brain is almost completed structurally (Coursin, 1965; Conel, 1963). Since brain components once laid down appear to have a remarkable stability in the face of metabolic stress, malnutrition, if it were to have permanent effects on brain size and composition, would be most likely to have an effect if it took place during the period of greatest brain growth, i.e., from the last trimester of pregnancy through the first years of life.

In investigations of the effects of nutritional inadequacy on brain growth and differentiation, two major types of dietary restriction have been imposed on laboratory animals. On the one hand, there is a quantitative type of restriction—i.e., starvation—in which the limiting factor appears to be the number of calories (McCance and Widdowson, 1966). On the other hand, there are various types of qualitative restrictions in which diets made imbalanced by a shortage of one or another nutrient are fed to animals to produce various deficiency diseases. Of late the nutrient whose lack has been most investigated is protein, the deficiency of which in young children produces kwashiorkor. Since prolonged protein lack, in contrast to simple starvation, depresses the appetite of animals (and children) more complex stratagems have been required to produce the second than the first form of malnutrition; and to date, the equivalence of the syndromes produced to those which occur in human infants, though increasing, is only partial (Kirsch *et al.*, 1968).

Diets deficient in nutrients other than protein, especially those missing various vitamins, were investigated in laboratory animals long before vitamins were even purified. But even more than the syndromes related to a shortage of protein, deficiency diseases in animals produced by artificial diets lacking a single pure substance have questionable relevance to man. Not only is man's diet seldom if ever singularly deficient, but there are also significant differences in the normal diets, the normal metabolisms, and hence in the characteristic vulnerabilities of man and his experimental animals. Thus a good deal of the literature on single deficiencies in animals tends to be more suggestive of types of possible effects rather than directly indicative of the results of specific nutritional shortages on growth and behavior in children.

In exploring the effects of starvation, McCance and his colleagues have successfully imposed really drastic quantitative restrictions on pigs—animals chosen because of a biochemical similarity to man more marked than is comfortable—(McCance, 1960; Widdowson, Dickerson, and McCance, 1960; McCance and Mount, 1960; Widdowson, 1966; Dickerson, Dobbing, and McCance, 1967). Piglets fed severely restricted quantities of a stock diet were held down in size and weight so that at a year of age they weighed 4–5 kilos, the weight of a normal pig when it is about 4 weeks old (McCance, 1960). The creatures so produced looked like "little old animals," with abnormal body proportions, croaking voices, and scaly itchy skins which they often abraded by rubbing against the walls of their pens. Subject to cold, to worms, and to severe infections, they mostly lay quietly in their darkened insulated cages; and when they walked, unlike normal pigs, they often walked on their heels. Animals who died naturally or were killed at intervals throughout the experiment were dissected and their organs weighed and analyzed. Table 8.1 compares brain and body size of a year-old undernourished pig weighing 5.4 kilos with those of two well-nourished pigs—one the same age but much bigger, and another of the same size but much younger. Brain growth in the undernourished pig was clearly much less retarded than body growth, so that his brain formed a larger proportion of his body weight; but there was a marked absolute reduction in both brain size and, as analysis of brain contents showed, in the number of brain cells in the undernourished animals—both of these reaching a level appropriate for a 10-week-old rather than a yearling pig (Dickerson, Dobbing, and McCance, 1967).

When these undernourished animals were rehabilitated they

TABLE 8.1

Effect of Severe Undernutrition on Body Weight and
Brain Weight of Pigs, 2 Weeks to 1 Year

	Age	Body Weight (kilograms)	Brain Weight (grams)	Brain Weight in Relation to Body Weight (percent)
Same weight				
Undernourished	1 year	5.4	75	1.4
Well-nourished	4 weeks	5.8	47	0.8
Same age				
Undernourished	1 year	5.4	75	1.4
Well-nourished	1 year	156.0	111	0.07

Widdowson, 1966

achieved by three and one-half years of age roughly 80% of the body, brain, and cord weights of litter mates who had grown normally throughout the period. Both the concentration of cholesterol and the absolute amount of DNA-P (indicating numbers of cells) were reduced in the rehabilitated pigs. Cholesterol was especially reduced in the forebrain, probably, as Widdowson (1966) has suggested, because the undernutrition, commencing as it did at weaning, came toward the end of the maximum period of growth, presumably producing the least effect on those lower portions of the central nervous system already developed and the greatest effect on those higher centers undergoing development during the period of deprivation.

The difficulty with studies of this type is, of course, the questionable applicability of the extreme starvation model to a human situation in which there is a more moderate degree of deprivation. The pigs in these studies were so severely restricted that at the end of 1 to 2 years they weighed less than 1/30 of the weight of a normally fed litter mate. These grossly deprived animals were difficult to raise, highly susceptible to cold, and prone to die suddenly from what would have been minor complications in more nearly normal animals. Humans so deprived from birth would probably fail to survive, though the accounts we now have of children who at 6 months or more merely maintain their birth weight have made the model seem a little less inapplicable (Hunger, USA, 1968).

Widdowson and her colleagues have induced a much more moderate level of food deprivation in young rats by altering litter size so that the number of pups in large litters exceed the number of teats, and those in smaller litters have an abundant supply of milk. In a series of papers, they have described the effects of such treatment on the growth and maturation of rat brain and body (Widdowson and McCance, 1960; Dickerson and Widdowson, 1960; Dobbing, 1964; Widdowson and Kennedy, 1962). As Figure 8.10 shows, the rate of

Widdowson, 1966

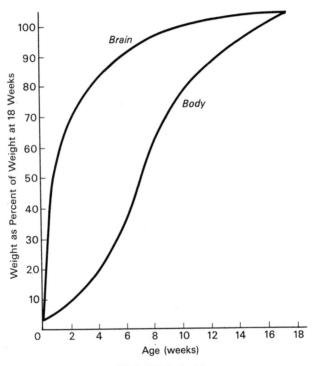

FIGURE 8.10

Weight of Brain and Body of Rat as Percent of Value at 18 Weeks

brain growth in rats during this 3-week suckling period exceeds the rate of growth of the body as a whole.

As was the case with the much more severely undernourished pigs, brain growth in rats was considerably less affected by undernutrition than was body growth. Table 8.2 compares undernourished rats with

TABLE 8.2

Effect of Undernutrition, from Birth, on Body Weight and Brain Weight of Rats

	Age (days)	Body Weight (grams)	Brain Weight (grams)	Brain Weight in Relation to Body Weight (percent)
Same weight				
Undernourished	10	10	1.0	10
Well-nourished	4	10	0.5	5
Same age				
Undernourished	10	10	1.0	10
Well-nourished	10	25	1.0	4

Widdowson, 1966

their age and weight controls, and shows that the brains of the under-nourished rats (like those of McCance's pigs) came to form an abnormally large percentage of their body weights. Brain size was, however, absolutely reduced in the slow growers; and Dobbing (1964) found the concentration of cholesterol even more reduced than the smaller brain size would suggest, because of a disproportionately high water content.

When the animals were weaned at 3 weeks and allowed to feed *ad libitum* on the stock diet, the previously undernourished animals gained weight more quickly than the fast-growing ones; but, like McCance's pigs, never recouped their early deficit (Widdowson and Kennedy, 1962). As Figure 8.11 shows, they remained stunted and became small adults with organ sizes, including that of brain, appropriate to body weight rather than to age. "If the rates of growth are compared simply on the basis of absolute gains during corre-

Widdowson and Kennedy, 1962

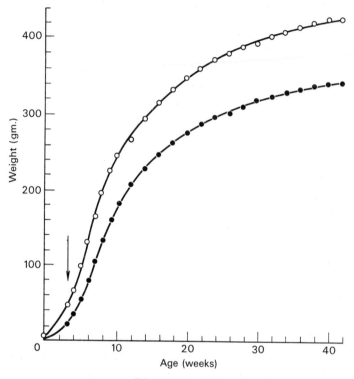

FIGURE 8.11

**The Effect of Suckling Rats in Small and Large Groups
on Their Subsequent Growth in Weight**

Arrow shows weaning. ○ = suckled in small groups; ● = suckled in large groups.

sponding weeks . . . they seem to have been permanently influenced or set by the nutritional experience of the first 3 weeks."

Widdowson and McCance (1963) found that undernutrition at any age *after* weaning appeared to make progressively less difference to the ultimate body size of the animal, and to have less lasting effects than deprivation imposed during suckling. Dobbing and Widdowson (1965) subsequently showed that brain size and brain cholesterol concentration were similarly sensitive to the age at which deprivation was instituted. Among rats exposed to severe deprivation, prolonged in some cases for as much as 8 weeks, reduction in brain weight was no greater, and ultimate recovery on rehabilitation was more complete, than it was among rats who had been exposed to a much milder level of nutritional deprivation during suckling —i.e., during the period of maximum brain growth.

It should be recalled that although a rat brain has achieved 80% of its growth by the end of the fourth week of postnatal life, that is, by about 1 week after weaning, a similar level of completion is not achieved in a human brain until around the age of 3 years. Thus the effects of restriction imposed on rats during suckling may well tell us something about the effect of similar restrictions in the early childhood of human infants. What is suggested by these experiments is that body size may be permanently stunted by early malnutrition, and that even relatively minor deprivation during critical periods of maximum brain growth may have permanent effects on brain size and cholesterol concentration far in excess of the most severe restrictions imposed in later life.

As we have seen earlier, evidence that human body size is reduced by early malnutrition is abundant; but our evidence with respect to the size and composition of the brain in malnourished children has, until very recently, been indirect—inferred from data on head-size differences in well and poorly nourished groups. Within the past few years, however, some direct evidence has accumulated to show that severe malnutrition may affect both brain size and cell number.

Brown, in 1966, analyzed data on the brains of 1,094 malnourished and nonmalnourished Ugandan children who at death ranged in age from birth to 15 years. His nutritional classification was rough since "many, if not most of the children dying in Mulago Hospital show suboptimal nutrition." However, children classified as malnourished fell below those not so classified at every age, in mean body weight as well as in the mean weights of the heart, liver, and spleen. Mean brain weights for both groups of children fell below a U. S. reference standard; but as the data in Figures 8.12 and 8.13 show, the curve for brain weight in malnourished children fell off far more sharply. When the individual brain weights were plotted against age, Brown found that most of the nonmalnourished children fell within the reference range for children of the United States; whereas most of the malnourished children fell outside of it.

If the growth of the human brain can indeed be influenced by postnatal undernutrition, the nutritional restriction could be affecting cell size or differentiation, cell number, the chemical composition of the brain, and the elaboration of its vasculature. Until recently, cell division was thought to be completed before birth and therefore not sensitive to deficiencies in the postnatal environment (Robinson and Tizard, 1966). More recent findings have suggested that this is not true, and that human brain cells increase in number until the fifth month of postnatal life. Winick (1969) has recently estimated cell number in the brains of children who have died of malnutrition by determining the DNA content of samples of such brains. His findings indicate that malnourished children have a significantly smaller number of brain cells than do normal children.

But the impact of nutritional stress on the nervous system is not limited to effects on the size of the brain, on its number of cells,

Brown, 1966

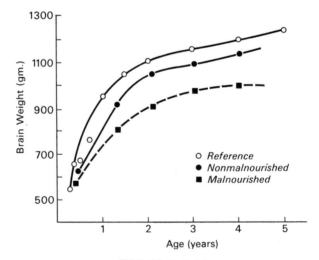

FIGURE 8.12

Mean Brain Weight for Age for Two Groups of Ugandan Children Compared to a U.S. Norm

Brown, 1966

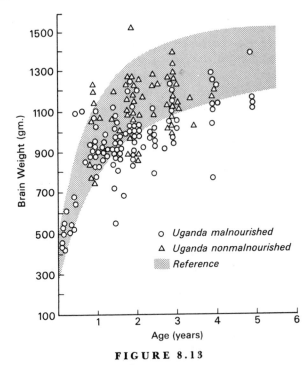

FIGURE 8.13

Individual Brain Weights by Age of Two Groups of Ugandan
Children Plotted Against a U.S. Norm

or on its maturational level. Although significant undernutrition
appears to delay growth and maturation to the point where the lost
growing time is never recouped, malnutrition (growth on an imbalanced diet) appears to have more generally noxious effects on
the brain. Brain substance appears to be much more vulnerable to
abnormal metabolic relationships than to absolute limitations in
nutrient levels. McCance's grossly undernourished pigs had normal
serum chemistries, and neither McCance nor Widdowson found
lesions in the central nervous system among underfed animals but
rather brains which were smaller and less mature. Such is not the
case with animals subjected to diets which are markedly unbalanced

by a serious lack of protein. Animals on such unbalanced diets, like the children hospitalized with kwashiorkor, have an abnormal number of red blood cells and abnormal serum chemistries, and they also show central nervous system changes at the cellular level.

Animals fed on "unbalanced" diets grow quite differently than those fed normally balanced rations in reduced quantities. McCance and Widdowson (1966) fed pigs the same basal diet used in the undernutrition experiment, but with additional calories in the form of fat or sugar. These pigs, unlike the famished ones, lost the desire to eat; and in spite of an unlimited supply of calories, grew so slowly that at the end of a year they weighed only 10–14 kilos. Some lost their appetites entirely and had to be force-fed with a stomach tube. Though they had normal body temperatures and, unlike the under-fed pigs, were not vulnerable to cold, their hematocrits and serum albumins were low and their plasma amino acid ratios were high just as they are in human kwashiorkor. Rats, given the same treatment, developed in much the same way—growing slowly, if at all, and accumulating more fat in their bodies and livers than did undernourished animals. When force-fed on such a diet they could after 6 weeks be brought to weigh twice as much as those on the same diet who were not force-fed, but their brain had a lower absolute weight and thus formed a very much smaller percentage of their body weight (Widdowson, 1966).

Lowrey et al. (1962) have also fed pigs on diets containing different qualities of protein and varying quantities of fat. Animals on high-fat diets tended to lose their appetites, failed to gain weight, and showed the most severe kwashiorkor-like symptoms. An analysis of the diets showed that the severity of the symptoms was inversely related to the absolute amounts of protein each group voluntarily consumed. When the animals were killed, those on a high-fat, poor-quality-protein diet had marked changes in the brain. Neurons were swollen and reduced in number throughout the gray matter, and Nissl substance was reduced or absent. Similar but less severe changes appeared in the brain tissues of the other groups.

The most extensive investigations of the effects of unbalanced diets on the growth and composition of animals have been carried out since 1954 by Platt and his colleagues in London (Meyer, Stewart, and Platt, 1961; Heard et al., 1961; Platt, 1962; Platt, Heard, and

Stewart, 1964; Platt, Pampiglione, and Stewart, 1965). In addition to studying prenatal malnutrition in dogs (earlier discussed in Chapter Six), these investigators examined the effects of protein-poor postnatal diets on tissues, structures, and organ systems as well as on the electrical activity of the brains of malnourished animals. In order to induce a kwashiorkor-like deficiency in pigs, Platt and his colleagues weaned normally born piglets onto diets containing various proportions of protein and carbohydrate. As the weight-age curves shown in Figure 8.14 demonstrate, all the low-protein diets resulted in abnormal growth. The animals' appearance was abnormal as well, and in the most severe cases an uncoordinated movement in the hind legs was observable. The extent of these abnormalities in growth and appearance was apparently related to the total quantity of protein consumed as well as its proportion in the diet, animals on low-protein diets tending to reduce their overall intake even further as a consequence of anorexia produced by the diet.

Differences between the animals were most marked when they were put on the diets at 10–12 days of age; animals started on experimental diets at a later period were less affected. Laboratory determinations taken on the various groups showed lowered hemoglobin, erythrocyte, and serum albumin levels in the blood of the low-protein groups as well as reduced levels of various nutrients, such as serum A, which depend on protein complexes for transport (Friend et al., 1961). The markedly reduced hemoglobin, always found in pigs fed diets low in protein or ones low in protein with added carbohydrate, was prevented by adding protein without adding extra iron. Thus the limiting factor in the synthesis of hemoglobin appeared to be the availability of protein. Carbohydrate metabolism was also deranged, and changes in the endocrine system produced an "altered and precarious endocrine balance."

When animals died or were killed, their brains and spinal cords as well as various other organs were examined for evidences of degenerative changes. All the deprived pigs showed increased brain-body ratios, but had smaller brains than their age controls. More significant were the changes in the spinal cord, especially in the gray matter of the anterior horn. "Chromatolysis, pronounced satellitosis, reduced staining of the nuclei, and occasionally Nissl's 'severe change' were seen in and around the motor cells" (Platt et al., 1965).

Platt *et al.*, 1965

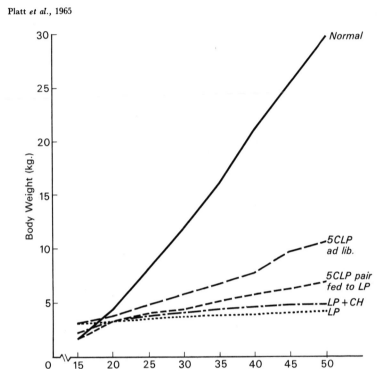

FIGURE 8.14

Typical Weight/Age Curves of Pigs Maintained on Diets of
Different Protein Values

LP = low protein diet; LP + CH = low protein diet plus 100 grams of carbohydrate; CLP = low protein diet with 5 grams of casein replacing 5 grams of
starch in every 100 grams of diet.

The structural abnormalities in the central nervous system appeared to have a parallel in abnormal electrical activity of the brain.
In a total of 157 electroencephalograms taken on experimental pigs,
Platt and his colleagues found a marked increase in the proportion
of slow components of the brain wave among the protein-deprived
animals, especially among those on low-protein diets with added
carbohydrate. Although control pigs showed a fairly constant pattern

in which mixed irregular frequencies between 20 and 40 cycles per second predominated, the dominant frequencies among the pigs fed diets low in protein and high in carbohydrate were between 4 and 15 cycles per second "even after alerting stimuli." These pigs also tended to fall asleep more readily than did those on low-protein or casein-enriched low-protein diets.

When brain and spinal cord findings on autopsy were compared with the findings of the last EEG taken before the animal's death, decreasing protein intake was reflected in increasingly severe abnormalities in both EEG and brain structure. It is notable that in rehabilitated animals the EEG appeared to return to normal on rehabilitation more rapidly than did the structure of the central nervous system. Moreover, clinical improvement, it had been found, was often even more rapid than the return to normal of the EEG, suggesting that lesions produced by protein deficiencies might persist even when grossly assessed physical disabilities have apparently disappeared.

Abnormal brain-wave activity has also been found among malnourished human infants (Sarrouy et al., 1953; Engel, 1956; Valenzuela et al., 1959; Nelson and Dean, 1959) with severe cases showing "abnormalities in the form, frequency and amplitude of electrical activity" (Cravioto, 1966). It is interesting to note that Valenzuela (1959) found records from malnourished children to be lacking a rapid rhythm characteristic of healthy children tested under the same conditions. Higher frequency waves were also absent in the EEGs of Platt's malnourished pigs. Though some investigators have found EEG abnormalities persisting in human beings even after rehabilitation is achieved (Engel, 1956; Nelson and Dean, 1959), Valenzuela in his series found normalization in the EEG to occur in all cases within 40 days after successful recovery from malnutrition.

There is little direct information on the brain functioning of malnourished children other than these abnormalities in electrophysiologic activity. Platt et al. (1964), reviewing the literature on central nervous system involvement, have observed that "neuropathological observations in cases of marasmus and kwashiorkor are few," and that "evidence of involvement of the central nervous system other than mental changes has been reported only rarely." Kahn (1954) and subsequently Kahn and Falke (1956) and Kahn (1957) described coarse tremors and periods of rigidity among a number of infants during recovery from malnutrition—a symptom not dissimilar, as Platt *et al.* (1964) have observed, from the acute exacerbations of nervous symptoms which occur when pups who have been congenitally malnourished (see Chapter Six) are weaned onto a diet having an adequate protein level.

Thus the evidence would seem to indicate that severe undernutrition during the early months of a child's life may reduce the number and size of cells in his brain as well as the extent of myelination; and that nutritional imbalance of severe degree may produce structural changes in the brain and spinal cord, abnormal electrical activity, and pathological lesions of the central nervous system. It must be recognized, however, that the relationship between these findings and children's mental development is an open question, because we know too little at present about the functional implications of most of what we can learn by looking at the brain, weighing it or its constituents, or reading the pattern of electrical activity on its surface. Delayed myelination, structural changes in the brain and spinal cord, and abnormal EEGs are unmistakable indicators of "something wrong," but there appears to be "no simple, direct relationship . . . between behavioral adequacy or intellectual capacity and any specific detail of structural integrity" (Birch, 1966). Therefore such abnormalities serve to tell us only that young animals who have been nutritionally deprived in infancy have nervous systems which are different from those of animals who have not been so deprived; and that where parallel evidence is available from deprived humans, similar kinds of effects are found. To move beyond this point and ask whether gross malnutrition or chronic poor feeding produce irreversible behavioral change requires that we look specifically at data from behavioral studies in nutritionally deprived organisms.

Table 8.3 summarizes the results of some of the recent investigations into the effects of various nutritional stresses on various testable capacities, primarily in the rat. If, assuming these to be representative studies, we tally the results like a baseball score, then it is clear that the "ayes" have won; and that nutritional restriction during the period of maximum brain growth has generally been found to alter the developmental rate, the neuromotor abilities, and the

TABLE 8.3

Nutritional Deprivation and Behavior in Animals

Study	Animal	Method of Deprivation	Test	Findings
Lát et al., 1960	rat	large litter size	activity	+ thru 49 days − at 500 days
Guthrie, 1968	rat	low protein at suckling < weaned to high protein 2 weeks low protein 4 weeks low protein 6 weeks low protein	exploratory activity neuromotor coordination avoidance	— — —
Barnes et al., 1966	rat	16/litter < postnatal low protein 8/litter > postnatal high protein	visual discrimination in Y maze	+ double-deprived males only
Barnes et al., 1967a	pig	low protein, high fat, postweaning	conditioned response	—
Barnes, 1967b	pig	low protein, low fat, postweaning	extinction of response	+
Simonson et al., 1967, 1968	rat	undernutrition during gestation and suckling	elevated multiple T maze	+

learning capacity of the rat and the pig. These studies *are* a representative sample of the work being reported, and we will examine them more closely before coming to a conclusion about what they prove.

There are two kinds of studies represented here: studies of a single generation of animals deprived usually only during suckling and then tested at maturity on various measures of functioning, and what might be called intergenerational studies which explore the effects of more extended deprivation involving both the mother and her offspring. The third major type of study involving deprivation during all or part of pregnancy but not after birth is, of course, relevant to prenatal undernutrition and has already been discussed. We have seen earlier that the suckling period in rats is the time of the most rapid brain growth and the time during which, therefore, experimental deprivation is most likely to have detrimental effects. Where subsequent behavior is being explored, the method of achieving undernutrition during suckling becomes critical.

The most obvious method is that which Jackson used almost 40 years ago in his classic inanition experiments: a simple separation of the pups from the mother at appropriate intervals. But although physical separation does reduce nutrient intake, it also introduces a number of other variables (such as removal from the nest and extra handling) which may in themselves affect subsequent behavior independently of the effect of the nutritional deprivation. Widdowson and McCance (1960) introduced another technique to reduce intake during nursing which has since been widely used: the alteration of litter size so that the number of pups exceeds the number of teats. In one of the earliest behavioral studies done on such animals, Lát, Widdowson, and McCance (1960) compared activity levels by observation of the animals' behavior in a two-compartment testing box. They found that the animals from small litters tended to be more alert and active during their period of growth and to mature earlier than those from large litters who had been more crowded during suckling and had grown more slowly.

Guthrie, who varied both litter size and protein quality to produce different levels of deprivation during and after suckling, found no significant differences between deprived and nondeprived rats (1968). Control pups were nursed 8 to a litter by a dam on an 18% protein diet, and weaned to the same diet. Deprived animals were nursed 16 to a litter by a dam on an 8% protein diet. Some of these pups were weaned to an 18% protein diet; others were maintained for a time on the 8% maternal diet and shifted onto the 18% protein diet at 2, 4, and 6 weeks after weaning. At 16 weeks all the deprived animals were smaller than the controls in proportion to their length of deprivation, but no differences were found in their ability to maintain balance on a rotating cylinder or to learn a shock-avoidance task.

On the other hand, Barnes and his associates at Cornell (Barnes et al., 1966; Barnes et al., 1967; Barnes, 1967) also used preweaning and postweaning deprivation and found some differences between deprived animals and their controls. Rats suckled in small or large litters were weaned onto either normal or low-protein diets. Eight weeks later, low-protein animals were shifted onto the normal diet to adulthood. All the deprived rats showed long-lasting growth retardation; and males deprived during suckling, especially those weaned onto low-protein diets, performed significantly more poorly than controls in a light-discrimination test in a water-filled Y maze. Barnes (1967) has also reported a curious long-term change in protein-deprived pigs. Pigs fed for 8 weeks on a low-protein high-fat diet which produced kwashiorkor-like symptoms were rehabilitated, and 6 months later subjected to a classical shock-conditioning situation. The formerly malnourished pigs established a response as rapidly as did normal pigs; but when the experimenters attempted to extinguish the response, it extinguished with difficulty and in some cases not at all during the period of the experiment. Similar results have been found with pigs on a marasmus-producing low-protein low-fat diet (Barnes et al., 1967).

The methods so far discussed for reducing the nutrient intake of suckling rats—that is, removal from the mother or changing litter size—have both involved major changes in the pups' environment. Putting 15 to 20 rat pups with 1 mother subjects them to markedly different degrees of relative deprivation depending on their success in laying claim to a teat. Physical crowding is considerably increased and results in more physical stimulation and elevated temperature levels for the animals in the high-density situation. Thus where litter size has been altered, the effects on growth and later behavior cannot be confidently ascribed to the impact of the early underfeeding alone.

Ideally, of course, nothing at all except the dietary intake should be changed when pups are being malnourished. The most effective approaches for achieving this ideal appear to be altering the mother's diet in such a way as to reduce the quantity or quality of her milk; or by removing teats surgically and maintaining a constant litter size, thus minimizing changes in the nonnutritional environment of the young rat which might affect his subsequent behavior. Chow and his group, it will be recalled (p. 141), achieved nutritional restriction by continuing into the nursing period the quantitative dietary restriction they had imposed on the mother prior to conception. They found that dietary restriction imposed during pregnancy was much more potent in reducing the size of rat pups than an equivalent restriction of the mother during lactation. Simonson *et al.* (1967, 1968) have shown that mother rats restricted during gestation and lactation to 50% of the overall *ad libitum* dietary intake of control rats, produce pups who show abnormal neuromotor development. When such rats were fed *ad libitum* after weaning and then tested on an elevated multiple T maze, they performed less well than controls who had experienced a normal gestation and nursing period. The mean time required to run the maze and number of errors made by the experimental animals were double those of the controls on the first trial, and the deprived animals also took longer to learn the task.

Although the studies of Chow and his associates are in some sense intergenerational—that is, they involve restriction both of the mother, and through the mother, of the pups—intergenerational effects have been much more extensively examined in the studies of Cowley and Griesel (1959, 1962, 1963, 1964, 1966) which were mentioned in Chapter Six. Initially, a group of female rats was maintained from weaning on a diet which was about 25% lower in protein than the rats' normal diet. At adulthood these animals, though smaller than their normally fed controls, showed no differences in either exploratory behavior or intelligence on the Hebb-Williams closed-field test. Female animals among this low-protein group were mated, their pups were nursed by these mothers on low-protein diets and then weaned onto the same low-protein diets.

Pups of the first filial generation (F_1/LP) were not only smaller than pups born to normally fed mothers and fed a normal diet, but were also slower and made significantly more errors on the Hebb-Williams test (1959).

Rehabilitating a group of these rats by weaning them onto a high-protein diet increased their size and improved their scores somewhat, but they still scored lower than controls born to a normally fed mother (1966). When low-protein females from this first filial generation were mated to produce a second filial generation (F_2/LP), these second generation pups showed a retardation on certain developmental measures: slowed emergence of some motor response patterns, delays in the unfolding of the pinnae of the ear and in the opening of the eyes, and a delayed initial reaction to sound. Raised to maturity on the same low-protein diet the males of this generation scored significantly more poorly on the Hebb-Williams than did their controls, and females scored more poorly though not significantly so. Finally a third generation of low-protein rats (F_3/LP) was bred from females of the second generation (Cowley and Griesel, 1966). Tested on the same developmental measures, they continued to show a marked retardation. Rats from a first and third low-protein generation were then compared with a group of third generation rehabilitated rats (F_3/R_1), that is, pups born to mothers of a low-protein second generation who had been weaned onto a stock diet and thus had grown to maturity and produced young while they were adequately fed.

The results of testing male animals of these groups on the Hebb-Williams at 105 days are shown in Table 8.4. The control group is superior to all the others; the third generation of low-protein rats the poorest. And though the rehabilitation treatment has resulted in the F_3/R_1 group scoring second best, their scores are clearly much below those of the controls. Rehabilitation for one generation did eliminate the size differences between the animals; but as the authors point out, such rehabilitation "does not entirely eliminate, in one generation, the effects of the low-protein diet."

From the standpoint of human nutrition, there are several things to be noted in these studies. To begin with, the handicaps of the rat pups quite obviously do not merely reflect the effects of a poor postnatal diet, since the mothers of the first filial and successive

TABLE 8.4

Mean Number of Errors on the Hebb-Williams Test

Group	N	Mean	S.D.	Scheffé's Multiple Comparisons Test		
				F_1/LP	F_3/LP	F_3/R_1
C	21	106.8	20.08	**	**	**
F_1/LP	17	145.1	19.77	—	ns	ns
F_3/LP	11	160.5	29.13	—	—	ns
F_3/R_1	18	137.0	26.26	—	—	—

Analysis of variance: $F_1 = 3$, $F_2 = 63$.
$F = 15.51$, $P = <0.01$.
ns = not significant; ** = significant at the 1% level.

low-protein generations were undernourished throughout pregnancy. But neither can the handicaps be thought to indicate solely the direct effects of prenatal malnutrition, for the F_3/R_1 rat pups scored lower than control rats on a number of measures though they were born of mothers who had had a fully adequate diet throughout pregnancy as well as throughout most of their lives. Moreover, in a cross-fostering experiment, Cowley and Griesel had control rats suckled by low-protein mothers and found some differences in their Hebb-Williams performances—under stress—from the performance of normally suckled controls. Thus the Cowley and Griesel studies suggest something significant about the nature of a poor diet, that is, that the diet and its effects will tend to be intergenerational, for the rats in these studies suffer from deprivation mild enough to permit them to mate and bear young, but from which there is no rehabilitation prior to testing—at least not for three generations. This is a circumstance more frequent than not in human affairs.

Although this is by no means a definitive survey of the results of animal studies in this area, it is a representative one. What does it tell us about malnutrition and learning? Unfortunately, less than we might hope. Where behavior is in question, the relevance of animal data to human beings is always questionable simply because there are such significant interspecies differences in the complexity of the finished product. It may well be, for example, that the most critical learnings of the child begin just about where the learning of a rat leaves off. Maier (1932) found that "reasoning" ability in the rat was affected when only about 3% of the cerebral cortex was damaged, but that the removal of up to 20% of the cortex left unaffected such apparently complex learning tasks as learning to run a maze. Added to this general difficulty in interpretation, however, is the specific fact that the animal nutrition studies have been characterized by a marked degree of behavioral unsophistication and a failure to specify what constitutes a significant behavioral change. It is clear that the types of behavioral differences identified among variably treated groups of animals will depend almost entirely on the measures used to discriminate among them. The more subtle the degree of dysfunction, the more subtle the measure required to identify it. It was earlier observed, in relation to studies on the intellectual and behavioral effects of prematurity, that global IQ scores are insensitive indicators of the varieties of neurological dysfunction which might be expected to result from the insult of premature birth.

Eayrs and his colleagues have called attention to the importance of determining the level of difficulty involved in any test situation where cerebral function is being assessed. In their own work on rats whose thyroids were removed at various ages, they found that replacement therapy almost fully restored performance on simple avoidance and maze-learning tasks in rats thyroidectomized at birth, but that medication could not overcome the handicap when rats so treated were faced with a more complex situation such as Maier's "reasoning" test (Eayrs and Lishman, 1955; Eayrs and Levine, 1963). "In a relatively uncomplicated situation where, presumably, the need for cortical integration is small, the efficiency with which cerebral tissues function provides the dominant factor regulating the animal's behavior; in more complex situations, such as where few constant environmental cues are available, or where frequent change of response is demanded, both the efficiency and functional potential of the nervous system are tested."

It is clear from all of this that failure to find differences between differentially treated groups of animals does not constitute proof that such differences do not exist and may, in fact, merely indicate that the measure is a poor discriminator. What is remarkable about the animal data is that they have demonstrated the existence of differences between malnourished and nonmalnourished animals on measures for which large portions of the brain appear to be redundant. As a group, then, these experiments allow for several conclusions: (1) that just as the size and composition of the brain can be altered by various kinds and degrees of nutritional restriction, so too does behavior appear to be affected by nutritional deprivation in young animals; (2) that animals raised on nutritionally inadequate diets may suffer from behavioral and learning difficulties, which appear even on relatively crude measures and which may persist after refeeding and rehabilitation; and (3) that when animals are maintained on a poor diet over several generations, the learning handicaps of the young may persist even after a generation of refeeding—mimicking a hereditary condition. Thus the intergenerational reproduction of an environment appears capable of producing a phenocopy of a genetic pattern.

What does this have to do with learning in children? We have found malnutrition in children to be associated with poverty, with disease, and with poor learning. When in animals who are genetically uniform we have removed the factors of disease and poverty, we have found nutritional deprivation to be associated with often persistent behavioral and learning changes. Epidemiology, as Dawber *et al.* (1963) have put it, is the science which establishes "guilt by association." In terms of such a definition, our available data are entirely sufficient to permit us to return a verdict for the plaintiff. In children, malnutrition probably does not act alone to interfere with learning but acts in concert with a number of social, cultural, and medical accomplices. We should be careful to recognize, however, that shared complicity does not imply innocence. It implies rather that the victim has been multiply assailed and needs multidirectional defenses.

We have examined the relationship between nutritional stress and learning through data drawn from animals and from populations far removed from our own, both culturally and geographically. To what extent is there hunger and disease among poor children in this country sufficient to produce learning handicaps? It is to this question that we now turn.

CHAPTER NINE

Malnutrition in American Children

In the Hippocratic treatise, *Ancient Medicine*, it was said that the gradual discovery of foods to suit all conditions of men finally resulted in the birth of medicine.

HENRY E. SIGERIST

CHILDREN, as growing organisms, are dependent on what they eat to a more immediate extent than are their elders. Consequently, as we have seen, their vulnerability to poor diet appears to be profound. We have presented evidence in a previous chapter that many poor families subsist on diets which are not only appallingly bad, but which, in many cases, have been so for generations. We wish to look now at the children of these families, and ask how widespread and how serious is this nutritional poverty among the young of the richest nation in the world.

We have been hearing a good deal lately in this country about hunger among our children. In 1967, six doctors, touring the Mississippi black belt to look at Headstart preschool children (New York Times, June 1967), reported that they found among the black children of that region "shocking" nutritional deprivation, so severe in some cases as to be properly described only by the term "starvation." Their appalled account (Southern Regional Council, 1967) received subsequent support from eyewitness newspaper and magazine reports (Bigart, New York Times, 1968; Coles and Huge, 1968a, 1969a, 1969b) and, most notably, from a series of public hearings held by the Citizens' Board of Inquiry into Hunger and Malnutrition in the U. S. and a TV documentary based on them (CBS Reports: Hunger In America, May 21, 1968). All these reports made it clear that the problem of hunger was not confined to one racial group or to one series of counties in one state, but was probably a much larger problem both geographically and numerically than anyone had previously imagined. The final report of the Citizens' Board, summarizing testimony at its own hearings as well as the available published and unpublished studies (Hunger, USA, 1968), concluded that there was a "shocking absence of knowledge in this country about the extent and severity of malnutrition," and that although there was certainly extensive hunger abroad in the land, its own report suffered from "the anomaly of asserting that a phenomenon exists, and that it is widespread, without being able to ascertain its exact magnitude or severity because no one ever believed it existed."

Although the committee report suffers from a somewhat uncritical approach to data, neither its scientific limitations nor the subsequent attack on its conclusions by various national and local officials (some of whom have, not surprisingly, denied the existence of starvation in the jurisdictions for which they are responsible—Coles and Huge, 1968b; New York Times, June 17, 1968, and August 18, 1968) should lead us to assume that the problem it has brought to light does not exist. As the report points out, the problem of acute hunger, which has attracted the widest attention, is undoubtedly but the extreme instance of much more widespread undernutrition among poor children in this country. We do not know the degree to which malnutrition—whether severe and clinically apparent or subclinical—occurs among children in the United States today; but so far as the poor in general are concerned the Citizens' Board of Inquiry concluded that from one-third to one-half of them, something on the order of 10 million persons, suffer from hunger and malnutrition.

The estimate was based on the impressions derived from the committee's own investigations, on the high level of postneonatal mortality in heavily poor areas of the country, on its own devastating review of the available assistance programs, and on the recent United States Department of Agriculture report showing a high prevalence of poor diets in families living on incomes of under $3,000 a year

(Dietary Levels of Households in the United States, 1968). This latter report showed that the adequacy of a family diet was directly related to income level. According to a household survey conducted in the spring of 1965, only 9% of families with incomes of $10,000 and over a year were judged as having "poor" diets. However, the proportion of poor diets increased regularly with each reduction in income level, with 18% of the families in the income range $5,000 to $6,999 having poor diets; and with 36% of families earning under $3,000 a year reporting poor diets, that is, diets containing less than two-thirds of the recommended allowance of one or more essential nutrients. Conversely, the proportion of "good" diets went from 63% in the $10,000-and-over category down to 37% in the under-$3,000 group. Of course, income alone is not an adequate indicator of socioeconomic status since in families with equal incomes more education appears to produce a better diet (Jeans, Smith, and Stearns, 1952; Murphy and Wertz, 1954; Hendel, Burke, and Lund, 1965). But, at the least such figures suggest that we must be seriously concerned with just how badly nourished are our poor in what we often claim is the "best-fed nation in the world."

How does one go about attempting to determine the degree to which malnutrition or the risk of being malnourished is present in a population? We will be looking in this chapter at four different kinds of studies which can be used as indicators of nutritional risk. As we will see, all these indicators—to the extent that they have been used to investigate those children who are most likely to be poorly fed—point to the existence of a high level of nutritional risk among them. The USDA household survey, though more extensive than most, is otherwise fairly typical of the type of study which has been most frequently used to assess nutritional status. Typically such a dietary survey attempts to determine through a variety of questionnaire and interview procedures how much of what food people actually do eat. Thus mothers may be asked what they feed their families, and how much of different kinds of food they purchase. Children in school may be asked whether they have had breakfast, whether meals are regular, or to describe the food they have eaten in the past 24 hours. Such a survey can provide information about general nutritional practices as well as actual food intake for a specified period, and thus permit us to define which segments of the population are likely to be at risk for the development of malnutrition.

Two other methods which deal somewhat more directly with nutritional status are clinical. In the first of these, a population which has not come to medical notice is screened for evidence of malnutrition. For example, presumably well children in schools or at home may be examined, weighed, and measured. If weight falls below a defined standard, if growth is below age expectancy, if muscle mass and subcutaneous fat are deficient, and if such clinical signs as pigmentation changes or inflammation of the mouth angles are observed, general undernutrition or a deficiency of particular nutrients is inferred. In more complete clinical surveys, samples of blood and urine may be obtained and analyzed for the presence or level of substances which may be affected by nutritional status. If hemoglobin levels are low, if blood proteins exhibit abnormal ratios, and if circulating ascorbic acid is depressed, further inferences of nutritional inadequacy may be made. At times nutrition studies may include x-ray examinations for the determination of bone age and deficient calcification.

The other clinical method extrapolates from cases of malnutrition which have come to medical notice, viewing such cases as but the visible peak of an iceberg, and assuming, with some justification, that a base of much larger size but lesser severity exists. If a high proportion of cases of malnutrition serious enough to have come to notice derives from particular economic or social groups, it can then be argued that such groups contain a far greater number of individuals who are malnourished though as yet without clinical symptoms.

One of the least direct, but on a large scale least difficult, methods of assessing nutritional risk in a population generally is economic analysis. Food costs money. Knowing how much it costs, we can determine the amount required to feed an adequate diet to a family of given size. Knowing overall income, we can estimate the funds available for food in various segments of the population. If any group has resources which fall significantly below the level required to provide adequate nutrition, we can infer that the members of that group are at risk of being malnourished.

Though government at all levels has tended until very recently to discount the reports of poverty-caused hunger, it is quite likely that

as a result of grossly inadequate welfare and food distribution programs, often reluctantly administered, the federal, state, and local
governments are themselves among the major contributors to dietary
inadequacy among children. In 1966, almost 15 million children,
1 in 5 of all children living in families, were living in poor families.
Of all children who had reached the age of 18 in 1963, 1 of 10 whites
and 6 of 10 nonwhites had been supported at some time during their
lives by Aid to Dependent Children programs (U. S. Dept. HEW,
Reference Facts on Health, Education and Welfare, 1967; Mugge,
1968). It is probably of significance to our present concern to note
that in January 1965, the median food-cost standard for the nation's
Aid to Dependent Children programs was $88 per month for a
mother and 3 children. Yet at the same time, under the Department
of Agriculture's own low-cost food plan, it was estimated that $102
a month would be required for that mother to buy the food which
would be needed for her family (Heseltine and Pitts, 1966). Moreover,
as of December 1966, only 3½ million children, less than one-fourth
of the children living in families below the poverty line, were receiving even this inadequate aid. The most recent reports (New
York Times, February 18, 19, 20, 1969) on families attempting to
use the government's food-stamp plan (which allows a family to
purchase stamps for a month's supply of food at a cost scaled to their
ability to pay) indicate that the food so provided is simply not
enough to carry the families who use it through a month, and that
a week or more of hunger often precedes the purchase of the next
month's stamps.

Intermittent marginal incomes are likely to provide marginal
diets: less often starvation than subclinical malnutrition, or what
Brock (1961) has called "dietary subnutrition . . . defined as any
impairment of functional efficiency of body systems which can be
corrected by better feeding." One detectable effect of such subnutrition appears to be the high level of iron-deficiency anemia,
which has been found by various investigators among lower-class
preschool children. Hutcheson (1968), reporting on a very large
sample of poor white and Negro children in rural Tennessee, found
the highest level of anemia among children around 1 year old. Of
the whole group of 15,681 children up to 6 years of age, 20.9% had
hematocrits of 31%, indicating a marginal status. Among the year-

old children, however, the incidence of low hematocrits was even higher: 27.4% of the whites and 40% of the nonwhites had hematocrits of 31% or less, and 10% of the whites and one-quarter of the nonwhites had hematocrits of 30% or under, indicating a more serious degree of anemia. Low hemoglobin level was also most common among the younger children in a group whom Gutelius (1969) examined at a child health center in Washington, D. C. Iron-deficiency anemia, determined by hemoglobin level and corroborative red cell pathology, was found among 28.9% of the whole group of 460 Negro preschoolers, but children in the age group 12–17 months had a rate of anemia of 65%. Gutelius points out, moreover, that these were probably not the highest-risk children, since the poorest and most disorganized families did not come for well-baby care at all, and of those who did attend, the test group included only children who had not previously had a hemoglobin determination— that is, they were children judged to be "normal" by the clinic staff. Thus "many of the highest-risk children had already been tested and were not included in this series."

Even in the summer 1966 Headstart program, in which the incidence of other disorders was surprisingly low (see p. 242), studies indicated that 20%–40% of the children were suffering from anemia, a proportion consistent with the findings of various studies summarized by Filer (1969) as well as with the level of anemia found in a random sample of predominantly lower-class children coming into the pediatric emergency room of the Los Angeles County Hospital (Wingert, 1968). Anemia rates as high as 80% among preschool children have been reported from Alabama (Mermann, 1966) and Mississippi (Child Development Group of Mississippi, 1967).

It is clear from such evidence that some degree of malnutrition is relatively widespread among poor children; but we have already seen that the effects of inadequate nutrition on growth and mental development depend to a very large extent on the severity, the timing, and the duration of the nutritional deprivation. Inadequate as are our data on the true prevalence of malnutrition among children in this country, we are even less informed about its onset or about its severity and quality. In the underdeveloped countries, where most of the research on the aftereffects of significant infantile malnutrition has been done, babies characteristically begin to show growth failure as a result of severe nutritional deprivation sometime between the fourth and sixth postnatal month; prior to this time they are fully and often quite adequately breast-fed (Jelliffe, 1952). The time when marked growth failure begins is not only the period when the child's muscle growth is accelerating (Jackson, 1964) and the output of breast milk begins to decline (Rao *et al.*, 1958), but also the period in which his inherited immunity runs out (McGregor, Billewicz, and Thomson, 1961) and when, as a consequence of his capacity to move about, his exposure to microorganisms increases (Gordon, 1964).

In the industrialized countries, where breast feeding is neither so universal nor so successful, it is possible that nutritional deprivation among poor children may begin at even earlier ages. Thompson, who has drawn a vivid picture of the rather unsavory ritual practices to which a newborn Gambian baby is subject (1966), has also noted that the baby is suckled immediately, repeatedly, and to satiation by any available lactating woman, and that as a consequence of this he gains weight rather more rapidly in early life than do children of similar birthweight in Aberdeen, Scotland.

It is difficult, however, to evaluate the actual nutritional significance of the marked drop-off in breast feeding among lower-class women in the U. S. (Sears *et al.*, 1957; Yankauer *et al.*, 1958; Salber and Feinlieb, 1966; Meyer, 1968). Breast milk from a well-fed mother is usually an adequate food for the very young, but certain nutrients may be at very low levels in the milk of a poorly nourished mother (Gopalan, 1962). Moreover, breast milk is not always "good for" an infant. Yankee, working in a migrant day-care center in Michigan, observed that "nearly all breast-fed infants had diarrhea because their mothers . . . had eaten too much fruit while they were picking" (1966). Even under more favorable circumstances, it has not been convincingly demonstrated that breast milk is superior to all other foods for infants (e.g., Aitken and Hytten, 1960; Gordon and Levine, 1947). Hytten and his colleagues found "tendentious" much of the evidence on the supposed superiority of breast-feeding mothers and breast-fed infants (Hytten, Yorsten, and Thomson, 1958; Aitken and Hytten, 1960). On the other hand, breast feeding may in many cases be superior to what is substituted for it.

In underdeveloped tropical countries, where hygiene tends to be poorly understood and difficult to maintain, "modern" bottle feeding may be strikingly dangerous. That it may be similarly dangerous in parts of this country was documented again only recently by French (1967) in his study of Navaho feeding patterns. Arizona Navahos, he found, suckled their breast-fed infants on unwashed nipples, and bottle-fed babies fared even worse. Bottles were infrequently washed and seldom if ever sterilized, and cans of milk from which the bottles were filled were opened in the morning and left to stand all day without refrigeration. Not surprisingly, the major cause of the high morbidity and mortality of the Navaho children was gastro-enteritis. Even in Aberdeen, Hytten found that many in a sample of 100 Aberdeen women were underfeeding their babies on improperly mixed formulas and that the underfed babies were in poorer condition and more vulnerable to infection than those adequately fed (Hytten and MacQueen, 1954). In this country, Woodruff (1957) attributed an increase in scurvy among infants in the Nashville, Tennessee, area to alterations in the traditional rural feeding patterns: not a shift from breast to bottle, but a shift from the use of milk direct from the cow to pasteurized milk in which the vitamin C had been destroyed, and a decline in the use of vitamin-C-rich pot liquor from the cooking of greens as a nutritional supplement for young babies.

The import of all these scattered findings is that poor infant nutrition may come from a breast, as a result of such factors as poor maternal condition, or from a bottle, as the result of poverty, carelessness, or ignorance of the nutritional needs of infants. If we assume that both poor maternal nutrition and lack of sophistication about infant nutrition are likely to be most prevalent in the lower classes, then it is fair to assume that there must be an increase in the incidence of inadequate primary feeding with declining socioeconomic status in this country. Our facts, however, are few (Heseltine and Pitts, 1966).

We do know that there appear to be significant social-class and educational differences in the tendency to provide solid food and nutritional supplements as opposed to keeping babies on "only milk" diets. Payton et al. (1961), for example, who found no social-class differences in the tendency to begin breast feeding among a group of Nashville Negro mothers, did find that more education and improved socioeconomic status within the Negro group was paralleled by an increasing tendency to provide nursing infants with both solid foods and nutritional supplements. Walter Boek *et al.* (1957), in a study of maternal and child health care in upper New York State, also found that low-income infants were kept on only milk diets for a longer time and received less vitamin supplementation than did those from upper-income families.

Just what an "only milk" diet means among the really poor can be judged from two recent observations. Studying living patterns among migrant families, Coles (1965) noted that most children were breast-fed for a year or more without the introduction of any food other than soft drinks; and French (1967) found that as bottle-fed Navaho babies grew older the amount of their formula was often increased simply by increasing the amount of water and using the same amount of milk, so that volume was increased but food value remained unchanged. He also observed that among breast-feeding mothers the breast was often used as a pacifier, that little attention was paid to alternating the breasts at successive feedings, and that the nutritional value of the sucking was often questionable. It must be kept in mind, however, that so long as a diet is supplemented with vitamins and minerals missing in milk, merely showing that a child is kept longer on an "only milk" diet is not equivalent to demonstrating that he is inevitably more poorly nourished than a child whose diet is varied.

Cravioto *et al.* (1967), studying weight gain of a complete birth cohort in a Guatemalan village, found that in children under 6 months of age "poorest gain tended to be associated not with the lowest levels of [extramaternal] supplementation, but rather with levels of supplementation of food intake that were equal to or greater than those found in the highest weight gain group." Among the explanations proposed for this surprising finding was the probability that the extramaternal food was not, in fact, supplementary, but rather substitutive for a reduced milk intake (caused, in this case, by a failing maternal milk supply).

That milk displacement may be the inadvertent effect of at least some infant dietary "supplementation" in this country is suggested by a recent questionnaire survey of the diets of 4,146 infants, aged 6 months, from a "nationally representative" sample (Filer and Martinez, 1964). As expected, the investigators found that "infants of mothers with least formal education and in families with lower incomes are fed more milk formula" and less solid foods than those from higher educational and economic groups. Since an unsupplemented diet consisting wholly or even predominantly of milk is iron-poor, deficiencies of iron intake were most severe among infants whose mothers were in low economic and educational levels. Those whose mothers had a grade-school education received a mean intake of only 6.7 mg. of iron a day, compared with the 9.11 mg. mean intake of infants whose mothers had been educated beyond high school; and there were similar, though less marked, differences related to income (9.8 vs. 9.4 mg.). Such a finding could account for at least some of the excess anemia often found among children from lower socioeconomic groups.

Yet, on the face of it, the Filer and Martinez data seem to bring into question the idea that "lower-class" infants are likely to be severely malnourished (at least at 6 months of age) as a consequence of their longer dependence on milk. The *highest* intakes of protein, calcium, phosphorus, and vitamins D and C were found among the infants of the poorest and least-educated mothers—a reflection of the superiority of milk formula to much that "supplements" it, even in a modern culture. Intakes of most nutrients were more than adequate for all the children in the study. Where, then, in the light of such findings, are the really hungry children? The data presented, which characterize the population in relation to a number of social-class variables, suggest an answer: namely, that the really poor are simply not represented in the study. Only 22% of the families in the Filer and Martinez sample had incomes as low as $4,000 a year; yet in the year the children were born more than 22% of *all* families in Georgia, Louisiana, North Carolina, Tennessee, Kentucky, South Carolina, Alabama, Arkansas, and Mississippi had incomes of *under $2,000* a year. It would appear, then, that the really poor children, like their pregnant mothers, are not included in nutrition studies or "national samples" because they are not seen by doctors, because their families move about, or because their mothers either do not supply reliable data or do not return questionnaires at all. The children of the migrant families studied by Delgado, with weekly earnings of $36 to $43, or of the Navaho families whose yearly cash incomes average less than $500, most certainly were living at a nutritional level which is not reflected in these data. The women whose traditionally poor diets we have examined in Chapter Seven are quite unlikely to provide their children with foods which meet the nutrient needs of infancy.

There is only a little to be found in the professional literature about the nutritional status of such children. Jones and Schendel (1966) examined 36 infants 4–10 months of age from low-income Negro families who were attending a well-baby clinic in Greenville County, South Carolina. They found 10 infants with serum albumin concentrations indicating marginal protein nutrition, and 1 additional child at a level indicating severe protein deficiency. Twenty-two of the infants (61%) had concentrations of total serum protein which were below normal. Measurements of serum ascorbic acid concentration revealed 12 infants (33%) with a suboptimal dietary intake of vitamin C, of whom 8 were judged to be severely deficient. French was unable to collect useful quantitative dietary information from the Navaho mothers, but the observed feeding practices, taken together with a sudden drop-off in growth rate among the infants around the middle of the seventh month of life, led him to conclude that nutrition was grossly inadequate. Such skimpy published findings must be considered in conjunction with testimony taken by the Citizens' Committee on Hunger and Malnutrition (Hunger, USA, 1968). They were told of Alabama babies whose mothers were unable to nurse them, who received only water as food; of children fed for months primarily on "soup" and soda water; and of babies 2, 4, and 5 months and even 1 year of age who weighed no more than they did at birth.

Our data on older children are only *relatively* more extensive. The Bryan and Anderson 1965 study, "Dietary and Nutritional Problems of Crippled Children in Five Rural Counties of North Carolina," examined family diet patterns of 164 handicapped children from low-income families. Basing their estimates on information about a child's daily food intake, day-to-day variations in diet, food shopping practices, adequacy of conditions for home food storage and preparation, and other relevant factors, the researchers estimated that fully 71% of the Negro children and 35% of the white children had diets which were "probably" or "obviously" inadequate. Inadequate diets among these children were not primarily related to their physical handicaps; for 9 out of 10 children, the cause of a poor nutrient intake was an inadequate family diet. Only a limited number of food items were used in these families. In many homes "only one food was cooked for a meal and . . . eaten with biscuits and water, tea or Kool Aid." Discussing the problems created by food dislikes when choices are so limited, the researchers quote the mother of one "poor eater" as saying, "Sometimes when there are two things in the house to eat, like potatoes and beans, I call out and give Alice Faye a choice."

North Carolina is a border state. The population studied was a group of families known to at least one agency. Other reports from the South have made it abundantly clear that there are thousands of less visible Southern families among whom deprivation is even more severe. The Child Development Group of Mississippi (1967), in a survey of family meal patterns, found that 47% of 118 families surveyed *never* served milk and that only 18% of the families had any fruit or fruit juices for the children.

Owen and Kram (1969) studied the nutritional status of 558 Mississippi preschoolers and found that the poorer children were on the average smaller than more affluent children and at greater nutritional risk. The nutrients most often in short supply in their diets were vitamin C, calcium, and riboflavin, and they suffered as well from a general shortage of calories. Preliminary findings from the National Nutrition Survey report similar levels of deficiency among children in other parts of the South (Nutrition and Human Needs, Part 3—National Nutrition Survey, 1969). There is no reason to suppose, however, that the problem is confined to the South. Indeed, several recent studies provide some insight into the risks for poor dietary status of low-income children in the urban North. Dibble *et al.* (1959) in Onondaga County, New York, found that among students drawn from a junior high school which was 94% Negro and predominantly laboring class, 41% had come to school without breakfast; but in two "overwhelmingly white" junior high schools, only 7% in one school and 4% in the other had skipped breakfast. In recent studies among teen-agers in Berkeley, California, Hampton *et al.* (1967) and Huenemann *et al.* (1968) have found intakes of all nutrients declining with socioeconomic status, with

Negro girls and boys having worse intakes than those in other ethnic groups. Huenemann also found that among junior and senior high-school students studied over a 2-year period 90% of the Negro teen-agers had irregular eating habits and many appeared to be "fending for themselves."

Two recent studies of school children in slum areas of New York and Boston once again show a high proportion of inadequate diets. Christakis *et al.* (1968), in the first diet study of New York school children in 20 years, examined the diet and clinical status of 642 children aged 10–13 from 6 Lower East Side elementary schools in Manhattan. Though the area investigated was poor, it should be noted that only 45% of the total fifth- and sixth-grade population received parental permission to participate in the survey, that only 19% of the parents participating were on welfare, and that the overwhelming majority of the children lived with *both* of their parents. Thus once again the highest-risk population was probably not adequately represented. Nevertheless, the diets of 71% of the children examined were judged to be poor, less than 7% had ex-cellent diets, and having a family on welfare increased the likelihood that a child would have an inadequate diet. In the light of recent reports about the unavailability of school-lunch programs in many poor areas, it is interesting to note that all 6 schools studied had school-lunch programs and that the children who ate lunch at school had significantly better diets than those who did not.

In the Roxbury section of Boston, the Harvard School of Public Health studied the diets and nutritional status of 332 fourth, fifth, and sixth graders, about two-thirds of them Negro (Myers *et al.*, 1968). Meals were ranked as "satisfactory" or "unsatisfactory." Four satisfactory ratings for a given meal over the 4-day period produced a "satisfactory" rating for the meal. Fifty-five percent of the children failed to get such satisfactory ratings for breakfast, 60% of them did not have satisfactory lunches, and 42% had less than four satis-factory evening meals in 4 days. "Satisfactory" scores declined with age for all meals, and Negroes generally had more unsatisfactory ratings than Caucasians. The schools had no school-lunch programs, and lunches were the poorest meals, with 33% of the children having two or more unsatisfactory lunch ratings in 4 days. During the 4-day period 64% of the children had less than two glasses of milk a day,

132 children had *no* citrus fruit, and only 1 child had a green or yellow vegetable; 37% of the Negro and 46% of the Caucasian children had "unsatisfactory" intakes of the protein foods in the meat, fish, poultry, eggs, and legume group. "It is evident," the authors concluded, "that many of these children were eating poorly."

We are fully aware that the data we have presented are severely limited for conveying a picture of the nutritional status of disadvantaged children in this country. Of themselves, the New York, Boston, Berkeley, and Onondaga studies, the data of Jones and Schendel, Bryan and Anderson, and Owen and Kram are as inadequate as would be a single tooth, a fragment of tarsus, and two caudal vertebrae of a brontosaurus in conveying to a layman the magnitude of the animal from which they came. Even the appalled reports in Hunger, USA, can only tell us how it really is where a few of the hungry have spoken up, and not how widespread such conditions are nor how many children are so afflicted. Yet to those concerned with nutrition and health in children, even these few data strongly suggest that the facts are limited not because the problem is small, but because it has not been studied. One can only hope that the concern generated by recent congressional hearings and the surveys now under way will remedy that lack.

CHAPTER TEN

Illness and Medical Care of Children

Mens sana in corpore sano.

W E H A V E already pointed out that where poor diet abounds, so will poor health and illness. The evidence presented in Chapter Nine, which suggests that many poor children may be badly fed in this country, would therefore lead us to anticipate that a high level of illness would exist among such children.

It must be acknowledged from the start that there really are no good national statistics on illness among poor children in the United States. Problems of ascertainment and classification make morbidity studies harrowing to carry out at best, and cross-class morbidity studies are especially complicated because classes differ in their knowledge of and attitudes toward symptoms as well as in their notion of what to do about them (Koos, 1954; Feldman, 1966). At best the relationship between the existence of a condition and its reporting is so complex that there is some question as to whether morbidity surveys are of any use at all in revealing actual illness rates (Sanders, 1962).

Inconsistencies between self-reported incidence figures and those based on clinical examinations are quite astonishing, even where the condition involved would seem to allow for little confusion. Lilienfeld *et al.* (1958), for example, found that 34% of a group of men who were asked (among other things) whether they were circumcised gave wrong answers, even though they knew that they were to be physically examined immediately afterward. Whether such mistakes arise from ignorance of the facts, from ignorance of the terminology, or from some more obscure motive, it is perfectly clear that survey data may be distorted by factors quite unrelated to actual rates of occurrence and can thus be seriously misleading—especially when different social groups have different perceptions both of illness and of interviewers.

The most serious and systematic distortion of morbidity data occurs, however, as a consequence of the inability of certain groups to pay for needed services and their reluctance or their inability to get care from public resources. In the U. S. this dominating economic factor interacts with the other variables affecting the identification of morbidity and its reporting to produce a particularly confusing national health picture. Before we attempt to sort out this confusion it will be useful to look at illness in children in a population where there are defined socioeconomic levels but where services for diagnosis and treatment are readily available to everyone regardless of income. Thanks to an administratively defined class structure and a National Health Service, Britain offers the opportunity to examine such a situation, and we turn once again, therefore, to statistics from that country for a first look at illness patterns in children.

The relative geographic unity of Great Britain and the residential stability of some sections of her population have made possible a number of careful longitudinal studies comparing illness rates among children of different social classes on both a national and a local level. In the largest such study, Douglas and Blomfield (1958) examined the pattern of illness in the first 5 years of life in a representative national sample consisting of more than 5,000 children drawn from all social classes. They found that illnesses requiring hospitalization were very much more frequent among poor children. In the first 9 months of their lives, hospital admission rates were four times as high among children of unskilled manual laborers as among those of professional and salaried workers, and at later ages admission rates in the lower classes were more than twice as high. Poor children also tended to stay longer in the hospital, once admitted, and were more likely to be readmitted within 12 months than were those of higher social and economic status.

Where unhospitalized sicknesses were concerned, there was also a social-class gradient. Specifically, morbidity increased with declining social class for such infectious illnesses as whooping cough, measles, mumps, bronchitis, pneumonia, and other respiratory infections. The excess of deaths from these causes among lower-class children was even greater than the excess of sickness incidents themselves. Taken together with the hospitalization data, these findings suggest that certain illnesses may be not only more common but also more often serious in the lower social classes.

Moreover, it must be recognized that the attention parents give to children's symptoms (and their recall of them) is affected by a number of factors which tend to vary with social class, such as the number of children in the family, the relative availability of the mother, or the presence in the household of other sick persons who need attention. Therefore it is possible that in the illness data from the Douglas and Blomfield study—drawn as they were from the mothers' recollections at the time of semiannual home visits—less serious illnesses were actually underreported by lower-class families.

In any case, a much more marked social gradient for illness was found by Grundy et al. (1957), who investigated illness and mortality experience in the first year of life for infants born in 15 areas of England and Wales. They found the numbers of illnesses and total days of illness to be markedly affected by social class. Overall, children experienced an average of just under one spell of sickness and just over 11 days of sickness per child per year. But spells of sickness were almost twice as frequent in the lowest class as in the highest—from 68 illnesses per 100 children per year in class I to 112 in class V, and days of sickness were more than doubled for children in the lowest as compared with the highest class. Fully half of the total sickness incidence among these infants consisted of respiratory infections, and most of the social-class gradient arose from a marked excess of respiratory and other infections among lower-class children. A particularly high incidence of illness was found to be associated with inadequate maternal care and bad housing, both of them characteristics more often found in the lower-class families.

Interactions between environment and illness were even more extensively investigated in the careful study of children's illness patterns in Newcastle-upon-Tyne, initiated by Sir James Spence in 1950. This study involved the continuous monitoring of the health and social circumstances of infants from 1,000 families living in a single community. In their first report, Spence and his colleagues reported finding a marked elevation in overall illness rates among infants in the first year of life in families having lower standards of living and/or lower social status (Spence *et al.*, 1954). The elevation of illness rate was especially marked in the case of multiple or

TABLE 10.1

Distribution of Respiratory Disease by Social Class

			Social Class			
Attacks	I	II	III	IV	V, N.C.	Total Children
0	0	3	18	4	9	34
1	2	7	31	9	22	71
2	3	14	77	20	26	140
3	4	10	70	21	28	133
4	2	6	57	16	22	103
5	1	11	73	15	20	120
6	2	7	31	11	18	69
7	0	5	36	8	20	69
8	0	4	20	5	6	35
9	1	2	16	4	6	29
10	0	0	6	1	1	8
11	0	0	8	3	4	15
12	0	0	2	2	2	6
13	0	0	3	1	1	5
14	0	0	0	1	3	4
15	0	0	1	0	1	2
16	0	0	2	0	0	2
18	0	0	1	0	1	2
Children at risk	15	69	452	121	190	847
Total attacks	54	271	2,006	543	862	3,736
Mean	3.6	3.9	4.4	4.5	4.2	—

$\chi^2 = 6.6$ n = 4   P = 0.2–0.1

Miller *et al.*, 1960

recurrent respiratory infections. The cumulative picture for the first 5 years (Miller *et al.*, 1960) confirmed the earlier findings. Once again there were more illnesses from all causes combined among lower-class children, with infectious illnesses—especially those reflecting severe infections of the respiratory tract—showing the most marked social-class gradient.

As Table 10.1 shows, when all respiratory infections were considered together, the mean number of attacks per year increased regularly though not significantly with declining social class. However, when consideration was limited to severe respiratory infections, as Table 10.2 shows, the incidence among children of unskilled laborers was more than double that of children of professional workers. Table 10.3 shows the effects of social class and various environmental variables related to social class on the occurrence of staphylococcal disease. Once more the trend is for the more adverse circumstances—declining social class, more crowding, and increasing size of household—to be associated with a significantly increasing level of infection.

Of all family members, preschool children appear to be the most vulnerable to infection. Brimblecombe *et al.* (1958), tracing the transmission of respiratory infection within families, found that the incidence of respiratory infection was the highest from birth until about 4 years of age, and that where families were living "in tenements, flats, or subdivided houses in crowded neighborhoods," preschoolers with older sibs were heavily exposed to infection within the family, from school-age siblings, and outside it, from neighboring peers. Altogether, then, these studies show that in Britain poor children are sick more often, and often more seriously sick, than are children of the more well-to-do, and that preschoolers, especially when they come from large families and overcrowded households, are particularly susceptible to illness.

In this country there is not merely a paucity of such longitudinal data on sickness among poor families, but a total absence of them. And the picture of child illness which emerges from such cross-sectional data as are available is quite descrepant with what the British studies would have led us to expect. Figures from the U. S. National Health Survey, for example, show that although poor persons over 15 years of age suffer considerably more disabling chronic illness than those who are not so poor, the difference does not exist among those under 15, and there is no correlation between either family size or income and the incidence of morbidity from episodes of acute illness among young people (NCHS, PHS 1000, 3:7, 1967). Indeed, the reported rates of both chronic conditions and of "medically attended" or "activity reducing" acute conditions among children under 15 rise

TABLE 10.2
Severe Respiratory Disease (Bronchitis and Pneumonia) and Social Class

	Social Class				
	I, II	*III*	*IV*	*V, N.C.*	*Total*
Attacks	35	367	106	197	705
Children	84	452	121	190	847
Rate per child	0.417	0.812	0.876	1.037	0.832

Variance analysis

	Sum of Squares	*Degrees of Freedom*	*Variance Estimate*
Between classes	22.9	3	7.63
Within classes	1,199.3	843	1.42
Total	1,222.2	846	1.44
F = 5.37	P <0.01		

NOTE: This significant difference is also demonstrable readily through the χ^2 test. This test, however, presumes all the events to be independent of each other when used as a test of the significance of differences between groups. With respiratory disease, it is unwise to presume that there is no functional relationship between successive attacks. Although the distribution of these illnesses is not normal, we have preferred analysis of variance. When all respiratory diseases are considered together the choice of test becomes critical.

Miller *et al.*, 1960

TABLE 10.3

Social Correlations of Staphylococcal Disease

SOCIAL CLASS AND STAPHYLOCOCCAL DISEASE

	Social Class				
	I, II	*III*	*IV*	*V, N.C.*	*Total*
Staphylococcal disease	17	128	38	63	246
No staphylococcal disease	67	324	83	127	601
Total	84	452	121	190	847

χ^2 (for linear trend of proportions) $= 4.28$ $n = 1$ $P < 0.05$

OVERCROWDING AND STAPHYLOCOCCAL DISEASE

	Mean Number of Persons Per Room					
	0–1	*1½*	*2*	*2½*	*Over 2½*	*Total*
Staphylococcal disease	61	74	48	28	35	246
No staphylococcal disease	193	176	139	47	46	601
Total	24.0	29.6	34.5	37.3	43.2	29.0

χ^2 (for linear trend of proportions) $= 10.26$ $n = 1$ $P < 0.005$

SIZE OF HOUSEHOLD AND STAPHYLOCOCCAL DISEASE

	Size of Household (Persons)				
	2–3	*4*	*5*	*Over 6*	*Total*
Staphylococcal disease	38	68	66	74	246
No staphylococcal disease	127	195	124	155	601
Total	165	263	190	229	847
Percent with staphylococcal disease	23.0	25.9	34.7	32.3	29.0

χ^2 (for linear trend of proportions) $= 6.22$ $n = 1$ $P < 0.025$

Miller *et al.*, 1960

with income (NCHS, PHS 1000, 10:9, 1964). Thus according to the survey sample, well-to-do children in this country are sick *more often* than poor ones. Similar findings have been reported from the California Health Survey, in which neither family income nor declining social class was noted to have any unfavorable effect on the illness or injury experience in children (Hornberger *et al.*, 1960).

The nationwide Headstart program has also failed to provide us with any convincing national data on rates of illness, chronic or acute, among poor children in this country. Because of the lack of a uniform method of recruitment or uniform bases for enrollment, not only is "extrapolation from Headstart prevalence figures nearly impossible" (North, 1967), but where generalizations are possible, they suggest that at least in the testing the highest-risk population was largely missed. Though there have been reports from individual Headstart centers which, as we shall see, show a high rate of morbidity of all sorts, the overall "incidence of . . . conditions in the *tested* Headstart population appears to be similar to the incidence in the general population as shown . . . in the National Health Survey" (North, 1967, italics added). In sum, then, the available national data all tend to point to the same conclusion: that poor children in the U. S. are not, like poor children in Britain or elsewhere, more likely to be sick than well-off children. On the contrary, growing up in poverty in the U. S. appears in some cases to be associated with lower recorded rates of illness than growing up in relative affluence.

There are several possible explanations for this "American exceptionalism." The first and most obvious possibility, of course, is that a much more marked social-class gradient exists in Britain than is present in the U. S.—i.e., that British children are, on the one hand, poorer and therefore sicker, and, on the other hand, wealthier and therefore healthier than the Americans. Without belaboring the point, it is common knowledge that such an explanation is untenable and that the real economic situation in the two countries is in fact the opposite—with extremes of wealth and poverty greater in this country than in England.

Granting the existence of a significant economic gradient, however, it is still possible to argue that for some reason this economic gradient is not paralleled in the U. S. by a health gradient among the young. For instance, class differences in the U. S. are complicated by ethnic differences in such a way that the lower socioeconomic group is heavily weighted with nonwhites. Perhaps the low reported illness rates among poor children in this country can be explained on some such basis as that "pigmentation protects," so that nonwhites do as well under poor conditions of life as whites do under less stringent circumstances. On the face of it, such an argument would appear to be nonsense, since on the basis of their survival record nonwhites as a group do not *seem* to be generally healthier. Whites live longer and have lower age-specific mortality rates for *all* the leading causes of death, including communicable diseases, cardiovascular-renal disease, cancer, motor vehicle accidents, and homicide. Only in regard to suicide is the nonwhite at significant advantage (Chase, 1965), and this only in certain age groups.

Moreover, the hypothesis that black is beneficent in infancy becomes even less credible if we consider the excessive exposure of black children to infection as a result of the chronically high levels of disease in the communities in which they live. The prevalence of tuberculosis, for example, is considered a good indicator of risk of illness in a population. Between 1965 and 1967, the national tuberculosis rate was 24.2 new cases a year per 100,000 persons. The rate in New York as a whole for this same period was 47.7 (Task Force on Tuberculosis in New York City, Dec. 1968). In the predominantly white, middle-class Flushing area of Queens, however, the rate was 20 per 100,000 (James, 1965). And a few miles away, in Central Harlem, the heart of New York's Negro ghetto, the new case rate was 226 per 100,000—more than 10 times as high. It is not surprising then that the new-case rate for tuberculosis, which between 1960 and 1964 was down 28% among whites and down 12% even among minority Puerto Ricans, was up 1% among Negroes. In Southern California, the incidence of tuberculosis is four times higher in the Negro ghetto of Watts than in the rest of Los Angeles County.

But TB is only one, albeit a significant and indicative, illness. Watts, with approximately 1% of Los Angeles County's population, also had the county's only diphtheria, brucellosis, and polio in 1966, about 45% of all the typhoid, and about 25% of all the mumps, measles, hepatitis, and bacterial meningitis (Tranquada, 1967; New York Times, Sept. 16, 1967). In Nashville, Tennessee, the rate of rheumatic fever between 1963 and 1965 was almost twice as high among Negroes as among whites (Quinn *et al.*, 1967). Since such data as these are repeatable whenever poor nonwhite populations are carefully studied, it is difficult to argue that black infants growing up in such circumstances are healthier and have fewer illnesses than white infants who are not so heavily exposed.

Moreover, if we can assume that excessive mortality implies either excessive morbidity or inadequate care or both, then any notion that black babies are no sicker than white ones is contradicted by the infant mortality data. These show that the excess of mortality among nonwhite infants relative to white infants—which is even higher in the postneonatal period than it is around the time of birth—results largely from deaths caused by infections and trauma. Table 10.4 (Hunt and Huyck, 1966) compares causes of death for white

TABLE 10.4

**Infant Mortality by Cause,
Ten Largest Cities,[a] 1962**

(Deaths per 10,000 live births)

Cause	White	Nonwhite	Percent Excess of Nonwhite
All causes	230.8	386.0	67.2
Prenatal and natal	154.6	230.4	49.0
Postnatal	76.2	155.6	104.2
Ill-defined, early infancy	18.0	30.6	70.0
Influenza and pneumonia (except newborn)	18.5	41.3	123.2
Certain infections	17.0	41.8	145.9
Accidents	3.8	10.1	165.8
Diseases of digestive system	7.8	11.7	50.0
Other postnatal causes	8.2	10.8	31.7
Symptoms and ill-defined conditions	3.0	9.5	216.7

[a] Baltimore, Chicago, Cleveland, Detroit, Los Angeles, New York, Philadelphia, St. Louis, Washington (1960 census)

Hunt and Huyck, 1966

and nonwhite infants in the 10 largest cities. Nonwhites experience excessive mortality for all causes, but the percentage of excess is more than twice as great in the postnatal period as it is in the period immediately around the time of birth when most deaths are the result of congenital defects or reproductive complications. And in the postneonatal period the factors accounting for the greatest white-nonwhite differential are infections, including influenza and pneumonia, accidents, and "symptoms and ill-defined conditions"—a classification most often representing undiagnosed disease complicating general debility.

Such facts would lead us to believe that the differences between patterns of child illness in the U. S. and Britain are more apparent than real, and that in both countries poor children suffer more (and more serious) illnesses than do their better-off contemporaries. The most likely explanation for the *apparent* discrepancy is that existing U. S. data are simply inadequate—and that they are inadequate largely because of the exaggerated degree to which the differing economic and social position of families in this country differentially affects their style of response to illness and to its reporting.

As we have earlier noted, the reporting of illness is remarkably vulnerable to distortions arising from a number of social and psychological factors. But of all the factors which will tend to reduce rates of reported illness in poor families, financial inability to seek care is probably the most potent, for it not only affects the extent to which illnesses are treated and so come to notice in the community, but also affects the extent to which the poor household can afford to acknowledge to itself the existence of physical symptoms which may prove to need medical attention. Koos (1954) found that the different social classes in the community he studied had very different attitudes toward what constituted an illness. His data in Table 10.5 show that for all the accepted symptoms of illness, declining social class was associated with diminishing concern about a symptom and a decreasing desire to see a doctor in regard to it.

Consequently, given the U. S. National Health Survey definition of an acute condition as one that has involved either restricted activity or medical attention, the finding of a higher prevalence rate for such conditions among children in higher-income families prob-

TABLE 10.5

Percentage of Respondents in Each Social Class Recognizing
Specified Symptoms as Needing Medical Attention

Symptom	High (N:51)	Middle (N:335)	Low (N:128)
Loss of appetite	57	50	20
Persistent backache	53	44	19
Continued coughing	77	78	23
Persistent joint and muscle pains	80	47	19
Blood in stool	98	89	60
Blood in urine	100	93	69
Excessive vaginal bleeding	92	83	54
Swelling of ankles	77	76	23
Loss of weight	80	51	21
Bleeding gums	79	51	20
Chronic fatigue	80	53	19
Shortness of breath	77	55	21
Persistent headaches	80	56	22
Fainting spells	80	51	33
Pain in chest	80	51	31
Lump in breast	94	71	44
Lump in abdomen	92	65	34

Koos, 1954

ably reflects not more illness but a different view of illness in these families, resulting in "the increased use of medical facilities and the reduction of usual activities among the higher income groups" (NCHS, PHS 1000, 10:9, 1964.)

In short, the findings of the National Health Survey and similar undertakings reflect poverty of data—not the real data of poverty. Children from well-off families turn out to have more *counted* illnesses and accidents than poor children. But as the National Health Survey data show, what counts and what gets counted as an illness varies with income group. In estimates of chronic illness, for example, hay fever, asthma, and other such conditions—often viewed by poor families as inevitable aspects of functioning rather than as diseases—accounted for only 20.2% of the chronic illnesses reported by those in the lowest income group compared with 40.1% of chronic conditions reported in the highest income group. The rate per 1,000 of such conditions in children from families with earnings of over $7,000 a year was more than two and one-half times the rate reported for children from poor families. On the other hand, the reported chronic illnesses of poor children include a higher proportion of the more seriously handicapping abnormalities of vision, hearing, or locomotion (Schiffer and Hunt, 1963).

Our information about the health of poor children, however, is not limited exclusively to "objective" national data like these in which such children appear to suffer from a relatively low prevalence of either acute or chronic illness. There also exists a body of concerned, if fragmented and sometimes anecdotal, literature from those who have looked at and worked among the poor. With few exceptions, this literature characterizes the health status of their children as appalling (e.g., Jeffery et al., 1963; Coles, 1965; Medical World News, 1965; Mermann, 1966; Yankee, 1966; Mico, 1966; Southern Regional Council, 1967; Hunger, USA, 1968). One such apparent exception is the report of Mico on the results of physical, dental, and mental health examinations given to some 1,400 preschool children for Boston's summer 1965 Headstart project. Eighty percent of the children were generally judged to be in "good" or "excellent" health. However, 77% of them required referral for treatment of one or more conditions. On the medical examination alone, 87% of the children were examined and 35% of these were referred for follow-up, with the ratio of previously unknown to previously known defects being 3 to 1. Though follow-up data were incomplete, known procedures required included treatment of 3 cases of active TB, 2 instances of open-heart surgery, and 12 operations for hernia. Moreover, family data suggested that like other self-selected Headstart populations, the children who participated were not the most needy, and the income which the average family earned "approached the upper limits" of the economic criterion of eligibility for the program. Among the most impoverished segments of the population, conditions appear to be proportionately worse. Widespread worm infestations have been reported among poor populations, both black and white. Half the children in Martin County, Kentucky, an area with a predominantly white population where the per capita income is $588, were found to have worm infestations (Appalachian Regional Commission Health Advisory Committee Report, 1966). And Jeffery *et al.* (1963), examining a group of 33 Negro families along the South Carolina coast, found one or more varieties of worms infesting over 70% of the population. Among children in the age group 0–5, 82% had ascaris infestations and 42.6% had trichuris; among the 6–11 year olds, the rate of infestation was even higher.

Robert Coles (1965), who has worked extensively with migrant families, has observed that children in these families face "from infancy onward through childhood a host of illnesses, uncorrected deformities, and congenital abnormalities or developmental disorders." Coles' more recent reports from poverty populations in West Virginia and Texas have served to confirm these findings on other groups, such as the Appalachian whites and Mexican-Americans (Coles, 1968; Coles and Huge, 1968, 1969).

Other accounts, like the report of the six doctors who toured the Mississippi black belt in 1967, sound more like reports of Biafra under siege than America in 1967. The physicians found hundreds of Negro children afflicted with suppurating sores, severe anemia, ear, eye, and bone disease, heart and lung ailments that had gone undiagnosed and untreated, chronic diarrhea, "appalling" tooth decay. "In almost every child," they wrote, "we observed one or another parasitic disease: trichinosis, enterobiasis, ascariasis, and hookworm disease. Most children we saw had some kind of skin disease: dryness and shrinkage of the skin due to malnutrition; ulcerations; severe sores; rashes; boils, abcesses, and furuncles; impetigo; rat-bites. . . . Many of these children were suffering from degenerative joint diseases. Injuries had not been treated when they occurred. . . . Now at seven or eight, their knee joints or elbow joints might show the 'range of action' that one finds in a man of seventy suffering from crippling arthritis. In child after child we tested for peripheral neuritis—and found it, secondary to untreated injuries, infections, and food deficiencies. . . . The children were plagued with colds and fevers—in a Mississippi late May—and with sore throats. They had enlarged glands throughout the body secondary to the *several* infections they *chronically* suffer" (Southern Regional Council, 1967).

The difficulty with such accounts is that they are not translatable into hard facts about the health of poor children generally, or even about the prevalence of poor health among the impoverished children of Mississippi or Boston. They are simply heartrending vignettes—illustrations for a chapter on the health status of poor children which, in the absence of useful national statistics, cannot yet be written. These isolated or anecdotal accounts are indications of a problem that cries out for what it has not had: a careful and systematic evaluation based on representative population samples. Lacking such detail, however, we have available to us yet a third kind of evidence—a large body of information on medical care from which inferences can be drawn about the health status of poor children. These data are probably more relevant to the population with which we are concerned than are the available national figures on sickness incidence, if somewhat less central; and they are more quantitative than the available anecdotal reports, if somewhat less dramatic. In the remainder of this chapter we shall focus on one major portion of this body of information, namely the kind and amount of medical and dental care which poor children receive relative to their more affluent peers.

Among the more widespread and consistent findings regarding the health care of children from different social and economic strata are those that show a much higher percentage of unimmunized children in these very lower-class groups which are most exposed to infection. Whether the variable that establishes social class is education, income, or occupational status, the children with parents having the least schooling, the least money, and the lower-status jobs are those most likely not to have had their "shots" (Hornberger *et al.*, 1960; North, 1967; Peters and Chase, 1967). In the California Health Survey, for example, Hornberger found that only 17% of mothers with more than 12 years of education had failed to get at least one triple-immunization for their infants; although among mothers with less than 12 years of education, 37% had failed to get such protection. Moreover, in families where mothers had less than 12 years of education or in which family incomes were under $5,000 a year, only half of the children had been vaccinated, a percentage consistent with the findings from the summer 1965 Headstart program in which only half of the participating children were found to have been immunized for diphtheria, pertussis, tetanus, polio, and smallpox. Among the most deprived families, levels of protection appear to be even lower. Walton (1964) found that only 18 in a group of 250 children (7.2%) in families who had been on "poor relief" in Ohio had received the full series of diphtheria, pertussis, and tetanus shots. And in some surveys among migrant workers, Siegel (1966) reports, no children are found who have completed their immunizations.

Though the fact that a child has been immunized does not necessarily mean that he has had adequate medical supervision (since some children apparently receive immunization who have little or no other care in the early months of life—e.g., Peters and Chase, 1967), the fact that he has *not* been immunized usually reflects a grossly inadequate level of medical care. The data on immunization, then, indicate that poor children receive significantly less medical care than their more affluent contemporaries—a suggestion that is confirmed by available national data on hospitalization and doctor visits. These tell us that children from poor families go to either doctors or hospitals much less frequently than do children whose families are better off. Poor children in Britain, it will be recalled, were more than twice as likely as their well-to-do contemporaries to be admitted to a hospital in infancy. Data from the U. S. National Health Survey, however, make it clear that in this country poor children are admitted to the hospital less often than the economically more privileged, and that the same relationship holds true for nonwhite children in relation to white children (NCHS, PHS 1000, 10:9, 1964). Once admitted, however (as was the case in Britain), poor children stay longer, as do those who are nonwhite. The average length of hospital stay was 9.8 days for nonwhites 0–14 years of age, and 5.6 days for whites, and the average stay for children whose family income was under $2,000 was almost twice as long as for those who had incomes of $7,000 or over.

The longer duration of stay for poor and nonwhite children may be partially explained by the fact that such children will often tend to have become sicker before they are brought to the hospital, and to be in worse general health and hence slower to recover. But there are a number of other variables which affect both the rates of admission and the duration of stay among different social and economic groups. One of these is the reluctance of many lower-class parents to have their children hospitalized at all, since on the basis of their experience hospitals are viewed as "places to die." Another is the much higher proportion of tonsillectomies among upper-income patients, which accounts for some proportion of the excess admissions and for the greater number of short stays among children in these groups. Still another is the tendency on the part of doctors to delay discharge to a later stage of recuperation for children whose home environments are thought to be unfavorable.

Thus hospitalization figures, like illness figures, tend to reflect social practices and prejudices as well as needs. The best evidence for such a statement comes from data on the health of premature infants. There is an abundance of evidence to the effect that premature infants have much higher rates of hospitalization in their early years than babies born at term (Douglas and Mogford, 1953; James, 1958; Drillien, 1964). Given the much higher rates of prematurity among nonwhites, one would expect to find a somewhat higher rate of hospitalization among nonwhite infants on this basis alone if care were actually distributed according to need. In fact the figures show a rate of admission of 79.9 per 1,000 children for whites in the age group 0–4 years, compared to a rate of only 63.1 for nonwhites.

The lower rate of hospital *admission* among low-income and nonwhite children, however, does not reflect a lower rate of overall hospital use. Indeed, for many of the urban poor, especially those in minority groups, hospitals represent almost the only source of medical care (Lesser, 1964). National Health Survey data show that nonwhites as a group are dependent on hospital out-patient clinic care to a much greater extent than whites. As the data in Table 10.6 (Gleeson and White, 1965) show, whites at all income levels were much more likely to seek care either in a doctor's office or by "other" means (primarily telephone contacts) than were nonwhites who, by contrast, were much more heavily dependent on clinics. The effect of the adoption of such patterns of care by nonwhites who have migrated to the central cities can be seen in some data presented by Tayback and Wallace (1962). They showed that despite an overall

TABLE 10.6

Physician Visits by Income, Color, and Place of Visit,
July 1963–June 1964

Percentage Distribution of Visits

	White				Nonwhite			
Family Income	Total	Office	Hospital Clinic	Other	Total	Office	Hospital Clinic	Other
All incomes [a]	100.0	71.0	10.0	18.9	100.0	57.0	31.8	11.2
Under $2,000	100.0	67.9	15.1	16.9	100.0	54.3	36.2	9.5
$2,000–3,999	100.0	68.3	16.8	14.9	100.0	56.3	34.7	9.0
$4,000–6,999	100.0	70.8	9.7	19.5	100.0	57.0	29.9	13.0
$7,000–9,999	100.0	72.5	7.3	20.2	100.0	66.0	15.9	18.0
$10,000+	100.0	73.6	6.2	20.2	100.0	68.9	22.4	8.7

[a] Includes unknown income

Gleeson and White, 1965

1.1% *decrease* in the total population of Baltimore between 1950 and 1960, the number of infants registered at well-baby clinics increased by 59% during the same 10-year period.

But increasingly, it is not only through the chronically over-crowded clinics that the urban poor make contact with hospitals. Rather they come in growing numbers to seek care from the hospital's emergency service. Weinerman *et al.* (1966) studied a sample of cases seen in the emergency services at Yale-New Haven Medical Center and found that 56% of them were classified by attending physicians as "nonurgent." Patients using the emergency rooms were found as a group to be younger, poorer, more heavily nonwhite, and more heavily in the lowest social class than the total population served by the hospital. Asked "Where do you usually go when you need medical help?" 25% of the sample said they came directly to the emergency room.

Ten years earlier Brown (1958) had already reported that non-whites were heavily overrepresented in the pediatric emergency room at Grace-New Haven, and that almost half the patients interviewed were bringing their children there for all care "as if the impersonal Emergency Room were their personal family physician." When Wingert (1968) questioned a sample of patients visiting the pediatric emergency room of the Los Angeles County Hospital, he found that almost half the patients were on welfare and that of the total group 14% of the Caucasian, 20% of the Negro, and 24% of the Mexican-American parents reported 12 or more prior visits. Moreover, only 32% of the children's parents had been referred to the service by a doctor or a health department; 49% of the whole group, 52% of the Negro group, were referred by friends or relatives or had "been coming a long time."

One result of this use, or misuse, of emergency and examining rooms as "their doctor" by low-income patients has been a heavy overburdening of these facilities with consequent deterioration in the quality of medical care. In Cook County Hospital in Chicago, for example, "in winter months . . . and at peak times, children with bronchopneumonia are given antibiotics and sent home and brought back daily for examination and further treatment." The special survey of health care in Chicago found that of 450 children seen during one 24-hour period in the summer on the admitting and examining service at Cook County Hospital, only 38 were actually admitted; the other 412 were "seen and advised." "The group identified as being seen and advised requires further comment. These are persons seen for a specific complaint [which] is handled and no provision for continuing care is made" (Chicago Board of Health, 1965). Obviously, then, the overdependence of low-income and minority-group parents on clinic or emergency room care for their children not only reduces the amount and quality of the care received, but—even more important in the long run—it almost inevitably affects the extent to which the children benefit from any kind of continuing supervision.

Given this pattern of care, it is not surprising that data from the National Health Survey show persons of all ages from low-income families consistently having fewer physician visits under any auspices than do those from better-off families. Such a finding does not, of course, indicate a lower level of illness among the poor; rather, it reflects a lack of preventive care—especially among poor children. Schonfield et al. (1962), in the New England community which they studied, found that a woman living in an area with the poorest housing was more likely to have made a physician visit for a sick child than was a woman living in a better housing area, but that the lower-class mother made fewer physician visits for infant health supervision than did the upper-class mother. Thus it is the failure of low-income families to obtain preventive well-child care which helps to explain why the differential in physician visits between high- and low-income families is greatest among children under 15 years of age—those from low-income families averaging only 3 visits a year, while those from high income families average 5.7. It is clear, then, that poor children differ from those who are not poor both in the source of their medical care—that is, public rather than private—and in the kind of care that they get—that is, emergency rather than preventive.

The major factors which influence this particular pattern of care are easily identified. Poor mothers seek what care they do, where they seek it, first because it is all they can afford and second because it is available. Private care almost always costs more than clinics or emergency services where fees are either uniformly low or graded on the basis of ability to pay. And in the short run, continuing preventive care, even at a clinic, is always more expensive if only in terms of time, energy, and carfare than a single emergency visit. For poor families, preventive care is a luxury. As it is, many of them spend more money on medical care than they do on clothing, furnishings, or transportation (Holmes, 1967).

Where availability of care is concerned, it is no mystery that few young physicians have in recent years sought to practice in poor areas, whether urban or rural. On a national level the 17 states with the lowest per capita income also have the smallest number of physicians per 100,000 population and the smallest number of pediatricians per 10,000 children. Table 10.7 (Chicago Board of Health, 1965) illustrates the differential at a local level. For every 1,000 people there are twice as many physicians in private practice and three times as many board-certified specialists in nonpoverty areas of Chicago as there are in poverty areas. It is important to emphasize that there is nothing intrinsically superior about care which comes from a physician in private practice, and nothing intrinsically inferior about clinic care. The difficulty is rather that as a result of

TABLE 10.7

Supply of Physicians in Private Practice in Poverty and
Nonpoverty Areas, Chicago, 1965

| | Practicing in | |
Physician Characteristics	Poverty Areas	Nonpoverty Areas
Physicians in private practice	807	2,652
Number per 1,000 population	0.62	1.26
Board-certified specialists	234	1,111
Number per 1,000 population	0.18	0.53
General practitioners	334	894
Number per 1,000 population	.25	.42

Chicago Board of Health, 1965

money shortages, both private and public, there is not enough of
either kind of care available to the poor. Robinson (1965), studying
the utilization of available medical facilities by children on urban
and rural welfare in Massachusetts, found that the rural children
had a smaller residue of untreated health problems and seemed to
have made better use of available services, but the differential was
at least partly due to the fact that the city children, for whom no
pediatric clinics were available, depended for care on aging prac-
titioners and on the emergency room of the city hospital.

Thus the frequent finding that families dependent on clinic care
have much less well-child supervision and lower levels of immunization than do private patients may often have little to do with the
potential adequacy of public medicine or with the "poor motivation" of the disadvantaged mother (Schonfield et al., 1962; Peters
and Chase, 1967). Peters and Chase found quite different levels of
well-child care among different socioeconomic groups in one Southern county. But they also found that the teaching-hospital pediatric
clinic registered fewer patients during summer and holiday periods
when medical students were not available to staff it, and that
none of the health department well-baby clinics was functioning
at all during the summer months. These findings led them to conclude that "extension and correlation of the data . . . to show the
actual amount of well-child care received by Negro infants and those

white infants in rural and lower socioeconomic groups would probably show that the recommended pattern of well-child visits *simply is not available from the sources their families utilize"* (italics added).

Lack of money and availability, however, do not fully explain the failure of poor mothers to get preventive medical supervision for their children. Even in situations where all care is both accessible and prepaid, some parents maintain patterns of behavior which interfere with regular well-child care. Nolan *et al.* (1967), who analyzed the pattern of attendance at two *prepaid* pediatric clinics in California, found that although more than half of the visits of white children were on appointment, 2 out of 3 visits of Negro children were "drop-in" visits. When visits were divided by cause, moreover, only 29.7% of the visits of Negro children to the clinic were primarily for health supervision—61% of them were for treatment of an "acute condition."

When further analyzed, this apparently racial pattern turned out to be predominantly a social-class pattern of behavior. The few "upper-class" Negroes included in the study had a greater proportion of appointment visits than did whites of equal class status. But declining social class within the Negro group was associated with a marked decline in the percentage of patients visiting the appointment clinic. Yet the persistence of an emergency pattern of care among these lower-class Negroes could not be explained simply as a class response because class status appeared to make little difference in the percentage of whites visiting the respective clinics. Nolan *et al.* suggested a variety of possible explanations for the Negro-white difference, including the fact that more of the Negro visits tended to occur during the evening hours when only drop-in clinics were available. Moreover, they pointed out that there may be more resistance among a discriminated-against minority to changing traditional methods of care, especially when there is not yet a clear understanding of the workings of prepaid medical services.

Though the effect of education was not directly examined in the Nolan study, it is another factor which appears to influence patterns of care. Ross (1962), analyzing National Health Survey data, found that, in general, highly educated persons made a much higher percentage of their physician visits for preventive care than did those with less education, and that there were marked differences in the total number of physician visits children received according to the educational level of the family head. Male children 0–4 years of age in families whose head had less than 5 years of education averaged 3.6 physician visits a year compared with 8.4 visits for children whose family head had some education beyond college. Other authors have found a similar relationship between amount of care and maternal education (e.g., Schonfield *et al.*, 1962; Peters and Chase, 1967). But in such studies the effect of education cannot be evaluated as a factor distinct from social class and financial status, and hence the availability of care to the poor. Stine *et al.* (1968) were able to examine the factor of education directly when they looked at the causes of broken pediatric appointments among a selected lower-class population at a free comprehensive clinic in Baltimore. They found that the level of the mother's education was the most significant single source of variation in the rate of broken appointments, and that it interacted in a variety of ways to exaggerate the effects of other, less independently influential variables.

But the behavior of groups faced with the relatively new option of taking advantage of available care cannot be viewed as the crux of the problem of the poor. The simple fact is that most of the poor do not have such an option. For most of them, all of the other variables —education, parity, social status, and the availability of care—which affect the use of doctors, tend to be closely tied to economic status. The result is that the average poor mother, multiply burdened not only by prejudice and lack of education but also by her impoverished status and a shortage of available medical facilities, often fails to seek not merely preventive care for her infant but care of any kind. Thirty-four percent of the children examined in the Headstart program through 1966 had not seen a doctor "for any reason" for 2 years (North, 1967). The children seen by the six doctors who toured Mississippi had, almost without exception, *never* before been seen by a doctor. The extent to which such a failure to seek care persists even where medical care is freely provided is merely an indication of the extent to which a pattern of nonutilization has been established among families who have been long conditioned by the realities of their social and, more specifically, their economic situation to ignore all conditions which "do not cause pain" (e.g., Jeffers, 1964).

A similar circumstance obtains with regard to dental care. National Health Survey data show that of all children between the ages of 5 and 14, 59.5% of those from families living on an income under $2,000 a year and 63% of those who are nonwhite have *never* been to a dentist. On the other hand, only 9.7% of children living in families earning over $7,000 a year and only 22.3% of white children on all income levels have failed to see a dentist some time before their fourteenth birthday.

Lack of dental care does not suggest a lack of need for it. In a study several years ago, a group of Chicago dental clinics participated in a survey of the needs of 2,564 children of indigent families. The children, aged 6 to 15 years, were brought to the dental clinics by their parents. Dentists found that although 97% of the children had decayed teeth, there was evidence of prior reparative or preservative dental treatment among only 8% of them. Twenty-two percent had missing permanent teeth, 25% had permanent teeth so decayed that extractions were indicated, and of 970 children in the age group 11 to 15 years, 12% had *ten or more* decayed permanent teeth and no fillings. When the results of the dental clinic survey were compared with those from an earlier school survey covering children of various economic groups, it was found that 75% of the children in the school survey but less than 8% of the indigent children in the clinic survey had fillings; and though indigent children by age 13 averaged 2 badly decayed teeth requiring extraction per child, the average for the school survey was one such tooth per 2 children. Decayed teeth averaged 2 per child in the school survey, 6 per child in the indigent survey (Chicago Indigent Dental Survey, 1960).

Although it may be argued that even among the poor, children who appear in a dental clinic have worse teeth than those who don't, the reverse is probably true—that children whose parents get them any dental care are at least better off than those who have never been seen. Moreover, what is at issue is not merely the amount of decay in a child's mouth, but the fact that the aftermath of decay among poor children is likely to be loss of teeth either as a result of total neglect or because saving poor teeth is a more prolonged and expensive process than extracting them. (Altogether, low-income dental patients need 14 times as many extractions due to decay and need dentures 20 times as frequently as do those with incomes of

$6,000 or higher—Survey of Needs for Dental Care, 1967.) National data show that of the total number of dental visits for children in the income group under $2,000—and only 40% of this population have ever seen a dentist—31.8% were for extractions and only 39.2% were for fillings, as compared with only 4.8% for extractions and just under 50% for fillings among children from families in the income group of $7,000 and over. In addition, preventive care accounted for just over one-fifth of the visits in children from high-income groups, and just over 1/20 of the visits of low-income children, and four and one-half times as many visits of high-income as of low-income children were for tooth straightening. For ages 15–44 the percentage of visits accounted for by extractions was $3\frac{1}{2}$ times as high among low-income as among high-income patients.

One aftermath of such deficient medical and dental care can be seen in the health and the care patterns of teen-agers in disadvantaged populations, many of whom came to notice as a result of Job Corps recruitment. For example, among 80 adolescents referred to a New York hospital for examination for Job Corps employment, 24% were found to have serious health problems requiring immediate treatment—disorders ranging from TB to severe cardiac conditions (Bernstein, 1965). In another city 41% of 165 boys and girls enrolled in a Job Corps program were found to need medical care, but less than 3% of them were found to be receiving it (Eisner et al., 1966). And when the records of Job Corps applicants in general were reviewed for a House committee (U. S. House of Representatives, Subcommittee on the War on Poverty, Program Hearings, April 1965), they showed that 50% of these 16- to 21-year-olds had never before been to a physician. In Boston, as a part of the same poverty program which turned up so many unwell preschoolers (p. 247), 98 of 159 school dropouts examined for the Job Corps were found to have some pathologic condition including asthma, disorders of the central nervous system, and defects in hearing and vision. Several of the teen-agers were toothless. "The older group," observed a health program physician, "was clearly a progression of the younger. It's just as if you were seeing the disadvantaged preschooler 10 years later . . ." (Medical World News, 1965).

The data we have examined on the nutrition of poor children in the United States and on their patterns of illness and medical care would seem to leave little doubt as to their poorer health status. Even on the basis of the scattered but provoking evidence that is available we can fairly infer that there exists a vast though largely uncharted region of undernutrition, malnutrition, and disease among the poor children in this country. At the very least it is clear that the infants and children in poor families are more often hungry, more often and more seriously sick, suffer more accidents, and receive less frequent and less skilled care both in sickness and in health than do children in families who are not poor. But our concern, of course, is not merely with the existence in an affluent society of children whose lives, quite literally, make them sick. Rather we are asking what is the effect of poor health status on the mental development and school learning of these children.

The evidence we have already considered suggests that there are at least two major routes by which a child's poor health in infancy and childhood can limit his competence as a learner. The first of these is direct. Children overexposed to accidents or illness, or to the effects of early or persistent nutritional deprivation, are clearly more likely to suffer direct interference with either the development or the integrity of the nervous system, whether from trauma, from poisoning, or from a variety of infective agents, nutrient lacks, or biochemical abnormalities than are children leading more protected, well-nourished, and medically supervised lives. Neurologically abnormal children, either those damaged by such postnatal conditions or those similarly traumatized by accidents of birth or abnormalities in the pregnancies which produced them, may well represent a much larger proportion of the failures and of the behavior problems among disadvantaged children than we have previously acknowledged or been prepared to cope with.

Pasamanick and Knobloch (1961; also Knobloch and Pasamanick, 1962a, 1962b), it will be recalled, found evidence of at least "minimal" neurological abnormalities among several groups of children suffering from behavioral or psychological impairments. Davidson and Greenberg (1967), attempting to discover the qualities which differentiated Harlem slum children "successful" in school from the great bulk of children in that community who were not successful, found a 10% prevalence of neurological impairment among the children whom they studied on the basis of a routine physical examination. Given the cursory nature of the examination, such a figure is almost certainly an underestimate. Thus it is highly likely that among children who are poor, some significant number will be found at school age to be damaged as a consequence of reproductive hazards, the assaults of a hostile postnatal environment, or the effects of a stressful environment acting on an already damaged organism.

But it is important to emphasize that the effects of a poorer health status in infancy and childhood are not necessarily confined to physical damage. Indeed, the adverse effects of early illness and malnutrition on a child's intellectual development need not be primarily or even most significantly the result of "brain damage" per se, but rather the consequence of any or all of a number of possible indirect effects. At least three of these are worth noting:

1. *Loss of learning time.* Since an unhealthy child is less responsive to his environment at the time he is ill or malnourished, he will have, at the very least, less time in which to learn. On the simplest basis, therefore—the loss of a certain number of months of experience —a child who spends his infancy in a chronic or frequent state of hunger or ill-health would be expected to show some developmental lags.

2. *Interference with learning during critical periods of development.* Learning is by no means simply a cumulative process. A considerable body of evidence indicates that interference with the course of the learning process at specific times may result in disturbances in function which are both profound and of long-term significance. What appears to be important is not the length of time the organism is deprived of opportunities for learning, but the specific stage of development at which a given set of experiences is missed—the so-called critical period (Bowlby, 1952; Scott, 1962, 1963).

Critical periods in human learning have not been definitively established, but some potentially useful hypotheses can be derived from several of the malnutrition studies. It will be recalled that Cravioto and Robles (1965) have shown that infants under 6 months of age recovering from kwashiorkor did not recoup their mental age deficit during the recovery period; and that although ultimate recovery was more complete in older children, the rate of recovery from the initial mental deficit among children who ranged in age from 15 to 41 months varied in direct relation to their chronological age at time of admission for malnutrition. Similarly, the findings of Barrera-Moncada (1963) and Keys *et al.* (1950) in adults indicate a strong association between onset and duration of malnutrition and the persistence of effects on subsequent mental performance.

3. *Motivation and personality changes.* It should be recognized that a mother's response to her infant is to a considerable degree a function of the child's own "personality" characteristics (Thomas, Chess, and Birch, 1968). One of the first effects of ill-health is an alteration in the child's responsiveness to stimulation and the emergence of various degrees of irritability or apathy. Such behavior on the part of an infant can function to reduce his value as a positive stimulus, diminishing the adult's responsiveness to him in turn and thus contributing to a cumulative pattern of reduced child-adult interaction. If this occurs, it can have consequences for stimulation, for learning, for maturation, and for interpersonal relations—the end result being a significant backwardness in performance on later more complex learning tasks.

It would be misleading, however, if one were to conclude from this line of argument that malnutrition and illness were significant hazards to children only in early infancy, or only as a consequence of their "permanent" effects. It must not be overlooked that a child's present hunger and illness also immediately affect his level of attention, his interest, his motivation to learn—in short, his achievement in the classroom. Unless we intend to feed children *today* t may be interesting, but unimportant to their prospects, to decide 'hether the effects of yesterday's hunger will continue to affect their mental development tomorrow. Since mental development is a process, perhaps only relatively more vulnerable to interruption at one point than at another, it is difficult to imagine that anything in the environment which interfered for a significant time with learning could fail to affect mental development. The real children in our classrooms are not like animals in the laboratory who can be rehabilitated at times appropriate to their development and convenient to a researcher. In the real world it may actually be quite unimportant whether the effects of nutritional stress are organic, biochemical, or emotional. Whether or not *damage* is permanent must be irrelevant in the face of a *deprivation* which is; the same children whose mothers were ill-fed and unready for pregnancy, who are born into poverty and survive an infancy of hunger and illness, are seldom miraculously saved in the third act. As Peachum says when the Queen's messenger saves Mack the Knife from the gallows at the end of the *Threepenny Opera:* "In real life . . . the glorious messenger does not come riding often."

CHAPTER ELEVEN

Retrospect and Prospect

. . . All do not develop in the same manner, or at the same pace. . . . Laws alone cannot overcome the heritage of centuries of broken families and stunted children, and poverty and degradation and pain. . . . We must first . . . demolish the . . . barriers of race and religion, social class and ignorance . . . , call upon common qualities of conscience and of indignation, a shared determination to wipe away the unnecessary sufferings of our fellow human beings. . . .

ROBERT F. KENNEDY

I have a dream. . . .

MARTIN LUTHER KING

WE BEGAN this book because we feared that attempts to remedy the school failure of disadvantaged children exclusively through educational intervention might well fail and, failing, revive the ancient claim that these children were genetically inferior. We did not doubt that educational achievement could be increased, probably for most children, by appropriate alterations in the educational system. However, we were concerned that children who had been repeatedly and excessively exposed to biological risk, both before and after birth, were unlikely to be dramatically helped solely by the application of "more schooling," no matter how early it was begun or how intensively it was pursued.

Unfortunately, what we and others before us feared (e.g., Gordon and Wilkerson, 1966) has come about. Programs enthusiastically initiated as certain to solve the learning problems of disadvantaged children are now being soberly reassessed in the light of reports showing that they have failed to do so. Though it is possible to question the accuracy of some of the most critical evaluations of such programs as Headstart, even the most optimistic proponents of compensatory education are forced to admit that the programs to date have accomplished but a fraction of what they had set out to do. Unquestionably some of these failures can be attributed to limitations in design, to shortages of funds, to impatience for results, and to a lack of clarity in defining both curriculum and objectives. Yet what we have seen of the physical risks to which poor children are subjected has made us more than ever certain that even the best of such programs cannot hope to succeed in fully averting, for those children now most likely to fail, the negative consequences of generations of exposure to poor conditions for health and growth.

It is essential to recognize this fact if we are not to be discouraged and misled, for the conclusions we believed would be drawn from the relative failure of compensatory programs have been drawn, and scientists such as Shockley (1966) and Jensen (1969) are now arguing that educational failure in socially disadvantaged children, especially among those who are nonwhite, must be viewed as deriving from an underlying genetic incompetence in interaction with an undeniably disadvantaged social environment. It is Jensen's claim that among students of the psychology of the disadvantaged there has been an increasing awareness "that the discrepancy in . . . average performance cannot be completely or directly attributed to discrimination or inequalities in education. . . ." Therefore, he argues, "in view of the fact that intelligence variation has a large genetic component," it is "not unreasonable . . . to hypothesize that genetic factors may play a part in this picture." We noted in the opening passages of this book, more prophetically than we then realized, that the genetic argument might be used to bolster the notion that we should accept a lower level of achievement from disadvantaged children. It seems appropriate to consider the merits of this argument once again, in the light of the conditions we have documented in the preceding chapters.

"The geneticist is constantly forced to remind his colleagues," Dobzhansky (1968) has written, "especially those in the social sciences, that what is inherited is not this or that particular phenotypic 'trait' or 'character,' but a genotypic potentiality for an organism's developmental response to its environment. Given a certain genotype and a certain sequence of environmental situations, the development follows a certain path. The carriers of other genetic endowments in the same environmental sequence might well develop differently. But also, *a given genotype might well develop phenotypically along different paths in different environments"* (italics added). Identical genetic constitutions, in other words, will result in different products when their development takes place under different environmental conditions.

It is essential to keep in mind that intellectual development does not take place in relation to some artificially isolated segment of the environment—the verbal environment, the social environment, the cognitive environment—but in relation to the child's total environment, physical as well as psychological, and prenatal as well as postnatal. The mind, we would once more observe, is an artifact of the workings of the brain, which is a part of the body. Given a wretched enough physical environment neither the body nor its brain will grow and develop normally—nor will the mind. Thus although it is entirely reasonable to wish to know more about the heritability of intelligence and learning capacity in human beings, the precondition for a serious consideration of this question is the equalization of the developmental environments of those whose genetic makeup we wish to compare.

The data we have presented in this book have made it abundantly clear that such equality does not exist, that the environments in which disadvantaged children develop from conception on are far less supportive to growth and health than are those of children who are not disadvantaged, and that this relative environmental impoverishment is exaggerated when the disadvantaged child is nonwhite. The differences are profound and prolonged. Mothers of such children tend to be less well fed, less well grown, and less well cared for before they reach childbearing age. When they reach it, they begin to bear children younger, more rapidly, and more often, and they continue to bear them to an older age. When such a mother is pregnant both her nutrition and her health will tend to be poorer than that of a woman who is better off, but she will be far less likely to get prenatal care and far more likely to be delivered under substandard conditions.

Children of such mothers are smaller at birth, die more readily, and are generally in poorer condition in infancy than are children born to the more affluent. If they survive the first month of life, their mortality thereafter is excessively high and their illnesses more frequent, more persistent, and more severe. Their early nutrition is negatively influenced by their mother's health, her age, her income level, her education, her habits and attitudes, so that among such children in the preschool years frank malnutrition, as well as subclinical manifestations of depressed nutritional status (reflected in anemia and poor growth), are markedly more prevalent. During the school years they eat irregularly, their health care continues to be almost totally inadequate, their housing is substandard, their family income is low, subsistence on public assistance is high, and family disorganization commonplace.

It is clearly absurd to argue that we can compare children such as these with the products of the average middle-class environment, and then make judgments about their genetic material. Children who have been conceived, brought to birth, and raised under such conditions must necessarily be very different from children who have not; and we are surely not yet in a position to assert that the sources of that difference lie in their genes.

We have tried to conceptualize the environmental relationships between poverty and educational failure by means of the flow diagram shown in Figure 11.1. Such a formulation makes it clear that the links which bind the poor into this repeating cycle of failure can be broken at any one of a number of points. Vocational training, for example, may interrupt the sequence that leads from school failure to unemployment, and adequate family allowances could break the link between unemployment and poverty. But while poverty persists, the failure of poor children in school is linked to it by a variety of environmental factors. Thus intervention at a single point must inevitably have a limited effect. Compensatory education may make up for a home in which the "cognitive environment" is restricted, but it cannot make up for a childhood spent with an empty belly.

One other fact is made clear by the flow chart, and that is that we cannot expect dramatic changes immediately from a program of health care. For any given child there are some adverse factors in his developmental environment which are contemporaneous with

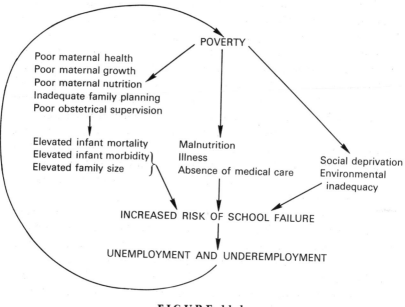

FIGURE 11.1

Environmental Relationships Between Poverty and Educational Failure

his own life, and some which are residues of environmental insults to which his mother has been subjected in the course of her own growth and development. Environmental improvement in the present generation, therefore, might be expected to make itself fully felt only when these children are having children of their own. However, animal studies, like those of Cowley and Grisell and of Chow and his associates, suggest that it may take even longer. They found that environmental insult not only accumulates across generations, but that it is not overcome by the rehabilitation of mothers for a single generation. Conversely, our height data on successive generations of immigrant groups indicates that improved environment continues to exercise its influence over several generations. Therefore environmental equalization must be viewed as a longer term process, stretching across two or three generations at least, and we must not expect to overcome within a single lifetime the entire consequence of 15 generations of suboptimal conditions for life. Our neglect will not be so cheaply or so hastily repaired.

If the scope and cost of reparations is so great as to tempt us to delay making them, recognition of the time scale involved should encourage us to begin. The sooner begun, the sooner effectively accomplished. Our traditions, however, are against us. Recognizing the existence of a problem and what will be required to eliminate it have been no guarantee in the past that something useful would be done. We have characteristically been unwilling both to acknowledge problems and to act on them. Only recently (1968) Sebrell, in a survey of 50 years of clinical nutrition in the United States, reviewed once again the story of Joseph Goldberger and pellagra as "one of the classical contributions to our knowledge of nutrition." It is a story which might stand as an uncomfortably appropriate warning.

When Goldberger began his work in 1908, pellagra, which was known to exist endemically in many parts of the world, was assumed to be rare in the United States. In that year, however, Searcy reported cases among the inmates of an Alabama insane asylum, and within a year a series of reports had made it clear that pellagra, far from being a rarity in America, was widely prevalent in the South. Vitamins were unknown at the time, and the disease was assumed to be infectious. When Goldberger began his studies of the problem, however, this hypothesis proved untenable because pellagra, though widely prevalent among inmates in various institutions, turned out to be virtually unknown among the professional staffs. Comparing the conditions of life of the patients and their caretakers, Goldberger found that although both had ample quantities of food, dietary quality for the two groups differed markedly. Patients subsisted on grits, syrup, fat pork, and gravy; the staff had additional quantities of milk, eggs, and lean meat. These findings led him to suspect, first, that pellagra was a nutritional disease and, second, that, as such, it should be correctable by improved diet.

In an orphanage in Jackson, Mississippi, where pellagra was particularly prevalent among the children, Goldberger carried out a clinical trial. Securing funds for research, he improved the institutional diet—with dramatic results. Existing cases of pellagra were cured, and no new cases appeared during the period of supplementation. As Sebrell points out, however, the story did not end happily. Goldberger's money ran out, the institution could not afford the supplementary foods, the children resumed their former diet—and pellagra reappeared. But the nutritional abandonment of the children of one orphanage was not the worst of it. Despite the fact that Goldberger soon showed the dietary cause of pellagra and suggested a number of cheap methods of preventing it, the peak year for cases of the disease in this country was 1929—20 years after both cause and cure were known. In that year some 200,000 people suffered from pellagra in the South, and 7,000 people died of it.

Like pellagra, serious poverty has long been considered rare in America. Acknowledging that there were children who were socially and culturally deprived, we have long failed to see that we also had children who were physically deprived. We do have such children— millions of them—and their future is not promising. The children growing up in poverty and deprivation today will not be easily rescued. Only by a massive investment of money and concern will we begin the long process of providing a decent life and an equal chance to learn for all our children. Goldberger's solution to the scourge of pellagra was cheap, quick, and simple to administer—yet society failed to apply it. None of the solutions to the deprivation of our children is cheap or quick, and surely none of them will be simple to administer. The question is, Can we afford *not* to begin?

The attitudes and values of more affluent segments of the population stand in the way of real action. Many of our attitudes toward poverty derived from historical periods in which our society's resources were limited—a time when this nation had neither its present affluence nor its technical scope. At the beginning of this book we noted that the nature of society has so changed and man's capacity for bettering his conditions has so improved that there are no longer sound social or economic reasons for the existence of chronic poverty. But as Moynihan (1968) has noted, poverty has increasingly become a way of life for nonwhites in rural backwaters and urban slums as well as for whites in areas like Appalachia. He notes that, in 1965, 288,624 children were on welfare in New York City alone, with the rate of welfare cases ranging from 1.8 per 1,000 in one health area to 718.1 per 1,000 in another. Needless to say the latter area was overwhelmingly nonwhite. By 1968 the total number of children in families receiving public assistance in New York had approached 500,000. the largest proportion of whom were nonwhite.

Thus conditions for children and particularly for nonwhite disadvantaged children are growing worse rather than better. It is fair to say that the situation today is significantly worse than it was in 1963, in which year, as we have earlier pointed out, one white youth in 10 and 6 nonwhite children in 10 reaching the age of 18 had at some time in their lives been supported by Aid to Dependent Children (Mugge, 1968). Thus a program begun in the 1930s to aid the children of widows has become a way of life for nonwhite disadvantaged families.

The social and economic disruption which underlies this change was foreseen by E: Franklin Frasier in 1939. Writing his classic study *The Negro Family in the United States,* Frasier forecast the economic exclusion of a large section of the Southern Negro population from agriculture, followed by the large-scale migration of these displaced populations to cities. The shift he predicted has come about. The central cities, faced with explosive increases in their nonwhite populations, have failed effectively to incorporate these newcomers into the economic structure. The consequences have included persistently high rates of unemployment, deteriorating conditions of life, and the expansion of ghettos as housing has failed to keep pace with population increase.

Education, too, has failed to keep up with changing times and shifts in the children who are being taught. As Gordon and Wilkerson (1966) have written: "Nowhere are the handicaps imposed by deliberate and accidental underdevelopment of human resources a greater source of embarrassment and concern than in the United States in the second half of the twentieth century. Faced with an embarrassing situation, public opinion has performed as it is wont to perform—it has looked for a scapegoat—and, in this situation, no one has seemed more available to bear the blame than the professional educator. The choice is not without justification. Granted that the school has not created the conditions that make for social disadvantage and economic deprivation. It is, nevertheless, quite clear that neither have professional educators done much to help significantly the children who are products of these conditions. . . ."

Zacharias (1964), reporting for the Panel on Educational Research and Development, has noted: "By all known criteria, the majority of urban and rural slum schools are failures. In neighborhood after neighborhood across the country, more than half of each age group fails to complete high school, and 5% or fewer go on to some form of higher education. Adolescents depart from these schools ill-prepared to lead a satisfying, useful life or to participate successfully in the community." Failure in these schools has been accompanied by high rates of maladjustment, behavioral disturbance, and physical disability. It has been preceded by conditions for health and development which were grossly suboptimal, and is succeeded by low levels of employability, and by the instatement of a life style destined to repeat the cycle of poverty.

It would be disastrous if our demonstration in this book that the problem of educational failure is multifaceted, chronic, and, indeed, multigenerational were used to support either delay or a counsel of despair. It is romantic to think that serious problems of social dislocation and deficit can be totally cured by single programs or actions. Their causes are complex, the paths to solution multiple.

There is much that can and should be done immediately. The health of children and their nutritional status can be immediately improved. It does not matter whether such action produces an immediate improvement in educational performance, since the likelihood that it will hurt performance is zero. Educational circumstances can be improved immediately, with the likelihoood that well-planned interventions will produce significant improvements in educational achievement. Compensatory education has not really failed; it has just not often been adequately tried. The conditions under which women bear their children can be immediately improved. Comprehensive health care can be provided for communities at risk through improving both the patients' economic status and the delivery of services. Family planning can be made available immediately, and women can be instructed in its utilization. All these things can be done—with the recognition that some of their consequences will be immediate and some will be long-range.

It is crucial to recognize, however, that none of these things can be done successfully as though by a laying on of hands. Social changes which improve health always occur within concrete historical and political atmospheres, and the best-intended plans are doomed to failure if they are politically and socially inappropriate. Thus a superbly equipped medical clinic will not positively affect the health of a community if its organization and the character of its services are unacceptable to the community it is designed to serve. Its utilization will be poor and unrepresentative, and its presence will be an invitation to disagreement and a focus for confrontation rather than a resource for the community.

If our government is based on the proposition that governmental soundness depends on the consent of the governed, then we must recognize that in the present period of history philanthropy and charity dispensed from above are no longer acceptable and must give way to service with the consent and agreement of those served. To recognize the present-day realities of history is to recognize that the planning of interventions to break the cycle of poverty, poor health, and educational failure must involve the fullest participation of the poor. Given this recognition and the willingness to act, much can be done both at once and over successive generations to remove historically induced ill health and inadequate learning as features of American life.

References

Abramowicz, M., and Kass, E. H.: Pathogenesis and prognosis of prematurity. New Eng. J. Med. 275:1001–1007, 1966.

Achar, S. T., and Yankauer, A.: Studies on the birth weight of South Indian infants. Indian J. Child Health 11:157–167, 1962.

Acheson, R. M., and Fowler, G. B.: Sex, socio-economic status and secular increase in stature: a family study. Brit. J. Prev. Soc. Med. 18:25–34, 1964.

Aitken, F. C., Hytten, F. E., Infant feeding: comparison of breast and artificial feeding. Nut. Abst. Rev. 30:341–371, 1960.

Aldrich, R. A.: Nutrition and human development. J. Amer. Diet. Ass. 46:453–456, 1965.

Ambrosius, D. K.: El comportamiento del peso de algunos organos en ninos con desnutricion de tercer grado. Bol. Med. Hosp. Infantil (Mexico) 18:47–53, 1961.

Anderson, Edith H., and Lesser, A. J.: Maternity care in the United States: gains and gaps. Amer. J. Nurs. 66:1539–1544, 1966.

Antonov, A. N.: Children born during the siege of Leningrad. J. Ped. 30:250–259, 1947.

Appalachian Regional Commission: Health Advisory Committee Report. Washington, D. C., 1966, p. 315.

Arnell, R. E., Goldman, D. W., and Bertucci, F. J.: Protein deficiencies in pregnancy. JAMA 127:1101–1107, 1945.

Asher, C., and Roberts, J. A. F.: Study on birthweight and intelligence. Brit. J. Soc. Med. 3:56–68, 1949.

Autret, M., and Behar, M.: Sindrome pluricarencial infantil (kwashiorkor) and its prevention in Central America. FAO Nutritional Series No. 13. Rome, 1954.

Aznar, R., and Bennett, A. E.: Pregnancy in the adolescent girl. Amer. J. Obstet. Gynec. 81:934–940, 1961.

Baird, D.: Variations in reproductive pattern according to social class. Lancet 2:41–44, 1946.

REFERENCES

Baird, D.: Social class and foetal mortality. Lancet 253:531–535, 1947.

Baird, D.: Social factors in obstetrics. Lancet 1:1079–1083, 1949.

Baird, D.: The cause and prevention of difficult labor. Amer. J. Obstet. Gynec. 63:1200–1212, 1952.

Baird, D.: The contribution of obstetrical factors to serious physical and mental handicap in children. J. Obstet. Gynaec. Brit. Emp. 66:743–747, 1959.

Baird, D.: The epidemiology of prematurity. J. Pediat. 65:909–924, 1964.

Baird, D.: A fifth freedom? Brit. Med. J. 2:1141–1148, 1965.

Baird, D., Hytten, F. E., and Thomson, A. M.: Age and human reproduction. J. Obstet. Gynaec. Brit. Emp. 65:865–876, 1958.

Baird, D., and Illsley, R.: Environment and childbearing. Proc. Roy. Soc. Med. 46:53–59, 1953.

Baird, D., Walker, J., and Thomson, A. M.: The causes and prevention of stillbirths and first week deaths. Part III. A classification of deaths by clinical cause; the effect of age, parity and length of gestation on death rates by cause. J. Obstet. Gynaec. Brit. Emp. 61:433–448, 1954.

Baker, P. T.: Human adaptation to high altitude. Science 163:1149–1156, 1969.

Bakwin, H., and McLaughlin, S. M.: Secular increase in height: is the end in sight? Lancet 2:1195–1196, 1964.

Balfour, M. I.: Supplementary feeding in pregnancy: the National Birthday Trust Fund Experiment. Proc. Nutr. Soc. 2:27–36, 1944.

Barnes, R. H.: Experimental animal approaches to the study of early malnutrition and mental development. Fed. Proc. 26:144–147, 1967.

Barnes, R. H., Cunnold, S. R., Zimmermann, R. R., Simmons, H., MacLeod, R. B., and Krook, L.: Influence of nutritional deprivations in early life on learning behavior of rats as measured by performances in a water maze. J. Nutr. 89:399–410, 1966.

Barnes, R. H., Moore, A. U., Reid, I. M., and Pond, W. G.: Learning behavior following nutritional deprivation in early life. J. Amer. Diet. Ass. 51:34–39, 1967.

Barrera-Moncada, G.: Estudios sobre alteraciones del crecimiento y del desarrollo psicologico del sindrome pluricarencial (kwashiorkor). Caracas, Editora Grafos, 1963.

Baumgartner, Leona: Health and ethnic minorities in the sixties. Amer. J. Public Health 55:495–498, 1965.

Baumgartner, Leona, and Pakter, Jean: The challenge of fetal loss, prematurity and infant mortality: assessing the local situation. JAMA 167:936–954, 1958.

Beasley, J. D., and Harter, C. L.: Introducing family planning clinics to Louisiana. Children 14:188–192, 1967.

REFERENCES

Beasley, J. D., Harter, C. L., and Fisher, Ann: Attitudes and knowledge relevant to family planning among New Orleans Negro women. Amer. J. Public Health 56:1847–1857, 1966.

Bedger, Jean E., Gelperin, A., and Jacobs, Eveline E.: Socio-economic characteristics in relation to maternal and child health. Public Health Rep. 81:829–833, 1966.

Benjamin, B.: Social and Economic Differentials in Fertility. In J. E. Meade and A. S. Parkes (Eds.) Genetic and Environmental Factors in Human Ability. New York, Plenum Press, 1966, pp. 177–184.

Benton, A. L.: Mental development of prematurely born children: a critical review of the literature. Amer. J. Orthopsychiat. 10:719–746, 1940.

Berger, G. C. A., Brummond, J. C., and Sanstread, H. R. (Eds.) Malnutrition and Starvation in the Western Netherlands, Parts I, II. The Hague, General Printing Office, 1947.

Bernard, R. M.: The shape and size of the female pelvis. Transactions of the Edinburgh Obstetrical Soc. Edin. Med. J. 59:2: 1–16, 1952 (Transactions bound at end).

Bernstein, Betty J.: Examination of Health Aspects in the Early Planning of the Poverty Program in New York City. Paper presented at annual meeting of APHA, Chicago, 1965.

Berry, Katherine, and Wiehl, Dorothy G.: Experiment in diet education during pregnancy. Milbank Mem. Fund Quart. 30:119–151, 1952.

Bibb, J. D.: Protein and hemoglobin in normal and toxic pregnancies. Amer. J. Obstet. Gynec. 42:103–109, 1941.

Bienstock, H.: Quoted in New York Times (Howard Rusk), "Poverty and Health," August 13, 1967.

Bigart, H: see New York Times, February 16–20, 1969.

Birch, H. G.: Research needs and opportunities in Latin America for studying deprivation in psychobiological development. In Deprivation in Psychobiological Development. Pan American Health Organization, Scientific Publication No. 134, pp. 77–84. Washington, D. C., WHO, 1966.

Birch, H. G.: Health and the education of socially disadvantaged children. Develop. Med. Child Neurol. 10:580–599, 1968.

Birch, H. G., and Cravioto, J.: Infection, nutrition and environment in mental development. In H. F. Eichenwald (Ed.) The Prevention of Mental Retardation Through the Control of Infectious Disease. Public Health Service Publication 1962. Washington, D. C., U. S. Government Printing Office, 1968.

Blake, W.: Infant Sorrow, from Songs of Experience (1791). In Poems of William Blake (selected by Amelia H. Munson). New York, Thomas Y. Crowell, 1964.

REFERENCES

Boas, F.: Changes in the Bodily Form of Descendants of Immigrants. Immigration Commission Document No. 208. Washington, D. C., U. S. Government Printing Office, 1910.

Boek, W. E., Lawson, E. D., Yankauer, A., and Sussman, M. B.: Social Class, Maternal Health and Child Care. Albany, New York State Department of Health, 1957.

Boutourline Young, H.: Epidemiology of dental caries: results from a cross-cultural study in adolescents of Italian descent. New Eng. J. Med. 267:843–849, 1962.

Bowlby, J.: Critical phases in the development of social responses in man and other animals. In J. M. Tanner (Ed.) Prospects in Psychiatric Research. Oxford, Blackwell Scientific Publications, 1952.

Boyne, A. W., and Leitch, Isabella: Secular change in the height of British adults. Nutr. Abstr. Rev. 24:255–269, 1954.

Braun, K., Bromberg, Y. M., and Brzezinski, A.: Riboflavin deficiency in pregnancy. J. Obstet. Gynaec. Brit. Emp. 52:43–47, 1945.

Brimblecombe, F. S. W., Cruikshank, R., Masters, R., Reid, P. L., Stewart, D. D., and Sanderson, Dorothy. Family studies of respiratory infections. Brit. Med. J. 1:119–128, 1958.

British Medical Journal: Low birth weight and intelligence. 2:401, 1964.

Brock, J.: Recent Advances in Human Nutrition. London, J. & A. Churchill, 1961.

Brock, J. F., and Autret, M.: Kwashiorkor in Africa. WHO Monograph Series No. 8. Geneva, 1952.

Brockman, Lois M.: The effects of severe malnutrition on cognitive development in infants. Ph.D. thesis, Cornell University, 1966.

Brown, S.: Regarding the emergency room (correspondence). New Eng. J. Med. 258:507–508, 1958.

Brown, R.: Organ weight in malnutrition with special reference to brain weight. Develop. Med. Child Neurol. 8:512–522, 1966.

Browne, T.: Religio Medici (1643). London, Cassell, 1905.

Browning, R., and Parks, L. L.: Childbearing aspirations of public health maternity patients. Amer. J. Public Health 54:1831–1833, 1964.

Browning, R. H., and Northcutt, T. J., Jr.: On the season: a report of a public health project conducted among Negro migrant agricultural workers in Palm Beach County, Florida. Florida Board of Health Monograph No. 2. 1961.

Bryan, A. H., and Anderson, Evelyn L.: Dietary and nutritional problems of crippled children in five rural counties of North Carolina. Amer. J. Public Health 55:1545–1554, 1965.

Buetow, Kathleen C.: An epidemiological approach to the problem of rising neonatal mortality in Baltimore. Amer. J. Public Health 51:217–227, 1961.

Burke, Bertha S., Beal, Virginia A., Kirkwood, S. B., and Stuart, H. C.: Nutritional studies during pregnancy. Amer. J. Obstet. Gynec. 46:38–52, 1943a.

Burke, Bertha S., Beal, Virginia A., Kirkwood, S. B., and Stuart, H. C.: The influence of nutrition during pregnancy upon the condition of the infant at birth. J. Nutr. 26:569–583, 1943b.

Burke, Bertha S., Harding V. V., and Stuart, H. C.: Nutrition studies during pregnancy. IV. Relation of protein content of mother's diet during pregnancy to birth length, birth weight and condition of infant at birth. J. Ped. 23:506–515, 1943c.

Butler, N. R., and Alberman, E. D.: Perinatal Problems. The Second Report of the 1958 British Perinatal Survey. Edinburgh, E. & S. Livingstone, 1969.

Butler, N. R., and Bonham, D. G.: Perinatal Mortality: The First Report of the 1958 British Perinatal Mortality Survey. Edinburgh, E. & S. Livingstone, 1963.

Cabak, Vera, and Najdanvic, R.: Effect of undernutrition in early life on physical and mental development. Arch. Dis. Child. 40:532–534, 1965.

Caldwell, D. F., and Churchill, J. A.: Learning ability in the progeny of rats administered a protein-deficient diet during the second half of gestation. Neurology 17:95–99, 1967.

Campbell, A. A.: Fertility and family planning among nonwhite married couples in the United States. Eugen. Quart. 12:124–131, 1965.

Campbell, A. A.: White-nonwhite differences in family planning in the United States. HEW Indicators, 1966, pp. 1–10.

C. B. S. Reports: Hunger in America, May 21, 1968.

Champakam, S., Srikantia, S. G., and Gopalan, C.: Kwashiorkor and mental development. Amer. J. Clin. Nutr. 21:844–852, 1968.

Chandra, R. K.: Nutrition and brain development. J. Trop. Pediat. 10:37–38, 1964.

Chase, Helen C.: White-nonwhite mortality differentials in the United States. HEW Indicators, 1965.

Chicago Board of Health: Preliminary Report on Patterns of Medical and Health Care in Poverty Areas of Chicago and Proposed Health Programs for the Medically Indigent. Chicago, 1965.

Chicago Indigent Dental Survey, 1960. Reported in Chicago Board of Health, 1965.

Child Development Group of Mississippi: Surveys of Family Meal Patterns. Nutrition Services Division. May 17, 1967, and July 11, 1967. Cited in Hunger, USA.

REFERENCES

Chow, B. F., Blackwell, R. Q., Blackwell, Boon-Nam, Hou, T. Y., Anilane, J. K., Sherwin, R. W., and Chir, B: Maternal nutrition and metabolism of the offspring: studies in rats and man. Amer. J. Public Health 58:668–677. 1968.

Chow, B. F., and Lee, C. J.: Effect of dietary restriction of pregnant rats on body weight gain of offspring. J. Nutr. 82:10–18, 1964.

Chow, B. F.: Growth of rats from normal dams restricted in diet in previous pregnancies. J. Nutr. 83:289–292, 1964.

Christakis, G., Miridjanian, Anoush, Nath, L., Khurana, H. S., Cowell, Catherine, Archer, M., Frank, O., Ziffer, H., Baker, H., and James, G.: A nutritional epidemiologic investigation of 642 New York City children. Amer. J. Clin. Nutr. 21:107–126, 1968.

Clark, M.: Kwashiorkor. E. Afr. Med. J. 28:229–236, 1951.

Clifford, S. H.: High risk pregnancy. I. Prevention of prematurity: the *sine qua non* for reduction in mental retardation and other neurological disorders. New Eng. J. Med. 271:243–249, 1964.

Coleman, J. S., *et al.*: Equality of Educational Opportunity. Washington, D. C., U. S. Government Printing Office, 1966, p. 737.

Coles, R.: Lives of migrant farmers. Amer. J. Psychiat. 122:271–284, 1965.

Coles, R.: Appalachia: hunger in the hollows. New Republic 159:16–19, 1968.

Coles, R., and Huge, H.: Strom Thurmond country. New Republic 159:17–21, 1968a.

Coles, R., and Huge, H.: FBI on the trail of the hunger-mongers. New Republic 159:11–13, 1968b.

Coles, R., and Huge, H.: "We need help," New Republic 160:18–21, 1969a.

Coles, R., and Huge, H.: Thorns on the yellow rose of Texas. New Republic 160:13–17, 1969b.

Conel, J. L.: The Postnatal Development of the Human Cerebral Cortex. Cambridge, Harvard University Press, 1963.

Conference on Prenatal Clinic Care in New York City. New York, Maternity Center Association, 1963.

Corkey, Elizabeth C.: The birth control program in the Mecklenburg County Health Department. Amer. J. Public Health 56:40–47, 1966.

Cornely, P. B., and Bigman, S. K.: Cultural considerations in changing health attitudes. Med. Ann. DC 30:191–199, 1961.

Cornely, P. B., Bigman, S. K., and Watts, Dorothy D.: Nutritional beliefs among a low-income urban population. J. Amer. Diet. Ass. 42:131–135, 1963.

Correa, P. G.: Que es la culebrilla? Rev. Med. Yucatan 3:No. 6, 1908.

Corsa, L.: Introduction: public health programs in family planning. Amer. J. Public Health 56: Suppl. 6–16, 1966.

REFERENCES

Co Tui: The fundamentals of clinical proteinology. J. Clin. Nutr. 1:232–246, 1953.

Coursin, D. B.: Effects of undernutrition in central nervous system function. Nutr. Rev. 23:65–68, 1965.

Cowley, J. J., and Griesel, R. D.: Some effects of a low protein diet on a first filial generation of white rats. J. Genet. Psychol. 95:187–201, 1959.

Cowley, J. J., and Griesel, R. D.: Pre- and post-natal effects of a low protein diet on the behaviour of the white rat. Psychologia Africana 9:216–225, 1962.

Cowley, J. J., and Griesel, R. D.: The development of second generation low protein rats. J. Genet. Psychol. 103:233–242, 1963.

Cowley, J. J., and Griesel, R. D.: Low protein diet and emotionality in the albino rat. J. Genet. Psychol. 104:89–98, 1964.

Cowley, J. J., and Griesel, R. D.: The effect on growth and behaviour of rehabilitating first and second generation low protein rats. Anim. Behav. 14:506–517, 1966.

Cravioto, J.: Malnutrition and behavioral development in the preschool child. In Preschool Child Malnutrition: Primary Deterrent to Human Progress. An International Conference on Prevention of Malnutrition in the Preschool Child, Washington, D. C., December 7–11, 1964. National Academy of Sciences–National Research Council Publication No. 1282. Washington, D. C., 1966.

Cravioto, J., Birch, H. G., DeLicardie, Elsa, R., and Rosales, Lydia: The ecology of infant weight gain in a pre-industrial society. Acta Paediat. Scand. 56:71–84, 1967.

Cravioto, J., DeLicardie, Elsa R., and Birch, H. G.: Nutrition, growth and neurointegrative development: an experimental and ecologic study. Pediatrics 38:No. 2, Part II, Suppl. 319–372, 1966.

Cravioto, J., and Robles, Beatriz: Evolution of adaptive and motor behavior during rehabilitation from kwashiorkor. Amer. J. Orthopsychiat. 35:449–464, 1965.

Crump, E. P., Horton, C. P., Masuoka, J., and Ryan, Donnalda: Growth and development. I. Relation of birth weight in Negro infants to sex, maternal age, parity, prenatal care, and socio-economic status. J. Pediat. 51:678–697, 1957.

Crump, E. P., Payton, E., and Horton, C. P.: Growth and development. IV. Relationship between prenatal maternal nutrition and socio-economic index, weight of mother and birth weight of infant. Amer. J. Obstet. Gynec. 77:562–572, 1959.

Crump, E. P., and Horton, C. P.: Growth and development in Negro infants and children. J Lancet 81:507–517, 1961.

Dann, Margaret, Levine, S. Z., and New, Elizabeth V.: The development of prematurely born children with birth weights or minimal postnatal weights of 1,000 grams or less. Pediat. 22:1037–1053, 1958.

Dann, Margaret, Levine, S.Z., and New, Elizabeth V.: A long-term follow-up study of small premature infants. Pediatrics 33:945–955, 1964.

Darby, W. J., Densen, P. M., Cannon, R. O., Bridgeforth, E., Martin, Margaret P., Kaser, Margaret M., Peterson, C., Christie, A., Frye, W. W., Justus, K., McClellan, G. S., Williams, C., Ogle, Pauline J., Hahn, P. F., Sheppard, C. W., Carothers, E. L., and Newbill, Josephine A.: The Vanderbilt cooperative study of maternal and infant nutrition. I. Background. II. Methods. III. Description of the sample and data. J. Nutr. 51:539–563, 1953a.

Darby, W. J., McGanity, W. J., Martin, Margaret P., Bridgeforth, E., Densen, P. M., Kaser, Margaret M., Ogle, Pauline J., Newbill, Josephine A., Stockell, Anne, Ferguson, Mary Ellen, Touster, O., McClellan, G. S., Williams, C., and Cannon, R. O.: The Vanderbilt cooperative study of maternal and infant nutrition. IV. Dietary, laboratory and physical findings in 2,129 delivered pregnancies. J. Nutr. 51:565–597, 1953b.

Darity, W.: Contraceptive education: the relative cultural and social factors related to applied health education with special reference to oral contraceptives. Ph.D. thesis, University of North Carolina, 1963. Cited in Corkey, 1966.

Davidson, Helen H., and Greenberg, Judith W.: School Achievers from a Deprived Background. New York, Associated Education Services Corp., 1967.

Davis, F.: Darkness on the delta, Reporter, 1967.

Davison, A. N., and Dobbing, J.: Myelination as a vulnerable period in brain development. Brit. Med. Bull. 22:1:40–44, 1966.

Dawber, T. R., and Kannel, W. B.: An approach to longitudinal studies in a community: the Framingham study. Ann. NY Acad. Sci. 107:539–556, 1963.

Dean, R. F. A.: The size of the baby at birth and the yield of breast milk. Great Britain, Medical Research Council Studies of Undernutrition, Wuppertal, 1946–49. Special Report Series No. 275. London, HMSO, 1951, pp. 346–376.

Dean, R. F. A.: The effects of malnutrition on the growth of young children. Mod. Probl. Pediat. 5:111–122, 1960.

De la Torre, J.: La infeccion enterica, agentes quimioterapicos y entibioticos. In Problemas en Pediatria. Mexico City, Ediciones Medicos, Hospital Infantil de Mexico, 1963.

Delgado, Graciela, Brumback, C. L., and Deaver, Mary B.: Eating patterns among migrant families. Public Health Rep. 76:349–355, 1961.

Densen, P. M., and Haynes, A.: Research and the Major Health Problems

REFERENCES

of Negro Americans. Paper presented at Howard University Centennial Celebration. Washington, D. C., 1967.

De Silva, C. C.: Common nutritional disorders of childhood in the tropics. Advances Pediat. 13:213–264, 1964.

Dibble, Marjorie, Brin, M., McMullen, Elsa, Peel, Annette, and Chen, Nancy: Some preliminary biochemical findings in junior high school children in Syracuse and Onondaga County, New York. Amer. J. Clin. Nutr. 17:218–239, 1965.

Dickerson, J. W. T., Dobbing, J., and McCance, R. A.: The effect of undernutrition on the postnatal development of the brain and cord in pigs. Proc. Roy. Soc. B 166:396–407, 1967.

Dickerson, J. W., and Widdowson, Elsie M.: Some effects of accelerating growth. II. Skeletal development. Proc. Roy. Soc. B 152:207–217, 1960.

Dieckmann, W. J., Adair, F. L., Michel, H., Kramer, S., Dunkle, F., Arthur, B., Costin, M., Campbell, A., Wensley, A. C., and Lorang, E.: The effect of complementing the diet in pregnancy with calcium, phosphorus, iron and vitamins A and D. Amer. J. Obstet. Gynec. 47:357–368, 1944.

Dieckmann, W. J., Turner, D. F., Meiller, E. J., Savage, L. J., Hill, A. J., Straube, M. T., Pottinger, R. E., and Rynkiewicz, L. M.: Observations on protein intake and the health of the mother and baby. I. Clinical and laboratory findings. J. Amer. Diet. Ass. 27:1046–1052, 1951a.

Dieckmann, W. J., Turner, D. F., Meiller, E. J., Straube, M. T., and Savage, L. J.: Observations on protein intake and the health of the mother and baby. II. Food intake. J. Amer. Diet. Ass. 27:1053–1058, 1951b.

Dietary Levels of Households in the United States, Spring, 1965. A Preliminary Report. ARS 62–17. U. S. Department of Agriculture. Agricultural Research Service. Washington, D. C., U. S. Government Printing Office, 1968.

Dobbing, J.: The influence of early nutrition on the development and myelination of the brain. Proc. Roy. Soc. B 159:503–509, 1964.

Dobbing, J., and Widdowson, Elsie M.: The effect of undernutrition and subsequent rehabilitation on myelination of rat brain as measured by its composition. Brain 88:357–366, 1965.

Dobzhansky, T.: On genetics, sociology, and politics. Perspect. Biol. Med. 11:544–554, 1968.

Donabedian, A., and Rosenfeld, L. S.: Some factors influencing prenatal care. New Eng. J. Med. 265:1–6, 1961.

Donnelly, J. F., Jr.: Etiology of prematurity. Clin. Obstet. Gynec. 7:647–657, 1964.

Donnelly, J. F., Abernathy, J. R., Creadick, R. N., Flowers, C. E., Greenberg, B. G., and Wells, H. B.: Fetal, parental and environmental factors associated with perinatal mortality in mothers under 20 years of age. Amer. J. Obstet. Gynec. 80:663–671, 1961.

Donnelly, J. F., Flowers, C. E., Creadick, R. N., Wells, H. B., Greenberg, B. G., and Surles, K. B.: Maternal, fetal and environmental factors in prematurity. Amer. J. Obstet. Gynec. 88:918–931, 1964.

Douglas, J. W. B.: Mental ability and school achievement of premature children at 8 years of age. Brit. Med. J. 1:1210–1214, 1956.

Douglas, J. W. B.: "Premature" children at primary schools. Brit. Med. J. 1:2:1008–1013, 1960.

Douglas, J. W. B., and Blomfield, J. M.: Children Under Five. London, Allen & Unwin, 1958.

Douglas, J. W. B., and Mogford, C.: Health of premature children from birth to 4 years. Brit. Med. J. 1:748–754, 1953.

Drillien, Cecil M.: Prematurity in Edinburgh. Arch. Dis. Child. 31:390–394, 1956.

Drillien, Cecil M.: The social and economic factors affecting the incidence of premature birth. I. Premature births without complications of pregnancy. J. Obstet. Gynaec. Brit. Emp. 64:161–184, 1957.

Drillien, Cecil M.: The growth and development of the prematurely born infant. Baltimore, Williams & Wilkins, 1964, p. 376.

Drillien, Cecil M.: Prematures in school. Pediatrics Digest, September 1965, 75–77+.

Duncan, E. H. L., Baird, D., and Thomson, A. M.: The causes and prevention of stillbirths and first week deaths. I. The evidence of vital statistics. J. Obstet. Gynaec. Brit. Emp. 59:183–196, 1952.

Dunn, L. C., and Dobzhansky, T. H.: Heredity, Race and Society. New York, Mentor Books, 1946, p. 115.

Eastman, N. J.: Prematurity from the viewpoint of the obstetrician. Amer. Practitioner 1:343–352, 1947.

Eastman, N. J., and DeLeon, M.: Etiology of cerebral palsy. Amer. J. Obstet. Gynec. 69:950–961, 1955.

Eayrs, J. T., and Levine, S.: Influence of thyroidectomy and subsequent replacement therapy upon conditioned avoidance learning in the rat. J. Endocr. 25:505–513, 1963.

Eayrs, J. T., and Lishman, W. A.: The maturation of behaviour in hypothyroidism and starvation. Brit. J. Anim. Behav. 3:17–24, 1955.

Ebbs, J. H., Tisdall, F. F., and Scott, W. A.: The influence of prenatal diet on the mother and child. J. Nutr. 22:515–526, 1941.

Edwards, Cecile H., McDonald, Solona, Mitchell, J. R., Jones, Lucy, Mason, Lois, Kemp, Alta Mae, Land, Doris, and Trigg, Louise: Clay and cornstarch eating women. J. Amer. Diet. Ass. 35:810–815, 1959.

REFERENCES

Eichenwald, H. F., and Fry, Peggy C.: Nutrition and learning. Science 163:644–648, 1969.

Eisner, V., Goodlett, C. B., and Driver, M. B.: Health of enrolees in Neighborhood Youth Corps. Pediatrics 38:40–43, 1966.

Eliot, J. W.: The development of family planning services by state and local health departments in the U. S. Amer. J. Public Health 56: Suppl. 6–16, 1966.

Eliot, Martha M.: Deaths around birth: the national score. JAMA 167:945–949, 1958.

Engel, R.: Abnormal brain-wave patterns in kwashiorkor. Electroenceph. Clin. Neurophysiol. 8:489–500, 1956.

Epitaph for a three-week-old child, Cheltenham Churchyard. Cited in J. Bartlett (Ed.) Familiar Quotations. Boston, Little, Brown, 1955.

Erhardt, C. L., Joshi, G. B., Nelson, F. G., Kroll, B. H., and Weiner, L.: Influence of weight and gestation on perinatal and neonatal mortality by ethnic group. Amer. J. Public Health 54:1841–1855, 1964.

Erickson, Roberta: Visiting wide neighborhoods. Nurs. Outlook 14:34–37, 1966.

Espinosa-Gaona, C.: Estudio del estado de nutricion y de algunos factores que lo determinan en Chilapa de Dias, Oaxaca, Mexico. Thesis, Escuela Superior de Medicina Rural I.P.N. Mexico, 1961.

Fairweather, D. V. I., and Illsley, R.: Obstetric and social origins of mentally handicapped children. Brit. J. Prev. Soc. Med. 14:149–159, 1960.

Feldman, J. J.: Dissemination of health information: a case study in adult learning. Chicago, Aldine, 1966, p. 274.

Ferguson, J. H., and Hinson, Mary L.: Importance of protein in maternal diets, and a charity hospital survey. J. Louisiana Med. Soc. 105:18–21, 1953.

Ferguson, J. H., and Keaton, Alice G.: Studies of the diets of pregnant women in Mississippi. I. The ingestion of clay and laundry starch. New Orleans Med. Surg. J. 102:460–463, 1950a.

Ferguson, J. H., and Keaton, Alice G.: Studies of the diets of pregnant women in Mississippi. II. Diet patterns. New Orleans Med. Surg. J. 103:81–87, 1950b.

Filer, L. J., Jr.: The United States today: is it free of public health nutrition problems?—anemia. Amer. J. Public Health 59:327–338, 1969.

Filer, L. J., Jr., and Martinez, G. A.: Intake of selected nutrients by infants in the United States: an evaluation of 4,000 representative six-months-olds. Clin. Ped. 3:633–645, 1964.

Five Million Women. Planned Parenthood Federation of America, 1967.

Frazier, T. M., Davis, G. H., Goldstein, H., and Goldberg, I. D.: Cigarette smoking and prematurity: a prospective study. Amer. J. Obstet. Gynec. 81:988–996, 1961.

Freedman, A. M. (principal investigator): The effect of hyperbilirubinemia on premature infants. New York Medical College, Department of Psychiatry, Progress Report, 1961.

French, J. G.: Relationship of morbidity to the feeding patterns of Navajo children from birth through twenty-four months. Amer. J. Clin. Nutr. 20:375–385, 1967.

Friend, C. J., Heard, C. R. C., Platt, B. S., Stewart, R. J. C., and Turner M. R.: The effect of dietary protein deficiency on transport of Vit A in the blood and its storage in the liver. Brit. J. Nutr. 15:231–240, 1961.

Fryer, J. H., Miller, D. S., and Payne, P. R.: A calorie paradox? Proc. Nutr. Soc. 20:xlix–l, 1961.

Galbraith, J. K.: The Affluent Society. Boston, Houghton Mifflin, 1958, p. 368.

Geber, M., and Dean, R. F. A.: The psychological changes accompanying kwashiorkor. Courrier 6:3–15, 1956.

Gleeson, G. A., and White, E. L.: Disability and medical care among whites and nonwhites in the United States. HEW Indicators, 1965.

Gold, E. M., Erhardt, C. L., Jacobziner, H., and Nelson, Frieda: Therapeutic abortions in New York City: a 20-year review. Amer. J. Public Health 55:964–972, 1965.

Goldstein, H., Henderson, Maureen, Goldberg, I. D., Benitez, E., and Hawkins, C.: Perinatal factors associated with strabismus in Negro children. Amer. J. Public Health 57:217–227, 1967.

Gollance, H.: Personal communication, 1966.

Gomez, F., Velaxco-Alzaga, J., Ramos-Galvan, R., Cravioto, J., and Frenk, S.: Estudios sobre el nino desnutrido. XVII. Manifestaciones psicologicas (communicacion preliminar) Bol. Med. Hosp. Infantil (Mexico) 11:631–641, 1954.

Gopalan, C.: Effect of nutrition on pregnancy and lactation. WHO Bull. 26:203–211, 1962.

Gordon, E. W., and Wilkerson, D. A.: Compensatory education for the disadvantaged. New York, College Entrance Examination Board, 1966, p. 299.

Gordon, H. H., Levine, S. Z., and McNamara, Helen: Feeding of premature infants: a comparison of human milk and cows' milk. Amer. J. Dis. Child 73:442–452, 1947.

Gordon, J. E.: Weanling diarrhea: a synergism of nutrition and infection. Nutr. Rev. 22:161–163, 1964.

Gordon, J. E., Guzman, M., Ascoli, W., and Scrimshaw, N. S.: La Enfermedad Diarreica en los Paises en Vias de Desarrollo. II. Sus Caracteris-

REFERENCES

ticas Epidemiologicas en la Poblacion Rural de Guatemala. Discusiones Technicas. XIV. Reunion del consejo de la OPS. Publicaciones Cientificas No. 11. 1964, p. 14.

Graham, G. G.: Growth during recovery from infantile malnutrition. J. Amer. Med. Wom. Ass. 21:737–742, 1966.

Graham, G. G.: Effect of infantile malnutrition on growth. Fed. Proc. 26:139–143, 1967.

Grant, Faye W., and Groom, Dale: A dietary study among a group of Southern Negroes. J. Amer. Diet. Ass. 35:910–918, 1959.

Greulich, W. W.: Growth of children of the same race under different environmental conditions. Science 127:515–516, 1958.

Greulich, W. W., Thoms, H., and Twaddle, R. C.: A study of pelvis type and its relationship to body build in white women. JAMA 112:485–492, 1939.

Griswold, D. M., and Cavanagh, D.: Prematurity: the epidemiologic profile of the "high risk" mother. Amer. J. Obstet. Gynec. 96:878–882, 1966.

Gruenwald, P., Dawkins, M., and Hepner, R.: Chronic deprivation of the fetus. Sinai Hosp. J. 11:51–80, 1963.

Grundy, F., and Lewis-Faning, E.: Morbidity and Mortality in the First Years of Life: A Field Enquiry in Fifteen Areas of England and Wales. London, The Eugenics Society, 1957.

Gutelius, M. F.: The problem of iron deficiency anemia in preschool Negro children. Amer. J. Public Health 59:290–295, 1969.

Guthrie, Helen A.: Severe undernutrition in early infancy and behavior in rehabilitated albino rats. Physiol. Behav. 3:619–623, 1968.

Guttmacher, A. F.: Prematurity: the obstetric viewpoint. New York J. Med. 53:2781–2784, 1953.

György, P.: Editorial: the late effects of early nutrition. Amer. J. Clin. Nutr. 8:344–345, 1960.

Hale, F.: Relation of Vitamin A to anophthalmos in pigs. Amer. J. Ophthal. 18:1087–1093, 1935.

Hale, F.: Relation of maternal vitamin A deficiency to microphthalmia in pigs. Texas State J. Med. 33:228–232, 1937.

Hall, R. E.: Therapeutic abortion, sterilization and contraception. Amer. J. Obstet. Gynec. 91:518–532, 1965.

Hamlin, R. H. J.: The prevention of eclampsia and pre-eclampsia. Lancet 1:64–68, 1952.

Hammoud, E. I.: Studies in fetal and infant mortality. II. Differentials in mortality by sex and race. Amer. J. Public Health 55:1152–1163, 1965.

Hampton, Mary C., Huenemann, Ruth L., Shapiro, Leona R., and Mitchell, Barbara W.: Caloric and nutrient intakes of teenagers. J. Amer. Diet. Ass. 50:385–396, 1967.

REFERENCES

Harper, P. A., Fischer, Liselotte K., and Rider, R. V.: Neurological and intellectual status of prematures at three to five years of age. J. Pediat., 55:679–690, 1959.

Harper, P. A., and Wiener, G.: Sequelae of low birth weight. Ann. Rev. Med. 16:405–420, 1965.

Harrell, Ruth F., Woodyard, Ella R., and Gates, A. I.: The influence of vitamin supplementation of the diets of pregnant and lactating women on the intelligence of their offspring. Metabolism 5:555–562, 1956.

Harris, J. W.: Pregnancy and labor in young primiparae. Bull. Johns Hopkins Hosp. 33:12–16, 1922.

Hartman, Evelyn E., and Sayles, Ethel B.: Some reflections on birth and infant deaths among the low socio-economic groups. Minn. Med. 48:1711–1718, 1965.

Haryou (Harlem Youth Opportunities Unlimited): Youth in the Ghetto: A Study of the Consequences of Powerlessness and a Blueprint for Change. New York, Haryou, 1964, p. 635.

Hassan, H. M., and Falls, F. H.: The young primipara. Amer. J. Obstet. Gynec. 88:256–269, 1964.

Havighurst, R. J.: The Public Schools of Chicago. Chicago, The Board of Education, 1964, p. 499.

Heard, C. R. C., Meyer, A., Pampiglione, G., Stewart, R. J. C., and Platt, B. S.: Clinical, electroencephalographic and pathological changes in the nervous system of experimental animals. Proc. Nutr. Soc. 20:1, 1961.

Heimer, C. B., Cutler, Rhoda, and Freedman, A. M.: Neurological sequelae of premature birth. Amer. J. Dis. Child. 108:122–133, 1964.

Hendel, Grace M., Burke, Marguerite C., and Lund, Lois A.: Socio-economic factors influence children's diets. J. Home Econ. 57:205–208, 1965.

Henderson, Maureen, Entwisle, G., and Tayback, M.: Bacteriuria and pregnancy outcome: preliminary findings. Amer. J. Public Health 52:1887–1893, 1962.

Herriot, A., Billewicz, W. Z., and Hytten, F. E.: Cigarette smoking in pregnancy. Lancet 1:771–773, 1962.

Heseltine, M. M., and Pitts, J. L.: Economy in nutrition and feeding of infants. II. Nutritional status of infants. Amer. J. Public Health 56:1760–1762, 1966.

Hiernaux, J.: Weight/height relationship during growth in Africans and Europeans. Human Biol. 36:273–293, 1964.

Hill, A. B., Doll, R., Galloway, T. M., and Hughes, J. P. W.: Virus diseases in pregnancy and congenital defects. Brit. J. Prev. Soc. Med. 12:1–7, 1958.

Hill, Adelaide C., and Jaffe, F. S.: Negro fertility and family size preferences: implications for programming of health and social services. In

REFERENCES

T. Parsons and K. B. Clark (Eds.) The Negro American. Boston, Houghton Mifflin, 1966, pp. 205–224.

Hinson, Mary L., and Ferguson, J. H.: Food habits of pregnant women in charity hospital clinics. Bull. Tulane U. of La. Med. Fac. 10:138–142, 1951.

Hollingsworth, M. G.: The birth weights of African and European babies born in Ghana. W. Afr. Med. J. 9:256–259, 1960.

Holmes, Emma G.: Spending patterns of low-income families. Adult Leadership 14:16–17 +, 1967.

Hornberger, R. C., Brown, Jean C., Greenblatt, H. N., and Corsa, L.: Health supervision of young children in California. Findings of the 1956 Child Health Survey. Berkeley, California Department of Public Health, Bureau of Maternal and Child Health, 1960.

Hsueh, A. M., Agustin, C. E., and Chow, B. F.: Growth of young rats after differential manipulation of maternal diet. J. Nutr. 91:195–200, 1967.

Huenemann, Ruth L., Shapiro, Leona R., Hampton, Mary C., and Mitchell, Barbara W.: Food and eating practices of teenagers. J. Amer. Diet. Ass. 53:17–24, 1968.

Hunger, USA. A Report by the Citizens' Board of Inquiry into Hunger and Malnutrition in the United States. Washington, D. C., New Community Press, 1968, pp. 1–100.

Hunt, E.: Some New Evidence on Race and Intelligence. Paper read at the meeting of the New York Academy of Science, Anthropology Section. New York, 1966.

Hunt, Eleanor: Recent Demographic Trends and Their Effects on Maternal and Child Health Needs and Services. U. S. Department of Health, Education and Welfare. Welfare Administration. Children's Bureau. Washington, D. C., U. S. Government Printing Office, 1966, pp. 1–20.

Hunt, Eleanor, and Huyck, E. E.: Mortality of white and nonwhite infants in major U.S. cities. HEW Indicators, 1966, pp. 1–19 (reprint).

Hutcheson, Hazel A., and Wright, N. H.: Georgia's family planning program. Amer. J. Nurs. 68:332–335, 1968.

Hutcheson, R. H., Jr.: Iron deficiency anemia in Tennessee among rural poor children. Public Health Rep. 83:939–943, 1968.

Hytten, F. E., and Leitch, Isabella: The Physiology of Human Pregnancy. Oxford, Blackwell Scientific Publications, 1964.

Hytten, F. E., and MacQueen, I. A. G.: Artificial feeding and energy requirements of young infants. Lancet 2:836–839, 1954.

Hytten, F. E., Yorston, Jessie, and Thomson, A. M.: Difficulties associated with breast-feeding: a sudy of 106 primipara. Brit. Med. J. 1:310–315, 1958.

REFERENCES

Illsley, R.: Social class selection and class differences in relation to stillbirths and infant deaths. Brit. Med. J. 2:1520–1531, 1955.

Illsley, R.: The duration of ante-natal care. Medical Officer 96:107–111, 1956a.

Illsley, R.: The social context of childbirth. Nursing Mirror, September 14 and 21, 1956b.

Illsley, R.: Early prediction of perinatal risk. Proc. Roy. Soc. Med. 59:181–184, 1966.

Illsley, R.: The sociological study of reproduction and its outcome. In S. A. Richardson and A. F. Guttmacher (Eds.) Childbearing: Its Social and Psychological Aspects. Baltimore, Williams & Wilkins, 1967, pp. 75–135.

Ingle, D. J.: Racial differences and the future. Science 146:375–379, 1964.

Insull, W., and Kenzaburo, T.: Diet and nutritional status of Japanese. Amer. J. Clin. Nutr. 21:753–777, 1968.

Jackson, C. M.: The effects of Inanition and Malnutrition upon Growth and Structure. London, Churchill, 1925.

Jackson, C. M., and Stewart, C. A.: The effects of inanition in the young upon the ultimate size of the body and of the various organs in the albino rat. J. Exp. Zool. 30:97–128, 1920.

Jackson, R. L.: Effect of malnutrition on growth in the preschool child. In Preschool Child Malnutrition: Primary Deterrent to Human Progress. An International Conference on Prevention of Malnutrition in the Preschool Child, Washington, D. C., December 7–11, 1964. National Academy of Sciences–National Research Council Publication No. 1282. Washington, D. C., 1966.

Jaffe, F. S.: Family planning, public policy and intervention strategy. J. Social Issues 23:145–163, 1967.

James, G.: Poverty and public health: new outlooks. I. Poverty as an obstacle to health progress in our cities. Amer. J. Public Health 55:1757–1771, 1965.

James, J. A.: The later health of premature infants: a field for further study. Pediatrics 22:154–160, 1958.

Jantzen, K., Michaelis, R., Ter Meulen, V., and Melichar, V.: Postnatale Besonderheiten hypotropher Neugeborener. Geburtsh. Frauenheilk 28:468–475, 1968.

Jeans, P. C., Smith, Mary B., and Stearns, Genevieve: Dietary habits of pregnant women of low income in a rural state. J. Amer. Diet. Ass. 28:27–34, 1952.

Jeans, P. C., Smith, Mary B., and Stearns, Genevieve: Incidence of prematurity in relation to maternal nutrition. J. Amer. Diet. Ass. 31:576–581, 1955.

REFERENCES

Jeffers, Camille: Three generations: case materials in low-income urban living. Life story of one family in Washington, D. C., 1964. Unpublished.

Jeffery, G. M., Phifer, K. O., Gatch, D. E., Harrison, A. J., and Skinner, J. C.: Study of intestinal helminth infections in a coastal South Carolina area. Public Health Rep. 78:45–55, 1963.

Jelliffe, D. B.: The African child. Trans. Roy. Soc. Trop. Med. Hyg. 46:13–41, 1952.

Jensen, A. R.: How much can we boost IQ and scholastic achievement? Harvard Educational Review 39:1:1–123, 1969.

Jerome, N. W.: Changing meal patterns among southern-born Negroes in a midwestern city. Nutr. News 31:9 +, 1968.

Jones, Rose E., and Schendel, H. E.: Nutritional status of selected Negro infants in Greenville County, South Carolina. Amer. J. Clin. Nutr. 18:407–412, 1966.

Jones, W. H. S.: Philosophy and Medicine in Ancient Greece. Baltimore, Johns Hopkins Press, 1946.

Kahn, E.: A neurological syndrome in infants recovering from malnutrition. Arch. Dis. Child. 29:256–261, 1954.

Kahn, E.: A neuropathy in children recovering from malnutrition (kwashiorkor). Cent. Afr. J. Med. 3:398–400, 1957.

Kahn, E., and Falke, H. C.: A syndrome simulating encephalitis affecting children recovering from malnutrition (kwashiorkor). J. Pediat. 49:37–45, 1956.

Kasius, R. V., Randall, A., Tompkins, W. T., and Wiehl, Dorothy G.: Maternal and newborn nutrition studies at Philadelphia Lying-in Hospital. Newborn studies. I. Size and growth of babies of mothers receiving nutrient supplements. In The Promotion of Maternal and Newborn Health. New York, Milbank Memorial Fund, 1955, pp. 153–168.

Kass, E. H.: Hormones and host resistance to infection. Bact. Rev. 24:177–185, 1960.

Kawi, A. A., and Pasamanick, B.: Association of factors of pregnancy with reading disorders in childhood. JAMA 166:1420–1423, 1958.

Keith, L., Evenhouse, H., and Webster, Augusta: Amylophagia during pregnancy. Obstet. Gynec. 32:415–418, 1968.

Kennedy, R. F.: Address at the University of Capetown, June 6, 1966.

Keys, A., Brozek, J., Henschel, A., Mickelsen, O., and Taylor, H. L.: The Biology of Human Starvation. Minneapolis, University of Minnesota Press, 1950.

Kimble, G. H. T.: Tropical Africa. New York, Twentieth Century Fund, 1960.

King, M. L., Jr.: Speech at the Lincoln Memorial, Washington, D. C., August 28, 1963.

REFERENCES

Kirsch, R. E., Saunders, S. J., and Brock, J. F.: Animal models and human protein-calorie malnutrition. Amer. J. Clin. Nutr. 21:1225–1228, 1968.

Knobloch, Hilda, and Pasamanick, B.: Genetics of mental disease symposium, 1960. II. Some thoughts on the inheritance of intelligence. Amer. J. Orthopsychiat. 31:454–473, 1961.

Knobloch, Hilda, and Pasamanick, B.: Etiologic Factors in "Early Infantile Autism" and "Childhood Schizophrenia." Preliminary draft read at Tenth International Congress of Pediatrics, Lisbon, September 9–15, 1962a.

Knobloch, Hilda, and Pasamanick, B.: Neurologic damage as a cause of disordered behavior. Paper read at Tenth International Congress of Pediatrics, Lisbon, September 9–15, 1962b.

Knobloch, Hilda, and Pasamanick, B.: Neuropsychiatric disorders: influence of pre- and perinatal trauma. Feelings and their medical significance. Ross 5:1–2, 1964.

Knobloch, Hilda, Pasamanick, B., Harper, P. A., and Rider, R.: The effect of prematurity on health and growth. Amer. J. Public Health 49:1164–1173, 1959.

Knobloch, Hilda, Rider, R., Harper, P., and Pasamanick, B.: Neuropsychiatric sequelae of prematurity: a longitudinal study. JAMA 161: 581–585, 1956.

Koos, E. L.: The Health of Regionville. New York, Columbia University Press, 1954.

Kumate, J., Mariscal, C., Hikimura, J., and Yoshida, P.: Desnutricion e inmunidad. I. Complemento hemolitico en ninos desnutridos. Bol. Med. Hosp. Infantil (Mexico) 21:427–434, 1964.

Langer, E.: Birth control: U. S. programs off to slow start. Science 156: 765–767, 1967.

Lát, J., Widdowson, Elsie M., and McCance, R. A.: Some effects of accelerating growth. III. Behavior and nervous activity. Proc. Roy. Soc. B 153:347–356, 1961.

Leitch, Isabella: Growth and health. Brit. J. Nutr. 5:142–151, 1951.

Lesser, A. J.: Accent on prevention through improved service. Children 11:13–18, 1964.

Lesser, A.: Health of Children of School Age. U. S. Department of Health, Education and Welfare. Welfare Administration. Children's Bureau. Children's Bureau Pub. No. 427. Washington, D. C., U. S. Government Printing Office, 1964 (reprinted 1965), pp. 1–31.

Liang, Pek Hien, Tjiook Tiauw Hie, Oey Henk Jan, Lauw Tjin Giok: Evaluation of mental development in relation to early malnutrition. Amer. J. Clin. Nutr. 20:1290–1294, 1967.

REFERENCES

Lilienfeld, A. M., and Parkhurst, Elizabeth A.: A study of the association of factors of pregnancy and parturition with the development of cerebral palsy: preliminary report. Amer. J. Hyg. 53:262–282, 1951.

Lilienfeld, A. M., and Graham, S.: Validity of determining circumcision status by questionnaire as related to epidemiologic studies of cancer of the cervix. J. Nat. Cancer Inst. 21:713–720, 1958.

Lilienfeld, A. M., and Pasamanick, B.: Association of maternal and fetal factors with the development of epilepsy. I. Abnormalities in the prenatal and paranatal periods. JAMA 155:719–724, 1954.

Lilienfeld, A. M., and Pasamanick, B.: The association of maternal and fetal factors with the development of cerebral palsy and epilepsy. Amer. J. Obstet. Gynec. 70:93–101, 1955.

Lilienfeld, A. M., and Pasamanick B.: The association of maternal and fetal factors with development of mental deficiency. II. Relationship to maternal age, birth order, previous reproductive loss and degree of mental deficiency. Amer J. Ment. Defic. 60:557–569, 1956.

Little, W. J.: On the influence of abnormal parturition, difficult labour, premature birth, and asphyxia neonatorum on the mental and physical conditions of the child, especially in relation to deformities. Trans Obstet. Soc. London 3:293–344, 1862.

Llewellyn-Jones, D.: The effect of age and social status on obstetrical efficiency. J. Obstet. Gynaec. Brit. Comm. 72:196–202, 1965.

Lowrey, R. S., Pond, W. G., Barnes, R. H., Krook, L., and Loosli, J. K.: Influence of caloric level and protein quality on the manifestations of protein deficiency in the young pig. J. Nutr. 78:245–253, 1962.

Lubchenco, Lula O., Horner, F. A., Reed, Linda H., Hix, I. E., Metcalf, D., Cohig, Ruth, Elliott, Helen C., and Bourg, Margaret: Sequelae of premature birth. Amer. J. Dis. Child. 106:101–115, 1963.

Lunde, A. S.: White-nonwhite fertility differentials in the United States. HEW Indicators, 1965.

Macy, Icie G.: Nutrition and Chemical Growth in Childhood. I. Evaluation. Springfield, Ill., Charles C Thomas, 1942, pp. 1–432.

Maier, N. R. F.: The effect of cerebral destruction on reasoning and learning in rats. J. Comp. Neurol. 54:45–75, 1932.

Marchetti, A. A., and Menaker, J. S.: Pregnancy and the adolescent. Amer. J. Obstet, Gynec. 59:1013–1020, 1950.

Mayer, J.: The nutritional status of American Negroes. Nutr. Rev. 23:161–164, 1965.

Mayo, C. W. Cited in New York Times (Howard Rusk), August 13, 1967.

McCance, R. A.: Severe undernutrition in growing and adult animals. I. Production and general effects. Brit. J. Nutr. 14:59–73, 1960.

REFERENCES

McCance, R. A.. and Mount, L. E.: Severe undernutrition in growing and adult animals. V. Metabolic rate and body temperature in the pig. Brit. J. Nutr. 14:509–518, 1960.

McCance, R. A., and Widdowson, Elsie M.: Protein deficiencies and calorie deficiencies. Lancet 11:158–159, 1966.

McCance, R. A., Widdowson, Elsie M., and Verdon-Roe, C. M.: A study of English diets by the individual method. III. Pregnant women at different economic levels. J. Hyg. (London) 38:596–622, 1938.

McCone Report. California Governor's Commission on the Los Angeles Riots: Violence in the City: An End or a Beginning? (commonly known as the McCone Report). Los Angeles, December 1965, p. 101.

McDonald, Alison D.: Neurological and ophthalmic disorders in children of very low birth weight. Brit. Med. J. 1:895–900, 1962.

McDonald, Alison D.: Cerebral palsy in children of very low birth weight. Arch. Dis. Child. 38:579–588, 1963.

McDonald, Alison D.: Intelligence in children of very low birth weight. Brit. J. Prev. Soc. Med. 18:59–74, 1964.

McGanity, W. J., Cannon, R. O., Bridgeforth, E. B., Martin, Margaret P., Densen, P. M., Newbill, Josephine A., McClellan, G. S., Christie, A., Peterson, J. C., and Darby, W. J.: The Vanderbilt cooperative study of maternal and infant nutrition. V. Description and outcome of obstetric sample, Amer. J. Obstet. Gynec. 67:491–500, 1954a.

McGanity, W. J., Cannon, R. O., Bridgeforth, E. B., Martin, Margaret P., Densen, P. M., Newbill, Josephine A., McClellan, G. S., Christie, A., Peterson, J. C., and Darby, W. J.: The Vanderbilt cooperative study of maternal and infant nutrition. VI. Relationship of obstetric performance to nutrition. Amer. J. Obstet. Gynec. 67:501–527, 1954b.

McGregor, I. A., Billewicz, W. Z., and Thomson, A. M.: Growth and mortality in children in an African village. Brit. Med. J. 2:1661–1666, 1961.

McMahon, B., and Sowa, J. M.: Physical damage to the fetus. In Causes of Mental Disorders: A Review of Epidemiological Knowledge, 1959. New York, Milbank Memorial Fund, 1961.

Mead, Margaret, and Newton, N.: Cultural patterning of perinatal behavior. In S. A. Richardson and A. F. Guttmacher (Eds.) Childbearing: Its Social and Psychological Aspects. Baltimore, Williams & Wilkins, 1967.

Medical World News: Major ailments affect one-third of poor children. November 5, 1965, pp. 64–65 +.

Mellanby, E.: Nutrition and childbearing. Lancet 2:1131–1137, 1933.

Meredith, H. V.: North American Negro infants: size at birth and growth during the first postnatal year. Hum. Biol. 24:290–308, 1952.

Mermann, A. C.: Lowndes County, Alabama, TICEP Health Survey, Summer 1966; and Statement Prepared for the U. S. Sentate Sub-Committee on Employment, Manpower and Poverty. Washington, D. C.

Meyer, A., Stewart, R. J. C., and Platt, B. S.: The spinal cord of pigs on low-protein diets. Proc. Nutr. Soc. 20:xviii, 1961.

Meyer, H. F.: Breast feeding in the United States. Clin. Pediat. 7:708–715, 1968.

Mico, R.: A look at the health of Boston's Project Headstart children. J. School Health 36:241–244, 1966.

Milam, D. F., and Darby, W. J.: The average diet of a southern county and its effects on nutritional status. Southern Med. J. 38:117–124, 1945.

Miller, F. J. W., Court, S. D. M., Walton, W. S., and Knox, E. G.: Growing Up in Newcastle-upon-Tyne. The Nuffield Foundation, Oxford University Press, 1960.

Miller, H.: Rich Man Poor Man. New York, Thomas Y. Crowell, 1964.

Mills, C. A.: Influence of environmental temperatures on warm-blooded animals. Ann. NY Acad. Sci. 46:97–105, 1945.

Mills, C. A.: Temperature dominance over human life. Science 110:267–271, 1949.

Mitchell, Helen S.: Nutrition in relation to stature. J. Amer. Diet. Ass. 40:521–524, 1962.

Mitchell, Helen S.: Stature changes in Japanese youth and nutritional implications. Fed. Proc. 23:877, No. 27, 1964.

Monahan, H. B., and Spencer, E.: Deterrents to prenatal care. Children 9:114–119, 1962.

Moore, Margaret C., Purdy, Maud B., Gibbens, E. Janis, Hollinger, Martha E., and Goldsmith, Grace: Food habits of women during pregnancy. J. Amer. Diet. Ass. 23:847–853, 1947.

Morris, J. N., and Heady, J. A.: Social and biological factors in infant mortality. I. Objects and methods. Lancet 1:343–349, 1955.

Morrison, S. L., Heady, J. A., and Morris, J. N.: Social and biological factors in infant mortality. VIII. Mortality in the post-neonatal period. Arch. Dis. Child. 34:101–114, 1959.

Moynihan, D. P.: The crises in welfare. Public Interest 10:3–29, 1968.

Mugge, R. H.: Children on ADC. Cited in Moynihan, 1968.

Murphy, Gladys H., and Wertz, Anne W.: Diets of pregnant women: influence of socio-economic factors. J. Amer. Diet. Ass. 30:34–38, 1954.

Myers, Madge L., O'Brien, Sheila C., Mabel, Judith A., and Stare, F. J.: A nutrition study of school children in a depressed urban district. I. Dietary findings. J. Amer. Diet. Ass. 53:226–233, 1968.

National Center for Health Statistics: Advance Report. Final Mortality

REFERENCES

Statistics, 1967. Monthly Vital Statistics Report 17:12: Suppl. 1–12, March 25, 1969.

National Center for Health Statistics: Advance Report. Final Natality Statistics, 1967. Monthly Vital Statistics Report 17:9: Suppl. 1–8, December 4, 1968.

National Center for Health Statistics: Infant, Fetal and Maternal Mortality, United States, 1963. Vital and Health Statistics. PHS Pub. No. 1000, Series 20, No. 3. Public Health Service. Washington, D. C., U. S. Government Printing Office, 1966.

National Center for Health Statistics: Infant and Perinatal Mortality in England and Wales. Vital and Health Statistics. PHS Pub. No. 1000, Series 3, No. 12. Public Health Service. Washington, D. C., U. S. Government Printing Office, 1968.

National Center for Health Statistics: Infant and Perinatal Mortality in the United States. Vital and Health Statistics. PHS Pub. No. 1000, Series 3, No. 4. Public Health Service. Washington, D. C., U. S. Government Printing Office, 1965.

National Center for Health Statistics: International Comparison of Perinatal and Infant Mortality: United States and Six West European Countries. Vital and Health Statistics. PHS Pub. No. 1000, Series 3, No. 6. Public Health Service. Washington, D. C., U. S. Government Printing Office, 1967.

National Center for Health Statistics: Medical Care, Health Status and Family Income, United States. Vital and Health Statistics. PHS Pub. No. 1000, Series 10, No. 9. Public Health Service. Washington, D. C., U. S. Government Printing Office, 1964.

National Center for Health Statistics: Natality Statistics Analysis, United States, 1962. Vital and Health Statistics. PHS Pub. No. 1000, Series 21, No. 1. Public Health Service. Washington, D. C., U. S. Government Printing Office, 1964.

National Center for Health Statistics: Natality Statistics Analysis, United States, 1964. Vital and Health Statistics. PHS Pub. No. 1000, Series 21, No. 11. Public Health Service. Washington, D. C., U. S. Government Printing Office, 1967.

National Center for Health Statistics: Selected Family Characteristics and Health Measures Reported in the Health Interview Survey. PHS Pub. No. 1000, Series 3, No. 7. Public Health Service. Washington, D. C., U. S. Government Printing Office, 1967.

National Center for Health Statistics: Vital Statistics of the United States, 1965. Washington, D. C., U. S. Government Printing Office, 1967.

National Office of Vital Statistics: Weight at Birth and Survival of Newborn by Age of Mother and Total-Birth Order: U. S. Early 1950. J. Loeb Vital Statistics—Special Reports 47 (2), PHS. Washington, D. C., 1958.

Neff, Mildred F.: Helping low-income families use donated foods. J. Amer. Diet. Ass. 45:358–361, 1964.

Nelson, G. K., and Dean, R. F. A.: The electroencephalogram in African children: effects of kwashiorkor and a note on the newborn. Bull. WHO 21:779–782, 1959.

Nelson, Marjorie M.: Production of congenital anomalies in mammals by maternal dietary deficiencies. Pediatrics 19:764–776, 1957.

New York Times: New criteria show 15 million children in poverty families. January 29, 1965.

New York Times (Nan Robertson): Severe hunger found in Mississippi. June 17, 1967.

New York Times (Jane Brody): Eating of starch linked to anemia. July 24, 1967.

New York Times: High prices found in poorer areas. July 24, 1967.

New York Times: Medical clinic opens in Watts. September 16, 1967.

New York Times (Joseph A. Loftus): House unit doubts report of starvation in U. S. June 17, 1968.

New York Times (Richard L. Madden): Poor food found in poverty areas. August 11, 1968.

New York Times: House panel finds acute hunger rare. August 18, 1968.

New York Times (Homer Bigart): Hunger in America: stark deprivation. February 16–20, 1969.

Nolan, R. L., Schwartz, J. L., and Simonian, K.: Social class differences in utilization of pediatric services in a pre-paid direct service medical care program. Amer. J. Public Health 57:34–47, 1967.

North, A. F.: Project Head Start and the pediatrician. Clin. Pediat. 6:191–194, 1967.

Northcutt, T. J., Browning, R. H., and Brumback, C. L.: Agricultural migration and maternity care. J. Health Hum. Behav. 4:173–178, 1963.

Nutrition and Human Needs. Hearings before the Select Committee on Nutrition and Human Needs of the U. S. Senate. Parts 1 et seq. Washington, D. C., U. S. Government Printing Office, 1969.

Obstetrical Statistical Cooperative. 1962 Combined Report for 18 Hospitals.

Ohlson, Margaret, Biester, Alice, Brewer, W. D., Hawthorne, Betty E., and Hutchinson, Marie B.: Anthropometry and nutritional status of adult women. Hum. Biol. 28:189–202, 1956.

Olarte, J., Cravioto, J., and Campos, B.: Inmunidad en el nino desnutrido. I. Produccion de antitoxina difterica. Bol. Med. Hosp. Infantil (Mexico) 13:467–472, 1956.

REFERENCES

Oppenheimer, Ella: Population changes and perinatal mortality. Amer. J. Public Health 51:208–216, 1961.

Orr, J. B.: Food, Health and Income. London, Macmillan, 1936.

Orten, A. U., Reidinger, A. A., Karo, J. J., and Doppke, H. J.: Absorption of amino acids in man: effects of infection and intestinal antiseptics. Fed. Proc. 21:260, 1962.

Owen, G. M., and Kram, K. M.: Nutritional status of preschool children in Mississippi: food sources of nutrients in the diets. J. Amer. Diet. Ass. 54:490–494, 1969.

Pakter, Jean, Rosner, H. J., Jacobziner, H., and Greenstein, Frieda: Out-of-wedlock births in New York City. I. Sociologic aspects. Amer. J. Public Health 51:683–696, 1961a.

Pakter, Jean, Rosner, H. J., Jacobziner, H., and Greenstein, Frieda: Out-of-wedlock births in New York City. II. Medical aspects. Amer. J. Public Health 51:846–865, 1961b.

Pasamanick, B., Constantinou, Frances K., and Lilienfeld, A. M.: Pregnancy experience and the development of childhood speech disorders: an epidemiologic study of the association with maternal and fetal factors. Amer. J. Dis. Child. 91:113–118, 1956.

Pasamanick, B., and Kawi, A.: A study of the association of prenatal and paranatal factors with the development of tics in children: a preliminary investigation. J. Pediat. 48:596–601, 1956.

Pasamanick, B., and Knobloch, Hilda: Brain damage and reproductive casualty. Amer. J. Orthopsychiat. 30:298–305, 1960.

Pasamanick, B., and Knobloch, Hilda: Epidemiologic studies on the complications of pregnancy and the birth process. In G. Caplan (Ed.) Prevention of Mental Disorders in Children. New York, Basic Books, 1961. pp. 74–94.

Pasamanick, B., Knobloch, Hilda, and Lilienfeld, A. M.: Socio-economic status and some precursors of neuropsychiatric disorders. Amer. J. Orthopsychiat. 26:594–601, 1956.

Pasamanick, B., and Lilienfeld, A. M.: Association of maternal and fetal factors with the development of mental deficiency. I. Abnormalities in the prenatal and paranatal periods. JAMA 159:155–160, 1955a.

Pasamanick, B., and Lilienfeld, A. M.: Maternal and fetal factors in the development of epilepsy. Relationship to some clinical features of epilepsy. Neurology 5:77–83, 1955b.

Pasamanick, B., Rogers, Martha E., and Lilienfeld, A. M.: Pregnancy experience and the development of behavior disorder in children. Amer. J. Psychiat. 112:613–618, 1956.

Payton, Eleanor, Crump, E. P., and Horton, C. P.: Growth and development. VII. Dietary habits of 571 pregnant southern Negro women. J. Amer. Diet. Ass. 37:129–136, 1960.

Payton, Eleanor, Crump, E. P., and Horton, C. P.: Growth and development. X. Feeding practices with Negro infants 6–8 weeks old and their relationship to various maternal factors. Amer. J. Obstet. Gynec. 81: 1009–1017, 1961.

People's League of Health: The nutrition of expectant and nursing mothers in relation to maternal and infant mortality and morbidity. J. Obstet. Gynaec. Brit. Emp. 53:498–509, 1946.

Peters, Ann D., and Chase, C. L.: Patterns of health care in infancy in a rural southern county. Amer. J. Public Health 57:409–423, 1967.

Pineda, Rebecca G., Desmond, Murdina M., Rudolph, A. J., Halleen, W., Rawls, W., and Ziai, M.: Impact of the 1964 rubella epidemic on a clinic population. Amer. J. Obstet. Gynec. 100:1139–1146, 1968.

Planned Parenthood: World Population, Annual Report, 1966.

Platt, B. S.: Protein in nutrition. Proc. Roy. Soc. B 156:337–344, 1962.

Platt, B. S., Heard, C. R. C., and Stewart, R. J. C.: Experimental protein-calorie deficiency. In H. N. Munro and J. B. Allison (Eds.) Mammalian Protein Metabolism, Vol. II. New York, Academic Press, 1964, pp. 445–521.

Platt, B. S., Pampiglione, G., and Stewart, R. J. C.: Experimental protein-calorie deficiency: clinical, electroencephalographic and neuropathological changes in pigs. Develop. Med. Child. Neurol. 7:9–26, 1965.

Pollin, W., Stabenau, J. R., Mosher, L., and Tupin, J.: Life history differences in identical twins discordant for schizophrenia. Amer. J. Orthopsychiat. 36:492–509, 1966.

Pontzer, Margaret E., and Dodds, Mary L.: Use of government-donated foods in a rural community. J. Amer. Diet. Ass. 42:128–130, 1963.

Poverty and High Fertility: The Crucial Link. Washington, D. C., Population Reference Bureau, 1965, p. 5.

Quinn, R. W., Downey, F. M., and Federspiel, C. F.: The incidence of rheumatic fever in metropolitan Nashville, 1963–1965. Public Health Rep. 82:673–681, 1967.

Raiha, C. E.: Relation of maternal heart volume in pregnancy to prematurity and perinatal mortality. WHO Bull. 26:2:296–300, 1962.

Ramirez, M.: Desarrollo y crecimiento de las minas de una colonia proletaria de la Ciudad de Mexico. Thesis, Facultad de Medicina Universidad National Autonoma de Mexico, 1960.

Ramos-Galvan, R.: Medidas convencionales de peso y talla para lactantes y pre-escolares. Bol. Clin. Ass. Med. Hosp. Infantil (Mexico) 1:19 +, 1960.

REFERENCES

Ramos-Galvan, R.: Communication to the PAHO Scientific Group on Research in Protein-Calorie Malnutrition. Bogota, 1964.

Ramos-Galvan, R., Perez-Navarrete, J. L., and Cravioto, J.: Algunos aspectos de crecimiento y desarrollo en el nino Mexicano. Bol. Med. Hosp. Infantil (Mexico) 17:455–474, 1960.

Randall, A., IV, Randall, J. P., Tompkins, W. T., and Wiehl, Dorothy G.: Maternal and newborn nutrition studies at Philadelphia Lying-in Hospital. Newborn studies. II. Clinical findings for babies of mothers receiving nutrient supplements. In The Promotion of Maternal and Newborn Health. New York, Milbank Memorial Fund, 1955, pp. 169–193.

Rao, K. S., Swaminathan, N. C., and Pathwardan, V. N.: Protein malnutrition in South India. Bull. WHO 20: 603–639, 1959.

Richardson, S. A.: Psychosocial factors contributing to deprivation. In Deprivation in Psychobiological Development. Pan American Health Organization Scientific Pub. No. 134. Washington, D.C., WHO, 1966, pp. 55–65.

Rider, R. V., Harper, P. A., Knobloch, Hilda, and Fetter, Sara A.: An evaluation of standards for the hospital care of premature infants. JAMA 165:1233–1236, 1957.

Rider, R. V., Tayback, M., and Knobloch, Hilda: Associations between premature birth and socio-economic status. Amer. J. Public Health 45:1022–1028, 1955.

Robinson, D.: The use of medical services and facilities by welfare supported children. Public Health Rep. 80:1055–1060, 1965.

Robinson, R. J., and Tizard, J. P. M.: The central nervous system in the newborn. Brit. Med. Bull. 22:49–55, 1966.

Robles, B., Cravioto, J., Rivera, L., Vilches, A., Santibanex, E., Vega, L., and Perez-Navarrete, J. L.: Influencia de Ciertos Factores Ecologicos sobre la Conducta del Nino en el Medio Rural Mexicano. Meeting of the Mexican Society for Pediatric Research. Cuernavaca, 1959.

Ross, J. A.: Social class and medical care. J. Health Hum. Behav. 3:35–40, 1962.

Russell, J. K., Fairweather, D. V. I., Millar, D. G., Brown, A. M., Pearson, R. C. M., Neligan, G. A., and Anderson, G. S.: Maternity in Newcastle-upon-Tyne: a community study. Lancet 1a:711–713, 1963.

Salber, Eva J., and Feinleib, M.: Breast-feeding in Boston. Pediatrics 37:299–303, 1966.

Sanders, B. S.: Have morbidity surveys been oversold? Amer. J. Public Health 52:1648–1659, 1962.

Sarrouy, C., Saint-Jean, M., and Clausse, J.: L'electroencephalogramme au cours de la dystrophie nutritionel le oedemateuse. Algerie Med. 57:584–588, 1953.

Schiffer, Clara G., and Hunt, Eleanor P.: Illness Among Children. Data from U. S. National Health Survey. U. S. Department of Health, Education and Welfare. Welfare Administration. Children's Bureau. Washington, D. C., U. S. Government Printing Office, 1963 (reprinted 1964), pp. 1–107.

Schonfield, J., Schmidt, W., and Sternfeld, L.: Variations in prenatal care and well-child supervision in a New England city. J. Pediat. 61:430–437, 1962.

Schrag, P. G.: Ghetto merchants: a study in deception. New Republic 159:17–19, 1968.

Schreider, E.: Recherches sur la stratification sociale des caracteres biologiques. Biotypiologie 26:105–135, 1964.

Scott, J. P.: Critical periods in behavioral development. Science 138:949–958, 1962.

Scott, J. P.: The process of primary socialization in canine and human infants. Monogr. Soc. Res. Child Develop. 28:1–47, 1963.

Scott, R. B., Cardozo, W. W., deG. Smith, A., and DeLilly, M. R.: Growth and development of Negro infants. III. Growth during the first year of life as observed in private pediatric practice. J. Pediat. 37:885–893, 1950.

Scott, R. B., Jenkins, M. E., and Crawford, R. P.: Growth and development of Negro infants. I. Analysis of birth weights of 11,818 newly born infants. Pediatrics 6:425–431, 1950.

Scrimshaw, N. S.: Evaluation of nutrition in pregnancy. J. Amer. Diet. Ass. 26:21–24, 1950.

Scrimshaw, N. S.: Malnutrition and infection. Borden Rev. Nutr. Res. 26:17–29, 1965.

Scrimshaw, N. S., Taylor, C. E., and Gordon. J. E.: Interactions of nutrition and infection. WHO Monograph Series No. 57, 1968.

Sears, R. R., Macoby, E. E., and Levin, H: Patterns of Child Rearing. White Plains, Row, 1957.

Sebrell, W. H., Jr.: Clinical nutrition in the United States. Amer. J. Public Health 58:2035–2042, 1968.

Shapiro, S.: Influence of birth weight, sex and plurality on neonatal loss in the United States. Amer. J. Public Health 44:1142–1153, 1954.

Shapiro, S., Jacobziner, H., Densen, P. M., and Weiner, L.: Further observations on prematurity and perinatal mortality in a general population and in the population of a prepaid group practice medical care plan. Amer. J. Public Health 50:1304–1317, 1960.

Shapiro, S., Ross, L. J., and Levine, H. S.: Relationship of selected prenatal factors to pregnancy outcome and congenital anomalies. Amer. J. Public Health 55:268–282, 1965.

Shockley, W.: Possible transfer of metallurgical and astronomical approaches to the problem of environment versus ethnic heredity. Presentation at the regional meeting of the National Academy of Sciences, 1966. Unpublished.

Siegel, E.: Migrant families: health problems of children. Clin. Pediat. 5:635–640, 1966.

Siegel, M., and Greenberg, M.: Fetal death, malformation and prematurity after maternal rubella: results of a prospective study. New Eng. J. Med. 262:389–393, 1960.

Sigerist, H. E.: Landmarks in the History of Hygiene. New York, Oxford University Press, 1956.

Simonson, M. R., Yu, W., Anilane, J. K., Sherwin, R., and Chow, B. F.: Studies of development in progeny of underfed mother rats. Fed. Proc. 26:519, No. 1464, 1967.

Simonson, M., Sherwin, R. W., Hanson, H. H., and Chow, B. F.: Maze performance in offspring of underfed mother rats. Fed. Proc. 27:727, No. 2872, 1968.

Simpson, D.: Dimensions of world poverty. Sci. Amer. 219:27–35, 1968.

Simpson, Winea J.: A preliminary report on cigarette smoking and the incidence of prematurity. Amer. J. Obstet. Gynec. 73:808–815, 1957.

Slatin, Marion: Extra protection for high-risk mothers and babies. Amer. J. Nurs. 67:1241–1243, 1967.

Smith, C. A.: Effects of maternal undernutrition upon the newborn infant in Holland. J. Pediat. 30:229–243, 1947.

Smith, C. A.: The valley of the shadow of birth. Amer. J. Dis. Child. 82:171–201, 1951.

Smith, C. A.: Prenatal and neonatal nutrition. Pediatrics 30:145–156, 1962.

Social and Economic Conditions of Negroes in the United States. Bureau of the Census and Bureau of Labor Statistics. Washington, D. C., U. S. Government Printing Office, 1967.

Sontag, L. W., and Wines, J.: Relation of mothers' diets to status of their infants at birth and in infancy. Amer. J. Obstet. Gynec. 54:994–1003, 1947.

Southern Regional Council: Special Report. "Hungry Children." Atlanta, Ga., 1967.

Speert, H., Graff, S., and Graff, Ada M.: Nutrition and premature labor. Amer. J. Obstet. Gynec. 62:1009–1019, 1951.

Spicer, C. C., and Lipworth, L.: Regional and Social Factors in Infant Mortality. Studies on Medical and Population Subjects No. 19. London, HMSO, 1966.

REFERENCES

Spence, J., Walton, W. S., Miller, F. J. W., and Court, S. D. M.: A Thousand Families in Newcastle-upon-Tyne. The Nuffield Foundation, Oxford University Press, 1954.

Stewart, W. H.: The unmet needs of children. Pediatrics 39:157–160, 1967.

Stine, O. C., Chuaqui, C., Jimenez, Consuelo, and Oppel, W. C.: Broken appointments at a comprehensive clinic for children. Med. Care 6:332–339, 1968.

Stine, O. C., Rider, R. V., and Sweeney, E.: School leaving due to pregnancy in an urban adolescent population. Amer. J. Public Health 54:1–6, 1964.

Stoch, M. B., and Smythe, P. M.: Does undernutrition during infancy inhibit brain growth and subsequent intellectual development? Arch. Dis. Child. 38:546–552, 1963.

Stoch, M. B., and Smythe, P. M.: Undernutrition during infancy, and subsequent brain growth and intellectual development. In W. S. Schrimshaw and J. E. Gordon (Eds.) Malnutrition, Cambridge, MIT Press, 1968, pp. 278–289.

Stockwell, E. G.: Infant mortality and socio-economic status in Providence. Rhode Island Med. J. 46:592–593, 1963.

Sundberg, Alice M.: Influencing prenatal behavior. Amer. J. Public Health 56:1218–1225, 1966.

Survey of needs for dental care, 1965. V. Dental needs according to income. (Bureau of Economic Research and Statistics.) J. Amer. Dent. Ass. 74:789–792, 1967.

Tanner, J. M.: Education and Physical Growth. London, University of London Press, 1961, pp. 1–144.

Task Force on Tuberculosis in New York City: A Modern Attack on an Urban Health Problem. City of New York. New York, 1968, p. 57.

Tayback, M., and Wallace, Helen: Maternal and child health services and urban economics. Public Health Rep. 77:827–833, 1962.

Tepper, Sheri E.: A "package" plan for extension of birth control services. Amer. J. Public Health 56: Suppl. II, 22–28, 1966.

Thomas, A., Chess, Stella, and Birch, H. G.: Temperament and Behavior Disorders in Children. New York, New York University Press, 1968.

Thompson, Barbara: Social study of illegitimate maternities. Brit. J. Prev. Soc. Med. 10:75–87, 1956.

Thompson, Barbara: The first fourteen days of some West African babies. Lancet 2:40–45, 1966.

Thompson, J. F.: Some observations on the geographic distribution of premature births and prenatal deaths in Indiana. Amer. J. Obstet. Gynec. 101:43–51, 1968.

REFERENCES

Thomson, A. M.: Diet in pregnancy. I. Dietary survey technique and the nutritive value of diets taken by primigravidae. Brit. J. Nutr. 12:4:446–461, 1958.

Thomson, A. M.: Diet in pregnancy. III. Diet in relation to the course and outcome of pregnancy. Brit. J. Nutr. 13:4:509–525, 1959a.

Thomson, A. M.: Maternal stature and reproductive efficiency. Eugen. Rev. 51:157–162, 1959b.

Thomson, A. M.: Prematurity: socio-economic and nutritional factors. Bibl. Paediat. 8:197–206, 1963.

Thomson, A. M., and Billewicz, W. Z.: Clinical significance of weight trends during pregnancy. Brit. Med. J. 1:243–247, 1957.

Thomson, A. M., and Billewicz, W. Z.: Nutritional status, physique and reproductive efficiency. Proc. Nutr. Soc. 22:55–60, 1963.

Thomson, A. M., and Duncan, D. L.: The diagnosis of malnutrition in man. Nutr. Abstr. Rev. 24:1–17, 1954.

Thurston, D., Graham, Frances K., Ernhart, Claire B., Eichman, P. L., and Craft, Marguerite: Neurologic status of 3-year-old children originally studied at birth. Neurology 10:680–690, 1960.

Timmer, M.: Prosperity and birth weight in Javanese infants. Trop. Geogr. Med. 13:316–320, 1961.

Tompkins, W. T. J.: The significance of nutritional deficiency in pregnancy. Int. College Surg. 4:147–154, 1941.

Tompkins, W. T.: The clinical significance of nutritional deficiencies in pregnancy. Bull. NY Acad. Med. 24:376–388, 1948.

Tompkins, W. T., Mitchell, R. McN., and Wiehl, Dorothy G.: Maternal and newborn nutrition studies at Philadelphia Lying-in Hospital. Maternal studies. II. Prematurity and maternal nutrition. In The Promotion of Maternal and Newborn Health. New York, Milbank Memorial Fund, 1955, pp. 25–61.

Tompkins, W. T., and Wiehl, Dorothy G.: Maternal and newborn nutrition studies at Philadelphia Lying-in Hospital. Maternal studies III. Toxemia and maternal nutrition. In The Promotion of Maternal and Newborn Health. New York, Milbank Memorial Fund, 1955, pp. 62–90.

Tompkins, W. T., and Wiehl, Dorothy G.: Nutritional deficiencies as a causal factor in toxemia and premature labor. Amer. J. Obstet. Gynec. 62:898–919, 1951.

Toverud, G.: The influence of nutrition on the course of pregnancy. Milbank Mem. Fund. Quart. 28:7–24, 1950.

Tranquada, R. E.: A health center for Watts. Hospitals 41:43–47, 1967.

Trowell, H. C., Davies, J. N. P., and Dean, R. F. A.: Kwashiorkor. London, Arnold, 1954.

REFERENCES

Turck, M., Goffe, B. S., and Petersdorf, R. G.: Bacteruria of pregnancy. New Eng. J. Med. 266:857–860, 1962.

Turnbull, E. P. N., and Walker, J.: The outcome of pregnancy complicated by threatened abortion. J. Obstet. Gynaec. Brit. Emp. 63:553–559, 1956.

Udani, P. M.: Physical growth of children in different socio-economic groups in Bombay. Indian J. Child Health 12:593–611, 1963.

U. S. Bureau of the Census: Current Population Reports Series P-60, No. 55. Washington, D. C., U. S. Government Printing Office, 1968.

U. S. Bureau of the Census: Trends in Social and Economic Conditions in Metropolitan Areas U. S. Current Population Reports Series P-23. Special Studies No. 27. Washington, D. C., U. S. Government Printing Office, 1969.

U. S. Dept. of Health, Education and Welfare: Reference Facts on Health, Education and Welfare. Washington, D. C., U. S. Government Printing Office, 1967.

U. S. House of Representatives: Subcommittee of the War on Poverty Program Hearings April 12–15, 29, and 30, 1965. Washington, D. C., U. S. Government Printing Office, 1965.

Valenzuela, R. H., Hernandez-Peniche, J., and Macias, R.: Aspectos clinicos electroencefalograficos y psicologicos en la recuperacion del nino desnutrido. Graceta Medica de Mexico, 89:651–656, 1959.

Vega, L., Ramirez, C., Maza, Z., and Cravioto, J.: "Operacion Nimiquipalg." IV. Influencia del estado de nutricion sobre el tipo y frecuencia de complicaciones en el sarampion. Guatemala Pediatrica 4:65–83, 1964.

Venkatachalam, P. S.: Maternal nutritional status and its effect on the newly born. Bull. WHO 26:193–201, 1962.

Verhoestraete, L. J., and Puffer, R. R.: The challenge of fetal loss, prematurity and infant mortality: a world view. JAMA 167:950–959, 1958.

Walton, W. P.: Effect on families and individuals in a rural community where poor relief was exhausted: a study of one hundred and sixty-two cases in Clermont County, Ohio, whose total poor relief grants were discontinued. Cincinnati J. Med. 45:226–227, 1964.

Warkany, J.: Congenital malformations induced by maternal nutritional deficiency. J. Pediat. 25:476–480, 1944.

Warkany, J.: Experimental studies on nutrition in pregnancy. Obstet. Gynec. Survey 3:693–703, 1948.

Warkany, J., and Nelson, R. C.: Congenital malformations induced in rats by maternal nutritional deficiency. J. Nutr. 23:321–333, 1942.

Watson, E. H., and Lowrey, G. H.: Growth and Development of Children. Chicago, Year Book Medical Publishers, 1951.

REFERENCES

Wegman, M.: Annual review of vital statistics. Pediatrics 42:1005–1008, 1968.

Weinerman, E. R., Ratner, R. S., Robbins, A., and Lavenhar, M. A.: Yale studies in ambulatory medical care. V. Determinants of use of hospital emergency services. Amer. J. Public Health 56:1037–1056, 1966.

Werner, Emmy: Cumulative effect of perinatal complications and deprived environment on physical, intellectual and social development of preschool children. Pediatrics 39:490–505, 1967.

When More Is Less. New York, Planned Parenthood World Population, 1969.

Whitley, J. R., O'Dell, B. L., and Hogan, A. G.: Effect of diet on maze learning in second-generation rats: folic acid deficiency. J. Nutr. 45: 153–160, 1951.

Whitridge, J., and Davens, E.: Are public health maternity programs effective and necessary? Amer. J. Public Health 42:508–515, 1952.

Whitsitt, A. F.: Nutrition services in a county public health program. The Child 6:16–19, 1941.

Widdowson, Elsie M.: Mental contentment and physical growth. Lancet 1:1316–1318, 1951.

Widdowson, Elsie M.: Nutritional deprivation in psychobiological development: studies in animals. In Deprivation in Psychobiological Development. Pan American Health Organization Scientific Pub. No. 134. Washington, D. C., WHO, 1966, pp. 27–38.

Widdowson, Elsie M., Dickerson, J. W. T., and McCance, R. A.: Severe undernutrition in growing and adult animals. IV. The impact of severe undernutrition on the chemical composition of the soft tissues of the pig. Brit. J. Nutr. 14:457–470, 1960.

Widdowson, Elsie M., and Kennedy, G. C.: Rate of growth, mature weight and life-span. Proc. Roy. Soc. B 156:96–108, 1962.

Widdowson, Elsie M., and McCance, R. A.: Some effects of accelerating growth. I. General somatic development. Proc. Roy. Soc. B 152:188–206, 1960.

Widdowson, Elsie M., and McCance, R. A.: The effect of finite periods of undernutrition at different ages on the composition and subsequent development of the rat. Proc. Roy. Soc. B 158:329–342, 1963.

Wiehl, Dorothy G., and Tompkins, W. T.: Maternal and newborn nutrition studies at Philadelphia Lying-in Hospital. Maternal studies. I. Method of study and description of sample. In The Promotion of Maternal and Newborn Health. New York, Milbank Memorial Fund, 1955, pp. 11–24.

Wiener, G.: Psychologic correlates of premature birth: a review. J. Nerv. Ment. Dis. 134:129–144, 1962.

REFERENCES

Wiener, G., Rider, R. V., Oppel, W. C., Fischer, Liselotte K., and Harper, P. A.: Correlates of low birth weight: psychological status at 6–7 years of age. Pediatrics 35:434–444, 1965.

Wiener, G., Rider, R. V., Oppel, W. C., and Harper, P. A.: Correlates of low birth weight: psychological status at eight to ten years of age. Pediat. Res. 2:110–118, 1968.

Willie, C. V.: Research note on the changing association between infant mortality and socio-economic status. Social Forces 37:221–227, 1959.

Wilson, D., Bressani, R., and Scrimshaw, N. S.: Infection and nutritional status. I. The effect of chicken pox on nitrogen metabolism in children. Amer. J. Clin. Nutr. 9:154–158, 1961.

Wingert, W. A.: The demographical and ecological characteristics of a large urban pediatric outpatient population and implications for improving community pediatric care. Amer. J. Public Health 58:859–876, 1968.

Winick, M.: Nutrition and cell growth. Nutr. Rev. 26:195–197, 1968.

Winick, M., and Rosso, P.: The effect of severe early malnutrition in cellular growth of human brain. Pediat. Res. 3:181–184, 1969.

Woodhill, Joan M., van den Berg, Anna S., Burke, Bertha S., and Stare, F. J.: Nutrition studies of pregnant Australian women. Amer. J. Obstet. Gynec. 70:987–1003, 1955.

Woodruff, C.: Infantile scurvy. JAMA 161:448–456, 1957.

Wortis, Helen, Bardach, J. L., Cutler, R., Rue, Rose, and Freedman, A.: Child-rearing practices in a low socio-economic group. Pediatrics 32:298–307, 1963.

Wortis, Helen, Braine, M., Cutler, R., and Freedman, A.: Deviant behavior in 2½-year-old premature children. Child Develop. 35:871–879, 1964.

Wortis, Helen, and Freedman, A. M.: Maternal stress and premature delivery. Bull. WHO 26:285–291, 1962.

Yankauer, A., Boek, W. E., Lawson E. D., and Ianni, F. A. J.: Social stratification and health practices in childbearing and child-rearing. Amer. J. Public Health 48:732–741, 1958.

Yankauer, A., Goss, K. G., and Romeo, S. M.: An evaluation of prenatal care and its relationship to social class and social disorganization. Amer. J. Public Health 43:1001–1010, 1953.

Yankee, Mildred: Migrant day care center. Amer. J. Nurs. 66:1756–1759, 1966.

Yerby, A. S.: The problems of medical care for indigent populations. Amer. J. Public Health 55:1212–1216, 1965.

Yerby, A. S.: The disadvantaged and health care. Amer. J. Public Health 56:5–9, 1966.

REFERENCES

Yerby, A.: Public policy in regard to birth-control services. New Eng. J. Med. 275:824–826, 1966.

Yerushalmy, J.: Neonatal mortality by order of birth and age of parents. Amer. J. Hyg. 28:244–270, 1938.

Yerushalmy, J.: Biostatistical methods in investigations of child health. Amer. J. Dis. Child. 114:470–476, 1967.

Yerushalmy, J., Palmer, C. E., and Kramer, M.: Studies in childbirth mortality, age and parity as factors in puerperal fatality. Public Health Rep. 55:1195–1220, 1940.

Young, P. T.: Affective arousal: some implications. American Psychologist 22:32–40, 1967.

Young, P. T., and Chaplin, J. P.: Studies of food preference, appetite and dietary habit. III. Palatability and appetite in relation to bodily need. Compr. Psych. Monogr. 18:1–45, 1945.

Zacharias, J. R. (Chairman) Innovation and Experiment in Education. A Progress Report of the Panel on Educational Research and Development. Washington, D. C., U. S. Government Printing Office, 1964, pp. 1–79.

Zamenhof, S., Van Marthens, Edith, and Margolis, F. L.: DNA (cell number) and protein in neonatal brain: alteration by maternal dietary protein restriction. Science 160:322–323, 1968.

Zitrin, A., Ferber, P., and Cohen, D.: Pre- and paranatal factors in mental disorders of children. J. Nerv. Ment. Dis. 139:357–361, 1964.

Author Index

AUTHOR INDEX

AUTHOR INDEX

Subject Index

SUBJECT INDEX

SUBJECT INDEX